How to Be Like
WOMEN
OF POWER

How to Be Like
WOMEN
OF POWER

Wisdom and Advice to Create
Your Own Destiny

Pat Williams
Ruth Williams
with Michael Mink

Health Communications, Inc.
Deerfield Beach, Florida

www.hcibooks.com

Library of Congress Cataloging-in-Publication Data

Williams, Pat, 1940-
    How to be like women of power / Pat Williams and Ruth Williams with Michael Mink.
      p. cm.
    ISBN-13: 978-0-7573-0650-1 (trade paper)
    ISBN-10: 0-7573-0650-0 (trade paper)
    1. Women—Life skills guides.   2. Women—Psychology.   3. Women—
United States—Biography.   4. Success.   I. Williams, Ruth.   II. Mink, Michael, 1958-
III. Title.
HQ1221.W674 2008
305.4092'273—dc22
    [B]

ISBN-10: 0-7573-0650-0
ISBN-13: 978-0-7573-0650-1

The How to Be Like Barbara Jordan chapter was written by Nancy Sokoler Steiner.
The How to Be Like Madeleine Albright chapter was written by Keith Rayve.
The How to Be Like Mary McLeod Bethune chapter was written by Amelie Frank.

Publisher: Health Communications, Inc.
        3201 S.W. 15th Street
        Deerfield Beach, FL 33442–8190

Cover photos: from left to right: 2007 WireImage, AFP/Getty Images, FilmMagic, 2007 Getty Images
Cover design by Justin Rotkowitz
Interior design by Dawn VonStrolley Grove
Interior formatting by Lawna Patterson Oldfield

To our four granddaughters,
Laila Kindy, Brianna Givans, and
Ava and Audri Joyce.

We hope that these four young ladies will grow up
to have an impact on the world.

—*Pat and Ruth Williams*

To Christy Jarvis and Becky Mintz,
two true Women of Courage who
have taught me a lot.

—*Michael Mink*

Contents

Introduction ix

1 **Rachael Ray: Enthusiasm** 1

2 **Barbara Jordan: Trailblazer** 13

3 **Danica Patrick: Fearless** 27

4 **Katharine Graham: Risk Taker** 39

5 **J. K. Rowling: Passion** 55

6 **Lucille Ball: Perseverance** 69

7 **Madeleine Albright: Activism** 85

8 **Estée Lauder: Quality** 101

9 **Jane Addams: Compassion** 119

10 **Meg Whitman: Collaboration** 135

11 **Shirley Chisholm: Maverick** 149

12 **Martha Stewart: Perfectionist** 163

13 **Mary McLeod Bethune: Education** 177

14 **Lorena Ochoa: Service** 197

15 **Condoleezza Rice: Optimism** 207

16 **Suze Orman: Financial Responsibility** 221

17 **Ruth Bader Ginsburg: Equality for Women** 241

18 **Ida B. Wells-Barnett: Courage** 255

19 **Mary Kay Ash: Dream Maker** 271

20 **Barbara Walters: Ambition** 281

21 **Rachel Carson: Naturalist** 297

Power Points 310

Epilogue 311

References 313

Acknowledgments 319

About the Authors 321

☙ Introduction ❧

You are looking at the ninth volume in the How to Be Like . . . series. The series had its inception in the fall of 1998 when Pat approached Peter Vegso, publisher of Health Communications, Inc., with a book concept. Michael Jordan had just led the Chicago Bulls to their sixth National Basketball Association title, and Pat had started giving a speech in the corporate world titled *How to Be Like Mike*. He suggested to Peter that this would be an ideal subject for a book, and Peter readily agreed.

In September 2001, *How to Be Like Mike* was published and sales and responses to the book were overwhelmingly positive. Shortly after *How to Be Like Mike* was released, Peter and Pat met for lunch to discuss future How to Be Like . . . projects. In the ensuing six years, How to Be Like . . . books have appeared regularly. Subsequent volumes have profiled Jesus, women of influence, Rich DeVos, Walt Disney, Jackie Robinson, John Wooden, women athletes of influence, and the book you are reading now, *How to Be Like Women of Power*, which profiles twenty-one amazingly powerful women from all walks of life—business, education, politics, sports, literature, finance, law, acting, publishing, and the environment.

Why are these women so powerful? Because they skyrocketed through the glass ceiling and catapulted themselves to the top of their professions, many times against incredible odds. But these women would not give up. A few were disadvantaged from the start. Some were homeless, some poor, some friendless, some outcasts. Others were brilliant, beautiful, talented, and privileged. Regardless of their station in life, they were passionate about their purpose. They were trailblazers, risk takers, activists, mavericks, naturalists, and servants. They were compassionate, optimistic, ambitious, and dedicated. They were driven to challenge the status quo, to push steadfastly towards their goal, to live their dream. They were innovative and possessed such a strong sense of self that they were able to defy conventional thinking and create new paths for others to follow. These women embraced the power of their dreams and dared to be different.

We are certain that the fascinating women that you will encounter on the following pages will have a positive impact on your life. They will challenge you and encourage you. They will inspire you and grab at your heart. And they will be dynamic, shining examples in a world where the lights have dimmed around many of our heroes. It is our hope that you will be inspired by these role models to forge ahead and leave your mark on the world.

Pat & Ruth Williams
Orlando, Florida

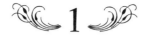

1

Rachael Ray
1968–

Enthusiasm

I don't want anything to separate me from
the viewers. I open the cans, I chop the onions myself,
and I wear street clothes. . . . I don't want people to look at
what I do and think that they can't do that too.
It's extremely important.

—RACHAEL RAY

Rachael Domenica Ray acknowledges that she has no formal culinary, business, broadcast, or writing training. But with her sheer determination, gutsy confidence, and passion for good food, Ray has built a cooking and media empire that reaches millions of loyal fans around the globe each day.

More than twenty million viewers watch her six television shows. More than five million copies of her cookbooks have been sold. Her bimonthly magazine has a circulation of one million.

Born the middle of three children on August 25, 1968, in Glens Falls, New York, Ray spent her first eight years in Cape Cod, Massachusetts. Her parents, James Claude Ray and Elsa Providenza Scuderi, owned four restaurants there. In 1976, the family moved to Lake George, New York, so Elsa could run several other restaurants.

Her early exposure to the restaurant business meant Ray encountered firsthand every aspect of food and hospitality service by the time she was ready for school. "My mother didn't like strangers watching her children, so we all were in the restaurants from the time we were born," Ray told *People* magazine. "We did every crap job there was—dishwasher, busgirl."

Despite the tough and gritty work involved, Ray became fascinated with the process of cooking. Every day, she watched as her mother or the restaurant cooks diced, chopped, marinated, and sautéed. She spent time with her father as he meticulously prepared the Cajun food he had grown up on. On Sundays, she watched carefully as her maternal grandfather, Emmanuel Scudari, gathered the extended family of twelve at his house and cooked specialties from his native Sicily.

The principle ingredient in her family's kitchens was enthusiasm, and Ray absorbed a crucial message: cooking should be easy, and it should be fun. "I was raised in a household that taught us that everybody has the right to have a lot of fun," she told writer Beverly Keel for *American Profile*.

She also soaked up the techniques they used to get the food on the table fast. Rather than measure out ingredients precisely, her mother and grandfather often happily improvised measurements while quickly pulling a meal together. They incorporated precooked, leftover, canned, or frozen foods into recipes to keep preparation simple.

They also encouraged the children to help, even if it resulted in mistakes or injuries. During her first kitchen foray at age three or four, Ray tried to emulate her mother's swift movements with a spatula "and I ended up grilling my thumb," she recalled in a Food Network biography. The experience only fired her determination to learn more.

After graduating from Lake George High School in Albany, New York, in 1986, Ray attended college. She had food on the brain, however, and decided real-life experience in restaurants suited her better than classroom theory. Eager for a big-city opportunity, she decamped in the early 1990s to New York City.

She landed a job at Macy's Marketplace helming the candy counter, but her hard work soon had her moving up to become the fresh-foods department manager. Two years later, armed with management experience, Ray left Macy's to become a manager and buyer at gourmet marketplace Agata & Valentina.

Ray engaged customers with her enthusiasm and breezy conversational style. To find out what they liked and didn't like about the store's offerings, she asked them directly and then listened intently.

But Ray yearned for the slower pace of upstate New York. After going through a bad personal breakup and getting mugged twice in one week—once in front of her apartment—Ray decided it was time to head home. She rented a cabin on three remote acres in the Adirondacks to make sure she had the peace she wanted.

Ray was confident that she wanted to stay in the food industry, so she took a series of local jobs, both to pay her $550 a month rent and to garner a solid array of experiences. She managed various pubs and the restaurant at Sagamore Resort in Lake George, ran food demonstrations at Price Chopper stores, and then took a job at the upscale Cowan & Lobel market as a buyer.

She kept careful tabs on trends and stocked the shelves at Cowan & Lobel with high-end, gourmet products that weren't widely available elsewhere and that she was sure customers would love—except these products weren't moving as fast as the premade chicken and pasta meals Ray cooked up herself and stocked in the deli case. What was up with that?

Ray loves a challenge. How could she move the shelf stock? She went right to the source for the answer, asking customers why they preferred the ready-made food. "They said they didn't have the time to cook or they didn't know how or they just didn't want to be bothered," Ray told the *Washington Post*'s Candy Sagon.

Ray's own early kitchen adventures sparked an idea—if she could learn, why couldn't others? She decided to use the products on the shelf for in-store cooking classes; she could both boost product sales and create a niche other stores didn't have. The focus? Easy and delicious meals customers could cook at home in less time than it took to have dinner delivered.

Her sincere zeal helped Ray sell the classes quickly, but she didn't have anyone to teach them. Making the rounds of local restaurants didn't help, either; her boss wouldn't pay enough to entice a trained chef to take on the job. Too bad, he told Ray—she'd have to do it herself.

Ray's first reaction was fear. She had never taught a cooking class. She didn't have a culinary degree. But a challenge means opportunity to Ray, so she went home and started researching. Digging through her own recipes, she looked for simple but tasty dishes that required little preparation.

I think she sees opportunity and goes for it.

—Doralece Dullaghan,
director of promotions for
Sur La Table

She decided to focus on Mediterranean-style dishes: they were healthy, they were usually the best-selling prepared foods at the grocery, and they cooked up in less than a half hour. She put together a three-hour class that yielded thirty dishes—six basic recipes that could each be prepared five different ways.

For the first class, Ray decided to stick with an approach she knew: warm, chatty, energetic, and casual. She talked throughout the demonstrations to encourage students and put them at ease, offering frequent tips she'd learned from her family and from watching the pros in restaurant kitchens. She laughed with students and poked fun at herself, keeping the mood lighthearted and positive. Her style proved to be a winner, and moms, scout groups, newlyweds, neighborhood groups, and senior citizens lined up for the classes.

The biggest demand was for Ray's thirty-minute meal classes, which often sold out. Their popularity snared the attention of a local newspaper and then Albany's WRGB-TV, where producers asked her to do a weekly "30-Minute Meals" segment on the evening news.

Confident she'd developed a winning formula in her cooking classes, Ray eagerly agreed. To make the point that her approach was different, she wanted to give her segment a unique hook. So instead of just whipping up a dish in the studio like every other TV chef, Ray decided to take her show to the audience—literally.

She hauled a television crew to a different location each week—a private home in the Albany area, a senior center, a firehouse, a college dorm—and showed the real people who lived there how to put a home-cooked meal on the table in half an hour.

During taping, she'd rattle off tips she'd relied on for years: use bagged baby carrots instead of wasting time peeling the large kind; try slicing chicken breasts while they're still partly frozen because they're easier to cut. They were all delivered with a toothy grin, frequent laughter, and a self-deprecating manner. She was unashamed about using boxed ingredients to speed up the process.

While the segment was taped, Ray refused to reshoot anything, to make sure it kept its straightforward, relaxed feel. If she burned a piece of meat, dropped her ingredients, or messed up a dish, she giggled through it and kept going.

She underscored the casual feel by generously sprinkling her narration with catchphrases she'd long made her own: "EVOO" for extra-virgin olive oil, "sammies" for sandwiches, "easy peasy" for a singularly simple technique. She shrugged off formal methods, urging the people she visited and viewers to just "run a knife through" whatever food needed cutting. "How cool is that?" she'd say when an item turned out well, or "What's up with that?" if it failed.

Ray's segments weren't scripted, but her delivery wasn't completely off-hand. Ray deliberately played up her average-goofy/cute-girl-next-door persona to connect with her audience and persuade them they could cook the same way she did. The segments pulled in more viewers, and Ray snared two regional Emmy awards.

Ray had nailed a niche—busy, frazzled people who wanted to cook but didn't have the time, knowledge, or confidence to do it. While gratified by the Emmys, Ray thought she could do more. Aware that her brief segments only reached a limited number of people, Ray decided to broaden her message and create more opportunities for herself.

In 1998, Ray gathered up her photocopied recipes and contacted Hiroko Kiifner, owner of independent publisher Lake Isle Press in Manhattan. Ray poured on the enthusiasm about her cooking approach and talked up her recent success. Then she pitched an unusual idea—why not do a cookbook and then sell it only in area grocery stores?

Her gutsy proposal persuaded Kiifner, and *30-Minute Meals* came out during the holiday shopping rush. In ten days, the book sold ten thousand copies.

Commitment and hard work are two of Ray's hallmarks, and her book's quick success didn't mean she was about to kick back. Instead, Ray kept running classes and demonstrations wherever she could to keep the momentum going. In 2000, a producer from NBC's *Today Show* read Ray's cookbook and invited her to come down to Manhattan to appear on the show and cook soup with its anchors.

The night before she was scheduled to appear, a heavy snowstorm hit upstate New York. Determined to make the appearance, Ray drove nine hours through heavy drifts to get to the studio. She made the soup in record time, her trademark wide grin never leaving her face.

The next day, Food Network came calling. The president had seen the *Today Show* spot and wanted Ray to come aboard for a national show.

Excited but nervous that she couldn't compare to the network's star chefs, the forthright Ray laid her cards on the table. She didn't want any misconceptions. "When I first heard from Food Network, I told them I was a beer in a bottle and they are champagne in a flute," she told *Investor's Business Daily*. The network was glad to hear it—and offered her a $360,000 contract.

> *This thing took on a life of its own. . . . It's my job to keep working because now there is this thing that people depend on.*
>
> —RACHAEL RAY

In 2002, *30 Minute Meals* debuted on the Food Network. She stuck to her format, keeping the show unscripted and relaxed. She still told stories about her family and friends. She still did all the chopping, opening, and struggling with packages, so viewers could see that the dishes really could be made quickly from start to finish. She refused to let a food stylist prepare items for the show: Ray wanted her dishes to look exactly as she made them—even if they were ugly.

The show was an immediate hit. Ray's instinct about just being herself on screen was further validated during the first of her several meetings with television megastar Oprah Winfrey, who told her to "be true to yourself and stay true to yourself," Ray said to *Investors' Business Daily*.

Recognizing the chance of a lifetime, Ray stretched to build her brand. And every time she met one goal, she set a new one. She expanded her TV offerings to six shows: Food Network's *30 Minute Meals, $40 a Day, Tasty Travels, Inside Dish,* and *Rachael's Vacation,* as well as her syndicated talk show *Rachael Ray.* She effuses on each show with her trademark patter but takes a slightly different focus so that viewers can look forward to a new angle. She added each show only after making sure the previous one was a hit. A total of more than twenty million viewers tune in to watch what she will do next.

You've got a great personality. . . . That's why you're such a hit. People like you.
—OPRAH WINFREY

She's churned out a stack of cookbooks that have sold more than five million copies in multiple languages. In 2005, she started a bimonthly magazine, *Every Day with Rachael Ray,* that has a circulation of one million.

The entrepreneurial Ray also sells knives, appliances, and cookware. Many of her products come out of her own cooking experience. For example, Ray designed an oval-shaped pot that comfortably handles spaghetti and fettuccine because she hated struggling trying to fit long pasta into a round pot.

Yet all of Ray's successes don't seem to impress a group of her detractors. They see her perky, amateur style as insulting and demoralizing to serious cooks and professional chefs. They shudder at her catchphrases and made-up words such as "yum-o." They ridicule her directions to viewers, such as using "half a palm-full" of an ingredient. They trash her on the Internet as a glib product of TV marketing, calling her names and spreading rumors about her personal and professional life.

Ray ignores the critics and keeps on working. To keep up with her varied projects, she sleeps just five hours a night. She constantly tests recipes, coming up with some six hundred new ones a year for her shows and cookbooks. She writes four columns for each edition of her magazine. She travels often and meets frequently with staffers from each of her ventures. She writes out her schedule daily in a small notebook to stay organized. And always, she keeps her audience's tastes in mind.

"The recipes I write are not always for my own taste," she told Keel. "Not everybody is interested in what I'm interested in. You have to have a small ego to write effective, everyday recipes. You can have a big ego and be a great chef, but that's not my job. It's my job to teach people and appeal to all different lifestyles, age groups and backgrounds."

Aware that work doesn't define a whole person, Ray also makes time to help others. In 2007, she founded the Yum-o! organization to help schools improve cafeteria food, create scholarships, educate parents about healthy food, and feed needy children. The foundation has already teamed with the Alliance for a Healthier Generation—an effort started by former President Bill Clinton and the American Heart Association—to improve school food.

Ray seeded the organization with $750,000 of her own money and plans to continue funding it. Following Paul Newman's model, she's currently developing products, including children's cookware and books, all profits from which will go to the foundation.

"She's a machine," Doralece Dullaghan, the director of promotions for Sur La Table, told the *New York Times.* "I think she's one of those for-the-moment people who never stops working."

Yet Ray understands the importance of balance. When she finds herself too stressed or exhausted, she heads up to her cabin in the Adirondacks (she bought it after signing her first Food Network contract) for some relaxation with family.

"My rule is that whenever I have off 36 hours or more, I go to my home upstate," she told Keel. "I like being home. I like a cozy life. The sky is darker, the stars are brighter, and things make more sense to me when I'm in the middle of the woods. You can play your music as loud as you want and nobody bugs you."

[Ray] has radically changed the way America cooks dinner. Her perky-girl-next-door swagger, her catchphrases for techniques and her dinner ideology of simpler, less expensive and just in time have sold [millions] of books and placed her at the top of the talent love heap at the Food Network, which has changed its focus from information exchange to helpful encouragement.

—Mario Batali, chef and author

Once she catches her breath, though, Ray resumes her busy schedule to keep her momentum. Her hard work has resulted in significant rewards: according to *Forbes* magazine, all Ray's ventures earned her an estimated $16 million in 2007. Yet she remains down-to-earth and dedicated.

Ray credits her mother for her inspiration and her motivation. Elsa often worked 80 to 100 hours a week, all while caring for her children. Though she's retired now, her mother handles all of Ray's fan mail and helps run her foundation.

"If anything, I'm a poor knockoff of her," Ray said of her mother to the *New*

York Times. Her strong relationship with her mother isn't an anomaly—Ray keeps close ties with all her family. It's clear they ground her. She cites her stonecutter grandfather—he of the Sunday meals that fed twelve—as another of her strongest influences and speaks glowingly of her father, sister, and brother as well. Her husband, attorney and musician John Cusimano, accompanies Ray to many of her location shoots and handles all her legal affairs. She also relies on her family to critique her work, frequently referring to them on her shows and in her books as her "research team."

Entertainment can be a tough business, so Ray depends on not only family but also trusted friends and employees to help her stay on an even keel. She spends time with girlfriends from her hometown. The makeup artist who works all of Ray's shows and appearances is one of her closest friends. She hired her public relations representative after befriending her: they met because Ray's PR rep is married to an old college friend of her agent.

Ray is loyal in return. She annually helps host a benefit for her high school. She's known to hurry to help a friend in need. She flew her family and about one hundred friends to Italy for her wedding to Cusimano, and a year later, flew them all to a resort to celebrate the couple's first anniversary.

"Her blend of dedication, hard work, humor, market awareness, and a keen eye for opportunity has made Ray one of the most appealing chefs ever," says Mario Batali, chef, restaurant owner, author, fellow Food Network star, and friend of Ray's. "She understands what people want, and she delivers."

"It's true that [Ray] dresses like a suburban American—not a chef," Batali told *Time* magazine. "[But] that is key. And her ease with basic kitchen techniques and a simple-to-find-in-Topeka ingredient list does not challenge viewers but entices them to join her in the famous 'carry the stuff from the fridge to the counter' move with her anti-food-stylist packaged groceries.' The promise of a meal in less than 30 minutes is

> *My life has been a total accident—a very happy, wonderful accident that I didn't and couldn't have planned.*
>
> —Rachael Ray

delivered every day and is calculated to hit all those who ever had a family or thought of having one, coaxing them to eschew the trap of fast-food facility and truly cook—even the easy fast stuff—at home."

But Ray thinks the real appeal is that she's an example of what you can do when you set your mind to it. "If I can do it," she says, "so can you if you only believe in yourself."

"I'm the everyperson," she told *Investors Business Daily*. "I'm very klutzy. I'm not a trained chef. I'm not a five-star traveler. I am a decent representative of what anybody could achieve in a kitchen or in their travels. Anyone can do it."

How to Be Like Rachael Ray

1) **Know your strengths.** Ray has no formal culinary, business, broadcast, or writing training, but that hasn't stopped her from building a cooking and media empire. Her strengths are her determination, confidence, and passion for good food.

2) **Have fun with what you do.** Ray does. The principle ingredient in her family's kitchens was enthusiasm, and Ray absorbed a crucial message: cooking should be easy, and it should be fun. "I was raised in a household that taught us that everybody has the right to have a lot of fun."

3) **Pay attention to trends.** Working as a buyer for the upscale market Cowan & Lobel, Ray discovered that her premade chicken and pasta meals were selling faster than anything else. She went right to the source to find out the reason, asking customers why they preferred the ready-made food. Her customers told her that they didn't have the time to cook or didn't know how or just didn't want to be bothered. That was the genesis of the staple of Ray's future empire, her thirty-minute meals.

4) **Be genuine.** It's one of the reasons Ray connects with her audience. While taping her weekly "30-Minute Meals" segment on the evening news in upstate New York, Ray refused to reshoot anything to make sure the segment kept its straightforward, relaxed feel. If she burned a piece of meat, dropped her ingredients, or messed up a dish, she giggled through it and kept going.

Ray further underscored the casual feel by generously sprinkling her narration with catchphrases she'd long made her own: "EVOO" for extra-virgin olive oil, "sammies" for sandwiches, "easy peasy" for a singularly simple technique. She shrugged off formal methods, urging the people she visited and viewers to just "run a knife through" whatever food needed cutting. "How

Cont'd

cool is that?" she'd say when an item turned out well, or, "What's up with that?" if it failed.

When the *Food Network* gave Ray her own show, Ray stuck to her format, keeping the show unscripted and relaxed. She did all the chopping, opening, and struggling with packages as she had always done so viewers could see that the dishes really could be made quickly from start to finish.

5) **Give back.** Ray founded the nonprofit organization Yum-o! in 2007 with an initial donation of $750,000. Teamed with the Alliance for a Healthier Generation, Yum-o! is dedicated to helping schools improve cafeteria food, educating parents about healthy food, and feeding children in need. Profits from products she is developing, such as children's cookware and books, will go to the foundation.

6) **Recharge your batteries.** Everybody has their own way of doing it. For Ray, it's heading up to her cabin in the Adirondacks. "I like a cozy life. The sky is darker, the stars are brighter, and things make more sense to me when I'm in the middle of the woods. You can play your music as loud as you want and nobody bugs you."

7) **Ignore destructive criticism and mean-spirited people.** As with anyone in the public spotlight, Ray has her detractors. She is criticized for everything from her perky style to her catchphrases and made-up words. She is routinely trashed on the Internet and a frequent subject of the gossip mills. How does Ray respond to such critics? She ignores them and keeps on working.

8) **Stay humble and grounded.** Ray keeps perspective on her success. By all accounts success hasn't changed her. According to *Forbes* magazine, Ray earned an estimated $16 million in 2007, yet she is down-to-earth, values her family and friends, and remains dedicated to her fans. "I never said I was the greatest thing ever. I just think people should be able to cook even if they don't have a bunch of time or money."

Barbara Jordan
1936–1996

Trailblazer

We live in this world in order to contribute
to the growth, the development, the spirit and the
life of the community of humankind.

—BARBARA JORDAN

On a July day in 1974, Americans were riveted by the sight of an African-American woman chastising the president of the United States for violating principles of the Constitution. The Civil Rights Act outlawing segregation had been passed just a decade earlier. Yet there sat freshman Congresswoman Barbara Jordan, eloquently articulating how President Richard Nixon's actions constituted the kind of "high crimes and misdemeanors" that constituted impeachable offenses.

Jordan was a member of the House Judiciary Committee, which was investigating Nixon's role in the Watergate scandal. Her powerful, reasoned remarks riveted the nation.

"My faith in the Constitution is whole. It is complete. It is total," she said. "I am not going to sit here and be an idle spectator to the diminution, the subversion, the destruction of the Constitution."

Nixon resigned days later.

Newsweek called Jordan's speech "the most memorable indictment of Richard Nixon to emerge from the House impeachment." Democratic strategist Ann Lewis told *USA Today* that Jordan "was the voice of moral authority."

Barbara wasn't really that concerned about the guilt or innocence of Nixon. . . . She was most concerned that the Constitution not be distorted for political reasons.

—CONGRESSMAN CHARLES B. RANGEL

Growing up in a poor, segregated, Houston ghetto, Jordan had overcome entrenched racial prejudice and sexism to become one of the most influential women in the United States. An outsider who was taken seriously by insiders, Jordan impressed supporters and detractors alike with her integrity, dignity, and commitment to upholding the values of the Constitution.

She was the first African-American to serve in the Texas State Senate since Reconstruction, the first African-American woman from the South to be elected to Congress, and the first African-American to deliver a keynote address at a party nominating convention. In 1984, Jordan received the Eleanor Roosevelt Humanities Award. The same year, she was voted "Best Living Orator" by the International Platform Association and elected to the Texas Women's Hall of Fame. She was awarded the Medal of Freedom by President Clinton in 1994.

It was just two years after the Watergate hearings that Jordan again electrified the nation with her majestic oratory when she delivered the keynote address at the Democratic National Convention.

"My presence here is one additional bit of evidence that the American Dream need not be forever deferred," she declared. The Democratic Party, she said, had "a positive vision of the future founded on the belief that the gap between the promise and reality of America can one day be finally closed."

In her biography *Barbara Jordan: American Hero,* author Mary Beth Rogers described Jordan's impact on the nation: "Barbara Jordan became a symbol of everything that was right about America at a time when so much seemed so wrong."

Jordan's faith in her own abilities and in the promise of America enabled her to open doors previously closed to those of her gender and skin color.

She was one of only two African-American women in her freshman class at Boston University Law School. There, she discovered that the schooling she had received in her all-black public schools and college did not measure up to the education received by her white peers. "I realized that my deprivation had been stark. . . . I realized that . . . separate was not equal; it just wasn't." This realization—and the desire to remedy it— fueled Jordan's political career.

After three terms in Congress, Jordan gave up what some might see as the trappings of power and retired from public office to become a teacher at the Lyndon B. Johnson School of Public Affairs at the University of Texas at Austin.

"I felt more of a responsibility to the country as a whole, as contrasted with the duty of representing the half-million people in the Eighteenth Congressional District," she said in her autobiography, *Barbara Jordan: A Self-Portrait.* "I thought that my role now was to be one of the voices in the country defining where we were, where we were going, what the policies were that were being pursued, and where the holes in those policies were."

In the academic setting, Jordan felt she could better influence the next generation of leaders. She told *Newsweek,* "I want my students to be premier public servants who have a core of principles to guide them. They are my future, and the future of this country."

Jordan faced numerous health problems and died at the age of fifty-nine. More than fifteen hundred people packed the church for her funeral, and hundreds more listened outside in the drizzling rain as speakers—including then President Bill Clinton—paid tribute. Former Republican Texas Governor Ann Richards summed up Jordan's life: "There was simply something about her that made you proud to be a part of the country that produced her."

Jordan had served as special counsel on ethics in Governor Richards's administration from 1991 to 1995.

Born on February 21, 1936, in Houston, Texas, Barbara Charline Jordan was the third of three daughters. Her father, Benjamin Jordan, was a laborer and Baptist preacher. Her mother, Arlyne Patten Jordan, cleaned houses. Both of Jordan's parents were well-known orators in their church, the Good Hope Missionary Baptist Church, and this skill would become one of their daughter's greatest attributes.

From birth, Jordan was encouraged to achieve, and she had numerous extended family members who served as examples. She was delivered by her cousin, Dr. Thelma Patten, the first black female physician in Houston. Her great-grandfather, Edward Patten, served as the only black member of the Texas House of Representatives from 1891 to 1893.

But the two people who had the greatest influence on young Jordan were her grandfather John Ed Patten, and her father, Benjamin Jordan. John Ed Patten had been convicted of trumped-up charges of assault and intent to murder. His unfair treatment by the Houston legal system was the first example Jordan was to witness of the double standards that applied to whites and blacks. Despite this negative experience, Patten maintained a strong self-image and tried to instill a similar sense of confidence and competence in his granddaughter.

Patten ran a junk business. While her sisters were busy with the Baptist Young People's Union, Jordan would spend afternoons helping her grandfather sort rags, papers, and scrap iron. He would read to Jordan and encourage her to "travel up from segregation."

He also discouraged his granddaughter from being like some of the other children in their neighborhood. "You just trot your own horse and don't get into the same rut as everyone else," he told her, according to Jordan's autobiography. And he made her memorize another adage that she would come to live by: "Just remember the world is not a playground, but a schoolroom. Life is not a holiday but an education. One eternal lesson for us all: to teach us how better we should love."

Jordan's father, Benjamin, insisted that his daughters "think, get good grades and speak properly," according to Laura S. Jeffrey, author of *Barbara Jordan: Congresswoman, Lawyer, Educator.* "He valued God, the Bible, his family, good music and the spoken and written word. He taught Jordan that race and poverty had nothing to do with her brain power or her ability to achieve lofty goals if she had the drive to work for them," Jeffrey wrote.

Jordan echoed his sentiment years later when she explained why she chose to work within the system to bring about change in the treatment of African-Americans in the United States. "Do not call for black power or green power," she said. "Call for brain power."

From her mother, Jordan learned the power of the spoken word. "She was the most eloquent, articulate person I ever heard; if she'd been a man, she would have been a preacher," Jordan said. Her grandfather also boosted Jordan's speaking abilities by reading to her from a pronunciation dictionary.

Jordan's gift for oratory soon became apparent at Phillis Wheatley High School in Houston. In 1952, she became Girl of the Year, placed first in the state Ushers Oratorical Contest, and won a trip to Chicago, where she won the national contest.

On "Career Day," a female African-American lawyer from Chicago spoke at Jordan's high school. Fourteen-year-old Jordan was so impressed, she decided right then to make law her profession. Later, Jordan would recall the decision: "I believed I was going to be a lawyer, or rather something called a lawyer, but I had no fixed notion of what that was."

After graduating from high school, Jordan attended Texas Southern University, an all-black college in Houston, where she was a star debater under debate coach Tom Freeman. Her team won many contests, and Jordan was particularly proud that their match against Harvard University was declared a tie.

In traveling with the team, however, Jordan became aware of prejudice and discrimination in the larger world. Until then, she had operated in an exclusively black milieu. The new experience was sobering.

In the Deep South, blacks could not find a public restroom to use, and they had to go to the back door of a restaurant to ask for a meal. Things were a little better in the North. "We could at least go in front doors to get something to eat. That was the main point: We could go in the front door," she said.

When Rosa Parks refused in 1955 to give up her seat on a city bus in Montgomery, Alabama, to a white person, it sparked organized boycotts of city buses and other civil disobedience actions. Watching these events, Jordan believed that integration could be achieved with less racial discord

The imperative is to if blacks proved they could make it in a "white man's
do what is right. world."

—BARBARA JORDAN   That became her goal. Jordan wanted to attend
Harvard Law School, which she felt was the best university in the country. Knowing that life at Harvard would not be pleasant for a black girl from a little-known southern college, Jordan's debate coach, Tom Freeman, encouraged her to apply to Boston University Law School instead.

She did and was accepted in 1956. At Boston University, Jordan discovered that she had not received the same education as her white peers. She spent a lot of time catching up. "I was doing sixteen years of remedial work in thinking," she recalled.

In law school, the work ethic she learned from her father served her well. Each night, she would stay up studying in an upstairs room of the graduate dormitory. "I didn't get much sleep during those years," she said. "I was lucky if I got three or four hours a night, because I had to stay up. I had to."

I had ambition, and The hard work paid off, and Jordan
I've always been willing to received her law degree in 1959. She passed
work, however many hours a the Massachusetts and Texas bar examina-
day would be required tions that same year.
for me to work.

          —BARBARA JORDAN   Jordan returned to Texas and opened a private law practice, working from her parents' dining room table. Eventually, she was able to open an office downtown. To supplement her income, she also worked as an administrative assistant to a county judge.

During the Kennedy campaign, Jordan volunteered to help appeal to the predominantly black precincts of Harris County. One night, when a Democratic speaker called in sick, Jordan was asked to address a local African-American church in his place. She electrified the audience with her deep voice, dignified manner, and heartfelt message.

"I was startled with the impact I had on people," said Jordan. "Those people were just as turned on and excited as if some of the head candidates had been there to talk about the issues. When I got back to the local headquarters that night . . . they said, 'We're going to have to . . . put you on the speaking circuit.'"

Jordan's efforts on Kennedy's behalf helped secure an 80 percent voter turnout. Her political career had begun.

With the civil rights movement in full swing, Jordan wanted to be part of the process of creating a truly integrated society. She felt politics was the best way to achieve this and ran for office in the Texas State House of Representatives. She lost two campaigns before winning a seat in the Texas Senate in 1966. This made her the first African-American woman ever to be elected to the Texas Senate, and the first African-American to serve since the Reconstruction period.

A former editorial writer for the *Houston Chronicle* was quoted in *Ebony* as saying, "If one wanted to think up the three handicaps with which one could enter a know-nothing, reactionary state senate of those days, it would be a person of liberal persuasion, a woman and a Black. Yet her intelligence and her commanding personality got her to the point where she had the Senate eating out of her hand."

Jordan was fully aware that her new colleagues might be wary of the only African-American and only woman in an otherwise all-white, all-male legislature. "There was some feeling that I would come in with bombast, mount the stump and curse the system. So I came in quietly. I attended the committee meetings, studied the legislation [and] developed professional friendships among senior members who felt most threatened by my presence. I gained their confidence. I singled out the most influential and powerful members and was determined to gain their respect."

Jordan said it was logical for blacks to want change given the oppression that marked their history in America, but that change is expressed in many different ways. She always chose substance over style. "I went to [the state legislature] to work, not to crusade," she said.

I have a tremendous amount of faith in my own capacity. I know how to read and write and think, so I have no fear.

—Barbara Jordan

In office, Jordan showed the same qualities that had served her well in school. "You work and you learn the rules and you keep your mouth shut until it is time to open it."

She worked on legislation to relieve the downtrodden, including the state's first minimum wage law, which encompassed provisions covering domestic workers, farm laborers, and laundry workers. She also sponsored much of Texas's environmental legislation and made the state place antidiscrimination clauses in all of its business contracts. Thanks to her political savvy and willingness to work with her colleagues, half the bills she submitted were enacted into law.

By this time in her career, Jordan had attracted the attention of the Democratic Party as well as President Lyndon B. Johnson, who invited her to the White House for a preview of his 1967 Civil Rights Message. He was to become a close political mentor and friend.

While Johnson's great and tragic failing was the Vietnam conflict, he was a giant in the area of civil rights. Jordan said: "Old men straightened their stooped backs because Lyndon Johnson lived; little children dared look forward to intellectual achievement because he lived; black Americans became excited about a future of opportunity, hope, justice, and dignity. Lyndon Johnson was my political mentor and my friend."

Her colleagues elected Jordan Outstanding Freshman Senator, the resolution reading in part: "[Jordan] has earned the esteem and respect of her fellow senators by the dignified manner in which she has conducted herself while serving in the legislature, and because of her sincerity, her genuine concern for others." In 1972, she was given the honor of "Governor for a Day," technically making her the first black woman governor of any state.

In 1972, after being elected to Congress, Jordan asked Johnson for advice. He recommended that she try to become a member of the House Judiciary Committee. Although he was no longer president by this time, Johnson helped secure Jordan's spot on the committee.

In an *Ebony* article entitled "Barbara Jordan: Texan Is a New Power on Capitol Hill," writer Charles Sanders describes Jordan's effectiveness as a politician:

> *She not only dazzled [members of the Texas delegation] with her intellectual brilliance but also with her knowledge of their kind of rough-and-tumble politics. . . . She never permitted the men of the "club" to feel uncomfortable around her. She could smoke and drink Scotch—just like them. She could tone down her Boston University kind of speech and talk Texas lingo—just like them. She knew as much as they did, or more,*

*about such things as oil depletion allowances and cotton prices and the
Dallas money market, but she never, says one member of the "club," made
men "feel like we had a smart-aleck, know-it-all woman on our hands."*

He added, "Now Barbara doesn't try to play possum on you; she doesn't
mind letting you know that she's got a very, very high I.Q. But she doesn't
embarrass you by making you feel that you're nowhere close to being as
smart as she is. It's an amazing thing how she can be standing there schooling you about something and still make you feel that you knew all that
right along."

In the same article, Texas Congressman Charles Wilson is quoted:

*In my view, Barbara Jordan is the most influential member of
Congress. If you're talking about the one person who is able to get just
about anybody . . . [to] stop and listen to what she has to say and convince
them that she's right, then you're talking about Barbara. . . . So what
makes Barbara so special? It's that along with her superior intelligence and
legislative skill, she also has a certain moral authority and a . . . presence,
and it all comes together in a way that sort of grabs you. . . . It's something
that God gave her, and it's something you really can't describe.*

The Watergate scandal erupted soon
after Jordan was elected to Congress, and
the Judiciary Committee took up the
matter of whether President Nixon
should be impeached. In a fifteen-minute
nationally televised speech, Jordan spoke
of the duty of elected officials to defend
the Constitution, and using her skills as a
lawyer, presented her argument detailing
how the Nixon administration had abdi-

*As we began to get into
impeachment she was articulate,
balanced, not extremist.
She began to display the ability
to be concise and precise,
but not aggressive.*

—SENATOR PETER RODINO ON
JORDAN DURING THE WATERGATE HEARINGS

cated those duties. On August 9, 1974, before the Committee made its
final decision, Nixon resigned.

Jordan's reputation as one of the great orators of the twentieth century
was cemented when she delivered the keynote address at the Democratic

National Convention in 1976. "We cannot improve on the system of government handed down to us by the founders of the Republic," she said in her deep, resonant voice. "But what we can do is to find new ways to implement the system and realize our destiny."

After the disillusionment caused by Watergate, Jordan offered a more hopeful vision of what leaders should be: "Those of us who are public servants must set examples. If we promise, we must deliver. If we propose, we must produce. If we ask for sacrifice, we must be the first to give. If we make mistakes, we must be willing to admit them."

She concluded her remarks by quoting Abraham Lincoln. "'As I would not be a slave, so I would not be a master.' This expresses my idea of democracy. Whatever differs from this, to the extent of the difference, is no democracy."

Pundits and the public alike called for Jordan to be named as Jimmy Carter's vice presidential candidate. "It's not my turn," she said. "You'll know when it's my turn."

Carter appeared to be considering appointing Jordan to the post of Health, Education, and Welfare secretary. Jordan seemed to want to be appointed Attorney General. In the end, she was not included in the Carter Cabinet.

She was, however, reelected to the House and continued to serve through 1978. She retired after serving three terms in Congress.

Jordan then returned to Texas as a full professor at the Lyndon B. Johnson School of Public Affairs, teaching political values and ethics. Her classes, which presented public service as the highest purpose of government work, became so popular that students had to be admitted by lottery.

She sought to both educate and inspire students who were considering political careers: "I tell them, don't expect to get rich—the public does not pay its servants a great deal of money. Go do this job because you want the government to run well and you think you can help it run well. And . . . if ever you decide you want to get rich then get out of government, because if you don't, I'll visit you in jail."

Her students fondly called her "BJ" and remember her as always carrying a copy of the Constitution in her purse.

"When I leave these classes, I'm just—I'm on the ceiling," she said. "And all I want to do is talk about what went on in class and how my students responded."

Jordan was committed to helping young people fulfill their roles in America's destiny. In an interview in Brian Lanker's book *I Dream a World: Portraits of Black Women Who Changed America,* Jordan said, "I am telling the young people that if you're dissatisfied . . . with the way things are, then you have got to resolve to change them. . . . It is a burden of black people that we have to do more than talk. We have somehow got to sacrifice our lives as an example to move young people along so that they will understand that it is a long, slow, tough road to really make it so that it lasts. I have got to offer myself as a role model to others so that perhaps something in my life will help move a young black person who might otherwise drop out to stay in school. That is part of my mission."

Speaking to high school students in Tennessee, Jordan said, "The American Dream is not dead. . . . Refuse to accept your present conditions as a permanent condition. . . . Believe that change is possible. . . . Believe in yourself first. . . . Recast the American Dream and make it yours. African/Black Americans are neither strangers nor guests here. This is our country, and we fully intend to make it work for us."

Jordan received more than twenty honorary doctorates. One of those was from Harvard, the school she refrained from applying to out of concern for its then unreceptive climate for a young black female student.

Jordan had learned back in 1973 that she had multiple sclerosis. By 1978, she was using a wheelchair. This did not stop her from giving numerous speeches and serving on corporate, governmental, and nonprofit boards. She repeated her role as Democratic National Convention keynote speaker in 1992, affirming that "America's strength is rooted in

If we are successful, we are going to make character the Number One call of young people in this country. They are going to think before they act because they know that if they do the wrong thing, that there are consequences, and they may not like these consequences. Kids must now understand that they are responsible for their actions . . . [and adults] are responsible for making sure that young people know what is expected of them.

—Barbara Jordan

its diversity." From 1994 to 1996, Jordan chaired President Bill Clinton's Commission on Immigration Reform.

Jordan died on January 17, 1996, from viral pneumonia caused by complications from leukemia. Shortly before her death, she summed up her life's mission: "We cannot stand to have, in a democracy, any significant portion of the people who do not have a voice in what happens to them. . . .We as a people, black, white, Asian, Hispanic, must keep scratching the surface until we get where we've got to be, and that's inclusiveness for all people."

How to Be Like Barbara Jordan

1) **Learn from role models.** Jordan was not only a great role model herself, but she benefited from examples in her own family. Although her grandfather, John Ed Patten, had been treated unfairly by the Houston legal system, he maintained his dignity and helped instill a similar sense of confidence and competence in his granddaughter. He read to Jordan and encouraged her to "travel up from segregation." He also made her memorize an adage that she would come to live by: "Just remember the world is not a playground, but a schoolroom. Life is not a holiday but an education. One eternal lesson for us all: to teach us how better we should love."

2) **Follow your passion.** Jordan was inspired when, as a fourteen-year-old, she heard a female African-American lawyer speak at her high school. She decided at that moment that she would become a lawyer.

   When she realized that she had not received as high quality an education as her white peers, she dedicated herself to remedying that situation for others. This became the catalyst for her political career. She felt politics was the best way to help create a truly integrated society.

   Jordan left elective office because of her passion for teaching young people the importance of selfless public service and social responsibility. "When I leave these classes, I'm just—I'm on the ceiling," she said. "And all I want to do is talk about what went on in class and how my students responded." Her classes became so popular that students had to be admitted by lottery.

3) **Never quit.** Jordan could have become discouraged after losing two elections in a row when she ran for a seat in the Texas House of Representatives. Instead, she ran for state senate and won.

Cont'd

4) **Pay your dues.** As the only African-American and only woman in an otherwise all-white, all-male legislature, Jordan began her legislative career quietly. Jordan gained her colleagues' respect and confidence by attending meetings, studying the legislation, and developing professional friendships among senior members. "You work and you learn the rules and you keep your mouth shut until it is time to open it," Jordan said.

5) **Set a dignified example.** This was the hallmark of Jordan's life and was illustrated by her remarks at the 1976 Democratic National Convention: "Those of us who are public servants must set examples. If we promise, we must deliver. If we propose, we must produce. If we ask for sacrifice, we must be the first to give. If we make mistakes, we must be willing to admit them."

6) **Be willing to work for your goals.** Jordan's father taught her that race and poverty had nothing to do with her ability to think or achieve lofty goals—if she had the drive to work for them. She followed his credo when she discovered that her education did not measure up to the education her white law school peers had received: "I was doing sixteen years of remedial work in thinking," she said. "I didn't get much sleep during those years. I was lucky if I got three or four hours a night, because I had to stay up. I had to."

7) **Refuse to accept a negative status quo.** Jordan was committed to helping young people fulfill their roles in America's destiny. "I am telling the young people that if you're dissatisfied . . . with the way things are, then you have got to resolve to change them."

As Jordan said to a group of high school students in Tennessee, "The American Dream is not dead. . . . This is our country, and we fully intend to make it work for us.

Danica Patrick
1982–

Fearless

I am living proof that if you work hard and aim high,
you can do whatever you set your mind to,
even if that makes you different.

—DANICA PATRICK

On April 20, 2008, Danica Patrick was a woman on a mission with something to prove. Her dedication, talent, and integrity had been doubted; she was determined more than ever to prove that women could race cars. Knowing that another loss would perpetuate the generalization that women are better off on the sidelines cheering rather than racing, she rose to the occasion. At the Indy Japan 300, in Motegi, Japan, Patrick accomplished something that no other woman had ever done in the world of auto racing—she became the first woman to win an IndyCar race.

"Hard work always pays off. Achieving a high level of success is a difficult process, but it is so worth the chance. Success doesn't just happen. You have to go out there and make it happen. If you sit around waiting for success, it'll never come," wrote Patrick in her autobiography, *Danica: Crossing the Line.*

For years, Patrick was criticized for attempting to break into a man's world. Critics gossiped that she was just another woman with a pretty face trying to do something meant for only males. Adding fuel to the fire was the fact that Patrick had never won a race. There was speculation that "the media frenzy that surrounded Patrick was completely unwarranted. Her perseverance, though, earned her a fourth place finish (the highest for a female driver) in the Indy 500, and she became the first female driver to lead a lap. Even then, people focused on her *Sports Illustrated* swimsuit shoot instead of her racing accomplishments. Finally, with Patrick's first-place win in Japan, she proved you can have it all: beauty, brains, and success.

I told her a long time ago that I thought a lot of her, and it's not because she's pretty. I respect her a lot more than some of the male drivers out here because she knows what she's doing on the track.

—HELIO CASTRONEVES

Growing up in Roscoe, Illinois, Patrick did not always have aspirations of getting into the male-dominated sport of racing. "She was a girlie girl," her mother, Bev, told Jill Inkrott of *Sports Illustrated.* "She didn't want grease under her fingernails." However, racing ran strong through her blood. "It's a good bet she inherited her need for speed," says neurologist Malcolm Stewart, medical director of the Human Lab at Presbyterian Hospital of Dallas. "She probably comes from a family of high dopamine producers."

Patrick came to the sport of racing naturally. Her parents met at a snowmobile race. As a child, she watched her father race snowmobiles and midgets and she went on frequent family outings to race go-karts. By the age of ten, young Danica knew there would be no other profession in her life than racing.

"Becoming a professional racecar driver is what I've worked for since the first day I sat behind the wheel of a go-kart in my hometown of Roscoe, Illinois," Patrick wrote. "I loved the feeling of driving—of being in control, of using my head and outsmarting the other drivers. From day one, I knew *this* was my calling, my destiny, my dream—and I knew that someday I would make it my dream come true."

Even though her brakes failed and she crashed into a concrete wall on her first ride, Patrick was not deterred. Instead, she began go-kart racing in 1992 at Sugar River Raceway in Wisconsin. At the beginning of her first race, the leaders lapped underdog Patrick six turns around the track. However, they had underestimated her talents. By the end of the twenty-two-race series, she stunned viewers by placing second and setting a new track record.

After her first success, she soon realized that not everyone was happy to see a girl triumph in what was considered by many to be a sport for boys. "It didn't take long for me to understand that being the only girl driver made me different, and my presence on the track would not always be welcomed with open arms. Almost imme-

Without bad days,
you can't appreciate the good.
Without defeat, you can't
appreciate victory. Being told
"no" should only be the
fuel to your fire.

—DANICA PATRICK

diately, the boys were intimidated by my success. Somehow I understood that this would be an ongoing battle and issue throughout my career. I didn't care. I adored what I was doing and was determined not to be deterred by their lack of enthusiasm or the teasing that would follow as I became a leader in karting."

By the age of sixteen Patrick had won three Grand National karting championships as she stayed focused of her big-picture dream. "The Indy 500 is the reason I started racing," she told ESPN. "The dream of winning this race has been my single focus since I was a kid. Through all the ups and downs, it's the one thing that kept me going."

It wouldn't be long until she started her drive down the long, arduous road to that dream. In 1998, she attended Track Speed School at Sebring International Speedway. She also attended two other driving schools, culminating in her driving a sedan at a Sports Car Club of America (SCCA) regional race at the Daytona International Speedway. The SCCA race, she told a reporter for the *Tampa Tribune,* was "the first step on the ladder in getting to Indy cars."

At sixteen, Patrick faced a difficult decision. John Mecom III, a team owner who has sponsored some of the biggest names in racing, including Mario Andretti, Graham Hill, A. J. Foyt, Roger Penske, Parnelli Jones,

Jackie Stewart, Rodger Ward, and Al Unser Sr., offered to sponsor her in England's Formula Vauxhall series. Knowing that her passion aligned with racing more than academics, Patrick decided to leave high school (she later completed her GED) and move to England to continue her training.

It's no secret in racing that to train with the best you travel to England. There, Patrick would learn one of the major lessons of her career: talent and drive are just the beginning; nothing comes easily. While sleeping on a living room couch at night and racing Formula Vauxhall during the day, Patrick would experience how taxing the profession could be. "I left home and went to England to make the leap from racing go-karts to driving Formula-style cars in the Formula Vauxhall circuit. . . . Bob Rahal refers to the Vauxhall and Formula Ford series as the 'equivalent of automotive gang warfare.' . . . It's a ruthless prep league for drivers from all over the world." Patrick adds, "This wasn't summer camp; it was boot camp— serious boot camp, Navy SEAL style."

Gentlemen, start your excuses! Quit your whining boys. Drive. Prove you're better or I will.

—Danica Patrick

Under great stress, Patrick became homesick. Things seemed to be taking a turn for the worse when she found herself once again fighting for respect in what felt like a boys-only club. "Being a girl described me, but it never defined me, at least not in my eyes," she wrote. The same wasn't true for everyone else, she discovered. British engineers and mechanics turned a cold shoulder, she said, employing a sink or swim mentality toward Patrick. Her ability to win a race was greatly tied to the amount of support she received from the engineers and mechanics. "They had little interest in seeing me break out as a driver. I would have been a 'frickin' girl' taking the place of one of the boys, and as I've said, racing in England was definitely a good ol' boys club."

According to Lars Anderson at *Inside Nascar*, this severely affected Patrick's mood. Attempting to fit in with the boys, she drank heavily in the pubs at night and gained weight. She got a reputation as a "party girl," and people began to question her dedication to racing. When rumors reached Mecom, he stopped funding her after one season. "I wasn't doing anything different than the guys were," Patrick says, "but because I was a girl, people started talking."

Despite the turmoil Patrick was dealing with, she knew that being in England was the best thing for her career. Her family had always been supportive of her career. Since the very beginning, both parents had been there to give advice. Patrick knew there would never be another career for her, and she knew how important it was to stay and train in England. So she asked her family for help, and with their support, she was able to remain in England for another two years.

England was not a total disaster, despite a bad first year and the overwhelming homesickness. Patrick earned second place in England's Formula Ford Festival. Not only was this the highest finish by a woman in the competition, but it was also the highest finish by an American. She came home a

Find what you're good at— do what you have a passion for. If you can make a living at it, you are among the luckiest people I know.

—DANICA PATRICK

winner, and she took what happened in England as an important life lesson. "My experience in England taught me how to deal with difficult people, characteristics, and circumstances. I learned whom I could trust and whom not to trust, and in the end one of my greatest lessons was learning you need to clear the path you walk on for yourself because no one else is really interested in clearing it for you."

Back in the United States, with her family financially tapped out and no racing sponsors, most critics thought Patrick's career was over. However, Patrick would remind us over and over again not to underestimate her. For some of the critics, this is the point where many people should just give up. But Danica Patrick's father taught her better than that, and she did not falter or quit.

Patrick and her father, T. J., started attending Indy races. As they followed the circuit from stop to stop in 2001, Patrick asked every owner in the garage for a chance to race, but no one gave it to her. Feeling sorry for the Patricks, owner Bobby Rahal, who had met Danica in England, let them hang out in his hospitality area whenever they were trackside. Then, before a race in Milwaukee in June 2002, Patrick got her big break. Never giving up, she popped the question once more to Rahal: "Will you let me drive for you?" Her persistence sparked a multiyear deal in 2002 to race for the team of Bobby Rahal, himself a former Indy 500 champion. She went on to compete in the Barber Dodge Pro Series and the Toyota Atlantic, finishing third in the Toyota Atlantic series in 2004.

It seemed as if Patrick would finally achieve her dreams on May 29, 2005, when she competed in the Indianapolis 500. What was especially monumental was that she was only the fourth woman in history to compete. This was more than just a chance for Patrick, this was the chance. This is what she had dreamed of since she first stepped into a go-kart. For Patrick, nothing but first place would do. "My dad taught me to never be satisfied with second place, and therefore I grew up believing you can always do better." Patrick was proving to the racing world she was a woman to be reckoned with.

During the race, it looked like Patrick was about to take first place. With nine laps left, she was leading and even pulling away from the field. But instead of first, she finished in a commendable fourth place. Under instructions from her pit crew, she had backed off the throttle to conserve fuel, allowing three cars to pass. Later, Patrick learned that she had 2.5 gallons of gas left at the end of that race. That 500, Lars Anderson wrote, was Patrick's to win. "Not going for the victory in '05 is the single greatest regret of my life," said Patrick. "I promise you I won't ever do that again. This year, I'm going for the win, no matter what."

Considering that fourth place was the highest a woman had ever reached in an Indy 500 up to that point, things were looking up for Patrick. However, with even minor success comes criticism. Some argued that her smaller size put her at an advantage in speed. Patrick argued that it might be true, but it is also true that male race car drivers make up for her speed in strength.

Then there were criticisms of a different kind: the daunting fact remained that she had not yet won a race. While her achievements should have garnered her some respect, many felt the only reason she was still around was because of her striking beauty. There was resentment from male drivers that she got the honor to grace the cover of *Sports Illustrated* in 2005. Furthermore, she was featured in a Secret Deodorant advertising campaign in 2005 and 2006, and she had a spot in a Honda Civic Coupe commercial. She even appeared in the Jay Z music video, *Show Me What You Got*. It seemed she was appearing just about everywhere in the media, which many male fans and racers attributed to her sex appeal and over-looked her talent.

Patrick realizes this is a result of being a female in a male-dominated sport. Yes, she will always be under the microscope because she is different, but she also sees this attention as positive. Sponsors want something different, so she gets noticed. Patrick says, "One of the most rewarding aspects of all the attention I've received . . . is showing the world that women can do anything, but it's not just about a woman competing in a male-dominated sport. It's about being the best at whatever you do, regardless of gender."

In July 2006, Patrick signed a deal to drive for Andretti Green Racing. Her first year with the new team was disappointing. It seemed as if with every step forward that came for Patrick, there was an eventual step back. In her first race with AGR at Homestead, she crashed into the pit wall on lap 15, sending her back to fourteenth place.

At the Milwaukee race, even though she had started second to last, she quickly moved up to fifth place. However, contact with competitor Dan Wheldon's car caused Danica to fall back to eighth place, the crash causing aerodynamic damage. Widespread coverage of the event caught on camera the heated exchange between Patrick and Wheldon after the race.

> *Her popularity has helped to grow the sport. We would not be as strong without her.*
>
> —Dan Wheldon

However, if there is one thing we can count on from Patrick, it is her ability to stand up for herself. Instead of letting the embarrassment bring her down, Patrick saw it as a way to empower herself. "I know my temper has gotten in the way from time to time, but I also know that as racers, we all have a responsibility to be careful on the track. I don't care if I am perceived as being rude—or a bitch. Let's face it: As the only girl out there racing, I am 'The Bitch' on the track whether I open my mouth or not! I have never cared what anyone else thinks or says about me."

Even though that first year with the Andretti Green racing team brought some successes (she scored her first three career podium finishes and had seventeen leading

> *She has fortune and fame, beauty and brains. She gives as good as she gets most times, powered by a ferocious competitive streak that doesn't care about stepping on toes.*
>
> —Dan Wetzel, Yahoo Sports

laps), critics still focused on her misfortunes. Again Patrick persevered. All the slipups and "almosts" were apparent during that first year: there was an accident in Nashville; her fuel troubles continued at the Michigan International Speedway; and in Kentucky, she spun out with less than fifty laps to go, only to have her tire blow, forcing her to give up the race.

However, her first year on the racing team was also a learning curve. According to Paul Newberry, her teammate Tony Kannan said she was eager to learn and work with her teammates. She was willing to listen and take the help she needed. For Patrick it wasn't a matter of talent, because she has that; it was a matter of experience. So that first year can be seen as preparation for the win at the Indy Japan 300.

Patrick has clearly learned the importance her team plays in her success as well. She realizes that it is a team effort. She may be the one in control on the track, but it is her team that is in control in the pit. Without a strong team, winning is that much harder. "All races involve a lot of communication between the driver and the crew. I don't pick my crew and they don't pick me," Patrick wrote. "As a driver, I'm ultimately hired by a team owner. The crew is hired by the COO of the team. We all trust that we're there because each of us is the best person for the job. This trust is what creates strength, energy, optimism, and that 'X' factor for a team. You can't buy true trust. It's essential."

Her former team owner Bobby Rahal has said of Patrick that she meets with success because she is not fearful of any challenge. In fact, she welcomes challenge. She has that "bring-it-on attitude."

There is no room for lack of confidence on the track. There are no "do-overs," no second chances, no second guesses. . . . Having the confidence to make those split second decisions in the moment is the difference between . . . winning and losing, and sometimes . . . between life and death.

—Danica Patrick

It was the attitude she took to the Indy 300 in Japan. Having learned from her mistakes, Patrick was ready to silence the critics and claim the respect she had been seeking from the male-dominated competition. Tired of being under scrutiny for her gender instead of her talent, Patrick did not buckle under the added pressure that male racers do not have to face.

When Patrick won the Indy 300 in Japan, she changed the face of race car driving forever. She showed girls everywhere that it is okay to dream about racing cars—or doing anything else formerly reserved for men. Patrick confirmed what the power of support can do for anyone chasing a dream. She proved that, although nothing comes easily, with hard work you can surmount any obstacle that comes your way. She also showed how important it is to be aware of your shortcomings, and continue to learn from your mistakes. Most of all, she has exemplified the power of determination and perseverance.

So what does she have to say now about all of those critics who accuse her of exploiting her good looks? Patrick said: "Some women in sports have remained reluctant to use their looks or their femininity to capitalize or exploit their roles. I say, don't be afraid. Use what God gave you—*You gotta rock what you've got.*"

I wasn't surprised to win. I expect to.

—DANICA PATRICK

How to Be Like Danica Patrick

1) **Work hard.** It always reaps rewards. At the Indy Japan 300 in Motegi, Japan, in April 2008, Patrick accomplished something that no other woman had ever done in the world of auto racing; she became the first woman to win an IndyCar race. Patrick said: "Hard work always pays off. Achieving a high level of success is a difficult process, but it is so worth the chance. Success doesn't just happen. You have to go out there and make it happen. If you sit around waiting for success, it'll never come."

2) **Pursue your goals with passion.** Patrick says it best in her autobiography: "Becoming a professional racecar driver is what I've worked for since the first day I sat behind the wheel of a go-kart. . . . I loved the feeling of driving—of being in control, of using my head and outsmarting the other drivers. From day one, I knew this was my calling, my destiny, my dream—and I knew that someday I would make it my dream come true."

3) **Develop a thick skin.** Patrick loves racing, but to pursue her passion, she had to deal with the slights and hostility directed toward her for being a woman in what has been a male-dominated sport. If she had let that stop her, she would never have achieved what she has.

   Of her experience in England, Patrick said it "taught me how to deal with difficult people, characteristics, and circumstances. . . . One of my greatest lessons was learning you need to clear the path you walk on for yourself because no one else is really interested in clearing it for you."

4) **Seek support.** Patrick has had the benefit of supportive parents. After losing her sponsorship from John Mecom, she turned to her parents, so she could stay in England and hone her skills.

Cont'd

Patrick's parents have always been supportive of her career, and with her family's help, she was able to stay in England for another two years. Having that kind of support can sometimes be the difference between achieving goals and dreams or giving up on them.

5) **Be persistent.** Upon returning from England and fresh out of funding, Patrick and her father started attending Indy races, following the circuit from stop to stop in 2001. She asked every owner in the garage for a chance to race, until Bobby Rahal finally agreed.

Patrick went on to compete in the Barber Dodge Pro Series, and she finished third in the Toyota Atlantic Championship. In 2005, she competed in the Indianapolis 500, becoming only the fourth woman in history to compete. She had persisted in asking for her chance, and when she received it, she made the most of it.

6) **Be yourself.** Patrick doesn't apologize for who she is. When a heated exchange between her and competitor Dan Wheldon was caught on camera, Patrick didn't back down. "I know my temper has gotten in the way from time to time, but I also know that as racers, we all have a responsibility to be careful on the track," Patrick wrote. "I don't care if I am perceived as being rude—or a bitch. Let's face it: As the only girl out there racing, I am 'The Bitch' on the track whether I open my mouth or not! I have never cared what anyone else thinks or says about me."

7) **Learn from others.** Very few novices or know-it-alls in any pursuit accomplish much. Besides her willingness to go to England to learn her craft, Patrick was eager to learn and work with her teammates. She was willing to listen and take the help she needed.

8) **Aim for the top.** Patrick learned from her father to never be satisfied with second place, always believing she could do better. Patrick says, "It's not just about a woman competing in a male-dominated sport. It's about being the best at whatever you do, regardless of gender."

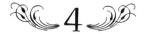

Katharine Graham
1917–2001

Risk Taker

*I cared so much about the [Washington Post newspaper]
and about keeping it in the family that, despite my
lack of knowledge and feelings of insecurity,
I felt I had to make it work.*

—KATHARINE GRAHAM

A gunshot wound that sadly ended one life, changed another: that of Katharine Graham.

She went from wife, mother, and part-time journalist to publisher of the *Washington Post*. She then changed the course of the newspaper, making journalism and business history in the process.

Born into extreme wealth as Katharine Meyer, the fourth of five children, she was more prepared for her moment than she realized. It was a time when women of her financial class, or any class for that matter, weren't expected to have careers. But her father, Eugene Meyer, was a self-made multimillionaire and power broker, and he and his wife placed high expectations on their children. Meyer, an investment banker who, among other things, had founded the Allied Chemical and Dye Corporation, purchased the *Washington Post* in a bankruptcy auction in 1932.

"The only discussions I do remember relating to wealth had to do with being told that you couldn't just be a rich kid, that you had to do something, to be engaged in useful, productive work. . . . Working was always a part of my life," Graham wrote in her autobiography, *Personal History*. That sense of purpose, once instilled, would serve her well during her life. Well educated at the best schools, Graham first worked at the *Post* as a copygirl and messenger before returning as a journalist.

When she married Philip Graham in 1940, he became the heir apparent to run the *Post*. Eugene Meyers's only son had chosen medicine over journalism and became a doctor. The thought of Katharine running the family newspaper was never considered by either father or daughter. In fact, Graham was pleased with her father's decision to anoint her husband.

In a sign of the chauvinistic times, Meyer gave his son-in-law a larger portion of stock in the paper than he gave to Katharine, because he believed no man should be working, in effect, for his wife. She, too, agreed with this.

Philip Graham, a law school graduate who possessed an intellect brilliant enough to have clerked at the U.S. Supreme Court for Justice Stanley Reed, joined the *Post* in January 1946 as the associate publisher. He'd been a major during World War II, stationed in the Pacific as an intelligence officer. When Meyer became president of the new World Bank in June 1946, son-in-law Graham ascended to the position of publisher of the *Washington Post*.

Phil Graham elevated the stature and quality of the *Post* and expanded the company's holdings by purchasing *Newsweek* magazine and two television stations. He was well regarded in Washington power circles and was a confidante of John F. Kennedy. But with all Graham accomplished, the *Post* was still thought of as just a typical, undistinguished, albeit successful, regional newspaper. Eventually, Graham became consumed by mental illness (what we know today as bipolar disorder). His mental condition deteriorated to such a degree that he was committed to a psychiatric institution. In August 1963, while visiting home on a weekend leave from the institution, he committed suicide.

Katharine Graham heard the shot and found her brilliant but troubled husband lying dead in a bathroom.

Phil was the love of Graham's life, and she remained devoted to him despite his often erratic conduct, which included abusive behavior that may have been triggered by his illness. Before anyone understood his condition, Phil was often verbally abusive to his wife in front of their friends and their children, belittling her intelligence, looks, and Jewish heritage. Among close friends and associates, there were whisperings of physical abuse when Graham occasionally appeared bearing bruises on her arms and face.

Phil Graham had not only emotionally tormented his wife; he'd even plotted to take her beloved *Post* from her. By this time, he was the paper's majority stockholder and, as such, planned to buy her out with *Post* money. Then, to add insult to injury, he plotted to run the paper with his mistress, a *Newsweek* reporter whom he planned to marry. Katharine Graham had resolved not to give up her family's paper without a fight, but Phil's suicide precluded any struggle for the *Post*. Later, Katharine generously blamed her husband's actions on his mental illness and even had kind words for his mistress in her autobiography.

After a funeral attended by such powerful figures as President Kennedy, Graham had a decision to make about the *Post*. Although she'd received numerous offers to buy the paper after her husband's death, the idea of letting go of the paper was out of the question to her. The *Post* was part of Graham. She had loved it from the first. It had been built up by her father and her husband, and ultimately, she intended for it to be passed on to her children. Graham's only question was who would run it until those children came of age.

Katharine Graham lacked confidence at that point in her life. In addition to her husband's belittling, she carried residual psychological baggage from her mother's incessantly critical and demanding nature. Agnes Meyer, Graham recalled, set impossibly high standards for her children that created pressure and insecurities. Her mother demanded perfection without considering the lifetime cost to her son and daughters.

Graham's father, however, had been her champion. He was kind and supportive, she said, even when he criticized her judgment. "He somehow conveyed his belief in me without ever articulating it, and that was the single most sustaining thing in my life. That was what saved me," Graham wrote.

She made her final decision to step in and become president of the Washington Post Company in September 1963, intending to run the paper until her children were ready to take over. Her professional experience had been limited to being a reporter in 1938 with the *San Francisco News*, and as a columnist and other assorted, minor positions with the *Post*. While Graham's editorial experience afforded her an advantage over her father and husband (neither of whom had any journalism experience before they became newspapermen), she also had another important asset that compensated for her lack of management and leadership experience: "My passionate devotion to the company and to the *Post*. I cared so much about the paper and about keeping it in the family that, despite my lack of knowledge and feelings of insecurity, I felt I *had* to make it work," Graham said.

She took up the reins of a newspaper that—despite ranking sixth in advertising nationally, and whose holdings included *Newsweek* magazine, two art magazines, several television stations, and a news service—had a cash-flow problem. Yet, under Graham's leadership, the *Washington Post* became one of the world's leading newspapers. She took the company public in 1971, and it still ranks as one of the fifty best-performing IPOs in the last century. The Washington Post Company hit the market at $6.50 per share in 1971, and it was trading at $222 a share on May 9, 1991, when Graham relinquished her duties as chief executive officer. The stock had increased 3,415 percent. During that time, the Dow Jones Industrial Average increased 227 percent. Revenue increased from $84 million in 1963 to $1.4 billion by 1991.

In 1972, Graham became only the second woman to head a company on the Fortune 500 list. Billionaire investor Warren Buffett, who put his money in the *Post* and eventually became Graham's friend, confidant, and mentor, wrote that she understood and practiced "the two most basic rules of business: First, surround yourself with talented people and then nourish them with responsibilities and your gratitude; second, consistently deliver a superior, ever-improving product to your customer. . . . If we look at newspaper and television profit margins on what I would term a 'quality-adjusted' basis, she took the Washington Post Company from near the bottom straight to the top."

Graham was named one of the "10 Greatest CEOs of All Time" in author Jim Collins's July 2003 cover story for *Fortune* magazine. Collins ranked Graham number nine. To make the list, Collins said a leader had to accomplish four tasks: produce exceptional results, make a distinctive impact on the world, preside over a significant crisis or renewal, and leave a legacy that transcends his or her own tenure or life. Not one, but two crises defined Katharine Graham: the Pentagon Papers case and the Watergate scandal.

Her sense of herself as an outsider, of not really belonging, was ultimately a key to her greatness. She often said she felt dowdy and dull next to her dashing, brilliant husband, the late Philip Graham. But she turned out to be a better journalist.

—Evan Thomas, *Newsweek*

"Katharine Graham accomplished all four objectives, becoming a role model not only for women, but for anyone—male or female—who aspires to effective leadership," Collins wrote in the forward to *Katharine Graham: The Leadership Journey of an American Icon* by Robin Gerber.

Graham had a penchant for asking the right questions and gathering information. This served her well editorially for the significant challenges the *Post* faced, and for her stewardship of the Post as a business. She recognized how little she knew about the world of business when she took over the paper, and she worked tirelessly to understand aspects of the newspaper business outside of her editorial purview. The Montessori method of learning by doing, she said, "Once again became my stock and trade."

Graham's mother, Agnes, did establish in her daughter's character one particular standard that Graham strove to uphold all her life: mediocrity was simply unacceptable. To that end, Graham said that in her early days of running the *Post*, she would often "lie awake at night reliving events of the day, going over and over certain scenes, wondering how I could have managed whatever it was differently."

Intellectual curiosity drove Graham to study what were considered good management techniques, both inside and outside the newspaper industry. "I began to do my homework in management. I must have driven everyone around me crazy by studying everything so intensely, but I was compelled to know more," Graham wrote.

While her background was in editorial writing, she realized she needed to have a comprehensive understanding of all newspaper operations. She learned how copy became a printed paper by visiting publishers in different cities to study newspaper production. Graham attended a weeklong, hands-on production process school, which was run by the publishers' association. Her attention to detail included learning how her paper's circulation department functioned.

"She would need to understand it all in order to track production costs and make financial decisions to underwrite news technology and machinery," Gerber wrote.

Graham also attended a seven-day IBM course to learn more about computers. She visited companies like Texas Instruments, Xerox, and NCR to glean from them what made a company successful.

The most important assets Graham brought into her new position were the high leadership standards of her father. Gerber wrote that Eugene Meyer gave his editors leeway and hired people for their character and intellect. Additionally, Meyer had instilled his newspaper values and social responsibilities in Graham. He emphasized to her that to make a newspaper a commercial success the paper had to tell the truth. He strongly believed a paper's civic duty was to align itself with the public good rather than the private interests of its owner or special interest groups.

"'If you give [people] the truth,' her father said, 'and back it up with clear explanations and sound arguments, you are exercising very great power in a very useful way,'" Graham recalled, as quoted by Gerber.

Graham ran the paper and the Washington Post Company as a news organization first. She embraced her father's notion that staying true to the paper's mission as a public trust was the best way to run it as a business enterprise. Her litmus test for reporting was simple, but solid: Did the *Post* get it right? Were they fair? Could they have done it better?

That ideal was put to the test with the Pentagon Papers case. The Papers were a U.S. Department of Defense study of United States involvement in the Vietnam War. The study was given to the *New York Times* by Daniel Ellsberg, a former Pentagon aide. The *Times* began publishing articles about it in June 1971. The Nixon administration, embroiled in the Vietnam War, but not in power at the time the study was done, immediately went to court to prevent the *Times* from publishing additional articles about the Papers. President Nixon claimed executive authority as his basis for suppressing the information, and his administration was granted an injunction in their favor to halt the *Times*'s publication of the Papers.

When the *Washington Post* came into possession of their own copy of the Pentagon Papers a couple of days later (courtesy of Ellsberg), Graham had a difficult decision to make. The court order against the *New York Times* said nothing about other newspapers publishing articles about the Papers, but the precedent had been set. Graham, who at one time held a personal and professional stance in favor of the Vietnam War, felt a responsibility to publish. The *Post*'s lawyers counseled Graham to wait until the *Times* case had run its legal course. Publishing could mean being prosecuted under the Espionage Act.

Graham also had to take into consideration the fact that the Washington Post Company had just gone public a couple of days earlier. The company had a plan in place to correct its financial troubles with this move, and bad publicity or prosecution could have potentially disastrous financial ramifications.

"Everyone understood that the danger to the company couldn't be over-stated. A decision to publish was a decision to risk everything," Gerber wrote.

In addition to Graham's own views, the editorial leaders wanted to publish. At a large meeting at managing editor Ben Bradlee's home, Graham made the final decision in Eisenhoweresque fashion. It was the *Post*'s D-day. "Go ahead, go ahead, go ahead. Let's go. Let's publish," Graham said.

She knew she'd "be risking the whole company on this decision."

Bradlee, one of the talented people Graham had brought to the *Post*, said she had the "guts of a cat burglar." Later, Bradlee himself would become a national figure during his professional collaboration with Graham.

One of the principles that Graham's father believed essential to running a newspaper was that "in pursuit of truth, the newspaper shall be prepared to make sacrifice of its material fortunes, if such course be necessary for the public good." Graham stayed true to that principle.

The Nixon administration sued the *Post*, who had to stop publishing after only two issues. The Supreme Court eventually heard the case, *New York*

Steadiness, decency, core journalistic values of public service, balance and fairness were the coin of the realm for Katharine. It wasn't just a business, but a calling to make society better.

—PAUL TAYLOR,
POST POLITICAL REPORTER

Times Co. v. United States, and ruled in favor of the newspapers. Justice Hugo Black echoed Graham's sentiments in his last opinion for the Court. He wrote "only a free and unrestrained press can effectively expose deception in government. . . . In revealing the workings of government that led to the Vietnam War, the newspapers nobly did precisely that which the Founders hoped and trusted they would do."

Graham's courageous decision to let the people know what their government, which is accountable to them, was doing ultimately gave the *Post* the prestige of a national paper, second only to the *New York Times*.

One person in particular wasn't applauding the *Post*: President Richard Nixon. He believed the *Post* wasn't just reporting the news, but was working an agenda against him. Secretary of State Henry Kissinger later told Graham personally that Nixon prohibited members of his administration from talking to the *Post*.

The Pentagon Papers case was, in some ways, only a warm-up for Graham's and the *Post*'s greatest challenge—the legendary and historic investigative reporting of the Watergate scandal that resulted in the August 1974 resignation of President Nixon.

In June 1972 five burglars were arrested at the Watergate Hotel Complex for breaking into the Democratic Party's National Headquarters located there. Nixon White House spokesman Ron Ziegler immediately downplayed the incident, calling it a "third-rate burglary attempt," of no significance to anything.

Washington Post reporters Bob Woodward and Carl Bernstein weren't taking that pronouncement at face value. They began investigating, and it soon came out the burglars belonged to a secret White House group known as "the plumbers." This revelation only led to more questions that uncovered more suspicious and overtly illegal administration activities. In some circles, including the *Post*'s own readers, the reporters' motives and those of the paper were questionable. Was the investigation unpatriotic? Was it targeting Nixon for political reasons? Much of what fueled this speculation for a while was the fact that the *Post* was the only paper investigating and covering the story.

Graham said she "loathed reports that personalized the whole dispute" and "detested" any belief that the *Post* was out to get Nixon. Graham had, in fact, been supportive of Nixon in the past.

"Many people misunderstood the role of the *Post*, believing that we got some sort of enjoyment out of kicking the president and the Republicans," Graham wrote. "Far from its being our aim or purpose, we got no pleasure from it. As I wrote someone, 'It's the only government we have, and it would be a lot bigger pleasure not to have to report the kind of things we do.'"

With intense criticism showered down on the *Post* from the Nixon White House and other conservatives, Graham and Bradlee held tough and backed Woodward and Bernstein. They remained steadfast in their conviction that the reporters should keep investigating the story—not out of any political or ulterior motives, but because it was the *Post*'s journalistic responsibility. Graham categorized her editorial leadership during this time as staying behind the scenes. She acted as the paper's "devil's advocate," challenging her editors and staff to make certain that what the paper was reporting on Watergate was factual, accurate, and well-sourced.

"We have been heavily attacked for biased reporting by many individuals, who, when confronted with the facts, have since resigned from the government," Graham wrote in response to a highly critical letter.

To a man who sent her an ad from a Miami paper suggesting that the *Post* people belonged in jail for their Watergate coverage, Graham wrote, "If we are exaggerating minor peccadilloes, why has the majority of the White House staff had to be unloaded?"

The *Post*, Graham said, was bearing the full brunt of Nixon's presidential wrath, and it took its toll. She felt the pressures "of living with an administration so completely at odds with us and determined to harm us." In one example of intimidation, Graham learned that White House aide Charles Colson wanted to know when the television stations owned by Graham's Washington Post Company were up for FCC renewal.

Colson was also quoted as warning that, after the 1972 election, the administration was going to "shove it" to the *Post* . . . "and that's only the beginning. After that, we're really going to get rough. They're going to wish on L Street that they'd never heard of Watergate." Graham even said a friend with administration contacts cautioned her that her own personal safety might be at risk, which she thought was melodramatic. Her friend reiterated that it wasn't.

After Nixon's Oval Office–taped conversations were disclosed, one tape revealed the president remarking that Graham had television stations coming up for renewal. "The game has to be played awfully rough," Nixon said.

Graham was informed about the threat to the stations while in Japan, dining with future prime minister Kiichi Miyazawa. "He remembered her fearless response," Gerber wrote. "'Well, if he dared to do that, just let him do it,' [Graham said.]) Nixon did dare, and Katharine met him head on."

After Nixon's reelection in 1972, the government posed license challenges to the Washington Post Company's television stations. Wall Street reacted, and the company's stock lost over half its value, plummeting in price from $38 a share to $16. One of Graham's lawyers advised cutting and running on Watergate for the financial sake of the company. But Graham wouldn't hear of it. Journalist Richard Reeves said Graham had "bet the company on journalism."

She was definitely her father's daughter.

The first mission of a newspaper is to tell the truth as nearly as the truth may be ascertained.

—EUGENE MEYER

With her newspaper under siege, Graham's mandate was to keep investigating for hard evidence, and then report it in detail and with accuracy. Given the stakes, *Post* editors demanded of themselves and their reporters an even higher standard for details, sources, and fairness in the stories they published.

"Throughout Watergate, I was amazed at the regular allegations that somehow we had created the agony of Watergate by recklessly pursuing certain stories and thereby causing the turmoil that the president was in. How could anyone make this argument in light of the fact that the stories we reported turned out to be true?" Graham wrote.

So true were the *Post*'s stories that they revealed the administration's cover-up of the initial Watergate burglary and its attempts to thwart ensuing investigations into the matter. Congressional investigations followed, and the *Post*'s pursuit of the truth ultimately climaxed in the unprecedented and historic resignation of an American president.

"Graham never awarded herself much credit, insisting that, with Watergate, 'I never felt there was much choice.' But of course, she did choose. Courage, it's said, is not the absence of fear, but the ability to act in its presence. By that definition, Katharine Graham may be the most courageous CEO on this list," wrote Collins in "The 10 Greatest CEOs of All Time."

Gerber, too, applauds Graham for her courage. She points out that Graham "could have insisted, especially when the *Post* was alone on the story and little new information was coming out, that continued investigation was a poor use of resources. When her television licenses were threatened and her stock price sank, she could have pressured Bradlee to back off. She wouldn't have been the first publisher to put profits over performance, especially when the continued existence of her company was at stake. Instead, she kept her fears mostly to herself, suffering long nights of doubt in private."

Between the Pentagon Papers and Watergate, Graham had lived up to the highest ideals that her father instilled in her about the public trust and the responsibility of running a newspaper. She never wavered in the face of financial ruin, because the people's right to know was more important.

"Watergate no doubt was the most important occurrence in my working life, but my involvement was basically peripheral, rarely direct. . . . What I did primarily was stand behind the editors and reporters, in whom I believed," Graham said.

Eugene Meyer would have been proud of his daughter in her finest moments. As he said, "The newspaper shall tell ALL the

> *If we were forced to pick only one business leader from whom to draw professional learning and personal inspiration, that one leader would very likely be Katharine Graham.*
>
> —JIM COLLINS, AUTHOR OF *GOOD TO GREAT*

> *At the* POST, *having regarded ourselves as doing the public's business, we were gratified by the results [of the Supreme Court's vote] and felt that the principle of no prior restraint of the press had been vindicated.*
>
> —KATHARINE GRAHAM

truth so far as it can learn it, concerning the important affairs of America and the world. . . . The newspaper's duty is to its readers and to the public at large, and not to the private interests of its owner."

How to Be Like Katharine Graham

1. **Embrace expectations or develop them.** Although Graham was born into wealth, her father was a high-achieving, self-made multimillionaire who had high expectations for his children. Graham remembered being told by her parents that she "couldn't just be a rich kid," that she had to do something useful and be engaged in productive work. Graham embraced that sense of purpose, and it served her well during her life.

2) **Find support.** Graham had been psychologically beaten down by her demanding mother and abusive husband, but her father was the shining light that encouraged and inspired her to become one of this nation's great business managers. Graham remembered him as kind and supportive even when he was critical of her judgment. "He somehow conveyed his belief in me without ever articulating it, and that was the single most sustaining thing in my life. That was what saved me."

3) **Follow your passion.** Despite her insecurities and lack of management experience, Graham had one important asset going for her when she stepped in to run the paper: her passionate devotion to the *Post*. "I cared so much about the paper and about keeping it in the family that, despite my lack of knowledge and feelings of insecurity, I felt I *had* to make it work," Graham said.

4) **Practice the two basic rules of business.** According to Warren Buffett, one of the richest men in the world and a mentor to Graham, she understood and practiced the two basic rules of business: "First, surround yourself with talented people and then nourish them with responsibilities and your gratitude; second, consistently deliver a superior, ever-improving product to your customer."

Cont'd

5) **Don't accept mediocrity.** Graham never did. It actually doesn't take much to be better than mediocre; just effort and caring will help people push past mediocrity and closer to excellence. While Graham said her mother placed impossibly high standards on her children that created pressure and led to insecurities, she did embrace her mother's ideal that mediocrity was unacceptable.

6) **Learn from your successes and failures.** In her early days of running the *Post*, Graham would often "lie awake at night reliving events of the day, going over and over certain scenes," wondering how she could have better managed them. While she didn't view this obsessing as a positive experience at the time, clearly it served her well to analyze and learn from her daily experiences. Along the same lines, one of her litmus tests for reporting was to ask how the *Post* could have done it better.

7) **Learn your business.** Graham studied management techniques both inside and outside her industry. "I began to do my homework in management. I must have driven everyone around me crazy by studying everything so intensely, but I was compelled to know more," Graham wrote.

   Although she had a background in the editorial field, she realized she needed to understand all aspects of newspaper operations to track production costs and make financial decisions. Along with studying printing production processes, Graham also attended a computer course at IBM and visited other top companies to learn what made them successful.

8) **Stay true to your business.** In the newspaper industry, a key element is objective reporting. Graham's father had instilled his newspaper values and social responsibilities in her. He believed that if a newspaper stayed true to the pursuit of the truth for the public good, the business side would take care of itself. "If you give [people] the truth," Eugene Meyer said, "and back it up with clear explanations and sound arguments, you are exercising very great power in a very useful way."

9) **Be brave.** By choosing to publish the Pentagon Papers in the face of a court injunction preventing the *New York Times* from doing so, Graham risked the financial future of the *Post*, as well as potential prosecution under the Espionage Act. "I would be risking the whole company on this decision," she said. So, why did she do it? The words of her father said it best: "In pursuit of truth, the newspaper shall be prepared to make sacrifice of its material fortunes, if such course be necessary for the public good."

10) **Lead, don't follow.** For a long period of time, the *Post* was the only paper writing and researching the Watergate story. This fueled speculation that the *Post* was going after Nixon and the administration by making news rather than reporting it. Graham had to ask herself the question: if there was a story, why wasn't any other paper working on it? Ultimately, she determined that the facts her team uncovered continued to speak for themselves. Administration officials were resigning from the government when confronted with these facts. "If we are exaggerating minor peccadilloes, why has the majority of the White House staff had to be unloaded?" Graham asked. Graham backed her editorial staff and reporters Woodward and Bernstein, and she made history in the process.

11) **Stand up to intimidation.** Bullies come in all shapes and sizes, and even in presidential administrations. Graham said she felt the pressures "of living with an administration so completely at odds with us and determined to harm us." As the *Post* investigated Watergate, they heard rumblings that the FCC renewals of their television stations were in jeopardy. White House aide Charles Colson threatened that, after the 1972 election, the administration was going to "shove it" to the *Post* and "get rough." One person close to the administration even warned Graham that her personal safety might be in jeopardy. Through it all, Graham stayed the course. She felt the *Post*'s most powerful response—and best display of strength—was to keep investigating.

J. K. Rowling
1965–

Passion

*Keep writing and throwing it away until
one day you do something that you don't think
belongs in the [trash bin]. Stick to writing
what you know about. Don't give up.*

—J. K. ROWLING

In the beginning of the wildly successful Harry Potter series, Harry is a young boy who has no idea of the power he possesses as the wizard he doesn't yet know he is. Likewise, there was an untapped magic and wonder in author Joanne Kathleen "J. K." Rowling. Rowling, although she had loved to write from the time she was a little girl, had no idea of the immense talent she possessed and the powerful influence she would have to change the literary world—and the real one. As a result, Rowling, through her Harry Potter books, has enriched the lives of children and adults alike worldwide.

She spent years writing the first Harry Potter book and plotting out the next six without knowing (not even having a hint) that her untold hours of hard work would amount to anything. She was unpublished, with no connections and no agent. Yet even as a financially strapped single mother, struggling to support herself and her child, she still made time to write. She wrote for the pure love of it. Her dream was to be a published writer, and she admits that she didn't think she had much of a chance to realize the dream.

Was she ever wrong!

"This is my life's ambition, and I've overshot the mark so hugely," Rowling said in Lindsey Fraser's *Conversations with J. K. Rowling.*

Born July 31, 1965 in Chipping Sodbury, England, Rowling's literary rise was meteoric. In July 1997, her first book, *Harry Potter and the Philosopher's Stone* (called *Harry Potter and the Sorcerer's Stone* in the United States), was published. By July 1999, there were 30 million copies of her first three books in print. By 2000, 76 million copies, and by 2004, the total had reached 250 million copies of the first five books. By her fortieth birthday, Rowling was one of the wealthiest people in the world with a fortune estimated at $1 billion. Today there are over 400 million copies of Rowling's seven Harry Potter books in print. According to *Forbes* magazine in 2006, she is the first author-billionaire.

"I still know that I'm an extraordinarily lucky person, doing what I love best in all the world," Rowling said.

Her secret to success, however, wasn't magic or luck. It was born instead of an old-fashioned work ethic.

Harry Potter was created on a train ride and, in a way, so was Rowling. Her eighteen-year-old parents met on a train departing King's Cross Station in London in 1964. They sat near each other on their nine-hour trip to Arbroath in Scotland and instantly fell in love. And like the magical train ride that Harry takes to the huge castle known as Hogwarts School of Witchcraft and Wizardry, Rowling, too, experienced a train ride that changed her life and the lives of her readers.

In June 1990, Rowling was returning to London from Manchester by train. As she gazed out the window and watched the countryside go by, she had what she says was the purest stroke of inspiration she had ever had in her life. At this point in her novice career, Rowling had written many short stories and two adult novels. She worked on the novels while supporting herself as a secretary, but she felt neither manuscript was good enough to warrant finishing.

Harry's story was different, however. She imagined an eleven-year-old boy wizard who lived among mortals, not knowing his true powers. Orphaned, Harry was raised in a heartless manner by his nonmagical aunt and her pompous husband.

With that idea to go on, Rowling said she needed to answer the question of why Harry is where he is when the story starts. Eventually, she developed the backstory about the lightning bolt–shaped scar on Harry's forehead and how it provided the key clue to his past. When the evil wizard Voldemort killed Harry's wizard parents, Lily and James, he didn't possess enough magical power to kill the infant Harry. Weakened in the attempt, the dreaded Voldemort did manage to leave the distinctive scar on Harry's brow. In the magical world yet unknown to him, the scar serves as proof that Harry is legendary among wizards as "the boy who lived."

The never-before-published Rowling decided by the end of that fateful train ride that she would write seven Harry Potter books. They would correspond to the seven years Harry spends at Hogwarts. She rode the enthusiasm of her vision and started writing that very night.

In a sense, Rowling had been preparing for that moment her entire life. Many of the greatest minds of civilization have written about the value reading played in their lives and successes. Rowling's parents served as an example to her because they both loved to read. "My mother was a huge reader and never happier than when she was curled up reading. That was a big influence on me," she recalled. In Rowling's case, reading certainly taught her how other writers told their stories, and these stories expanded her own imagination.

Today, with her busy schedule, Rowling still makes time to read. When O, The Oprah Magazine asked, "With so much on your plate, when do you find time to read?" Rowling responded, "I never need to find time to read. When people say to me, 'Oh, yeah, I love reading. I would love to read, but I just don't have time,' I'm thinking, how can you not have time?"

Early in her life Rowling was not only reading children's books but also books such as Little Women by Louisa May Alcott, which she tackled at age eight. She was nine when she read Ian Fleming's James Bond thriller

Thunderball. By her late preteens, she had read Jane Austen's *Pride and Prejudice,* and by age fourteen she conquered William Thackeray's *Vanity Fair*—all very sophisticated fare for a young girl. One book series that impacted her writer's imagination greatly was *The Chronicles of Narnia* by C. S. Lewis. Other favorite childhood authors included Paul Gallico, Noel Streatfield, and E. Nesbit.

As a young adult, she was moved by Charles Dickens's *A Tale of Two Cities* and inspired by the *Lord of the Rings* trilogy by J. R. R. Tolkien. Dickens's works frequently concerned matters of social injustice, and Tolkien wrote of epic battles between good and evil in imaginative realms. Both of these are important and recurring themes in the Harry Potter series.

Rowling says she was most influenced by the writings of Jessica Mitford. Her great aunt gave her Mitford's autobiography, *Hons and Rebels,* when Rowling was fourteen years old. Known as the "queen of the muckrakers," Mitford wrote extensively about social injustice. Rowling admired the way she lived her life and the courage she displayed as a human rights activist— courage that sometimes put Mitford in harm's way.

"[Mitford] showed her passion by acting on what she believed, not preaching. . . . I think I've read everything she wrote. I even named my daughter after her," Rowling noted. Mitford's courage ultimately permeated Rowling's novels as an essential character trait of Harry Potter and his two best friends, Ron Weasley and Hermione Granger.

Another key book Rowling read during childhood was Elizabeth Goudge's *The Little White Horse.* Rowling remarked that the more she read this book, the more clever it became. Likewise, surprises abound on each page of the Harry Potter books. Rowling says of *The Little White Horse* on her website, "Perhaps more than any other book, it had a direct influence on the Harry Potter books. The author always included detail of what her characters were eating, and I remember liking that. You may have noticed that I always list the food being eaten at Hogwarts."

Like Goudge, Rowling meticulously planned her books. She created all of her characters and their backstories as if she knew them as living, breathing people. "Sirius Black is a good example," Rowling wrote, "I have a whole childhood worked out for him. The readers don't need to know that, but I do. I need to know much more than them because I'm the one moving the characters across the page."

She filled one notebook with nothing but notes about Quidditch, a thrilling wizard's team sport that Harry and his classmates play at Hogwarts. Rowling also put extensive effort into naming the unique places and things surrounding her characters and very carefully selected the names of her characters.

As she wrote *Harry Potter and the Philosopher's Stone*, she also planned

Like Sir Arthur Conan Doyle, Ian Fleming, and any major mystery novelist who has successfully sustained a character-driven book series, Rowling has brought to life compelling people—heroes, their friends and allies, and their nemeses—whom we wish existed in the real world.

—AMELIE FRANK,
POET AND JOURNALIST

the plotlines for the next six novels. In addition, as she worked on the early novels, she wrote the last chapter of the seventh book—before the first novel was even close to completion. This prewriting of the final chapter of the last book served as Rowling's tangible commitment to herself that all the books would be completed. Her tremendous love of her work and belief in her ability to bring it to fruition drove her to invest significant time and energy to write her story the way she wanted it to be written. This is especially exceptional given the bleak financial circumstances she endured while she was writing.

In the summer of 1991, Rowling moved to Oporto, Portugal. After the death of her mother and the loss of her job, she wanted to get away. She found a position in Oporto teaching English in the afternoon and evenings and devoted her free mornings to continuing the work on the first Harry Potter book.

Drawing from her real-life experience of losing her mother, who was only forty-five, Rowling said that Harry's feelings about his dead parents became "much deeper, much more real. In my first weeks in Portugal, I wrote my favorite chapter in *Philosopher's Stone*, 'The Mirror of Erised.'" In the magic mirror, young Harry sees himself living happily with his parents. His greatest childhood desire (the mirror's name, Erised, is the word *desire* spelled backward) can be reflected back to Harry, but—like all illusions— it can never be realized.

At this time, Rowling realized her own desire for a family. While in Portugal, she married and gave birth to her daughter Jessica. The marriage soon failed. Rowling returned to Great Britain with Jessica, her unfinished manuscript, and boxes of Potter ideas in hand. In December 1994, she settled in Edinburgh, Scotland, where her sister, Di, lived with her husband.

Rowling had very little money and applied for and received welfare. It was depressing for the single mother. She never forgot that humiliating experience and the struggles that financial hardship brought. At one particularly low point, she settled in an unheated, dilapidated apartment where she could hear the pitter-patter of little feet, but they weren't Jessica's. They belonged to a community of mice running through the walls.

She stretched her dollars as far as she could and even frequented children's clothing stores to get the free diapers provided in their dressing rooms under the guise of shopping for her daughter. It broke her heart that she couldn't provide more for Jessica.

Very few people succeed in a vacuum without the care and concern of friends and family. In Rowling's case, she asked for help from her friend Sean Harris, who came through and lent her money, so she and her daughter could move to a better apartment. Rowling says that Harry's best friend, Ron Weasley, shares many of the traits of her friend Harris, including the fact that both are funny and loyal.

Rowling wanted to start teaching again but needed to get a teaching certificate to do so. She set her mind to finishing *Harry Potter and the Philosopher's Stone* before she started teaching full-time because she knew that teaching and taking care of a small child wouldn't leave her any spare time to write. She worked at a frenzied pace. Whenever her daughter fell asleep during the day, Rowling would take her to a café and write "like mad." In the evenings, she wrote still more. Initially, everything she produced was written in longhand.

In January of 1995, she began working toward her teaching certificate at a school called Moray House. When the school stopped offering child care, which Rowling needed for Jessica, a friend stepped forward and offered her a large loan that made it possible for her to continue her studies while Jessica was cared for.

"I broke down and cried when my friend offered it to me," Rowling said in Colleen Sexton's *J. K. Rowling*. "It was this enormous sum of money. I think we both thought I would never be able to pay it back. The friend was saying in effect: 'Here is a gift to help you.'"

She eventually typed the entire ninety-thousand-word book on a secondhand manual typewriter, then retyped it on public computers in a college library. By 1995, Rowling finished the first draft of *Harry Potter and the Philosopher's Stone*.

After the first three chapters were rejected by the first agent she sent them to, Rowlings sent out the package to an agent who had a name she liked: Christopher Little of the Christopher Little Literary Agency. Office manager Bryony Evens initially rejected the manuscript because Little didn't represent children's books. But then, fate intervened. Evens was drawn to the interesting folder the three chapters came in. When she read the synopsis, she felt the book had the elements of "a classic." She then read the first three chapters and was so impressed that she received Little's okay to request the rest of the manuscript.

When Rowling received that letter, she read it several times, calling it the second best moment in her life, after the birth of Jessica. When the manuscript arrived at the agency office, Evens, and then Little, read it in one night. Little immediately decided to represent Rowling. Over the course of the next year, twelve publishers would reject her first Harry Potter book. The thirteenth publisher was Bloomsbury, and the head of their children's division, Barry Cunningham, was drawn to Rowling's detail.

"What struck me first was that the book came with a fully imagined world. There was a complete sense of Jo knowing the characters and what would happen to them," Cunningham recalled. Rowling's intense work on the backstories of her characters paid off when it mattered most, at match point in her fledgling career.

In August 1996, magic happened:

Rowling's attention to small detail separates her from other authors. There are so many times in the Harry Potter series where a minute, seemingly insignificant detail in an early book becomes a major storyline factor later on. Adding characters is one thing, but being able to weave important storylines from previous background info makes Rowling stand out.

—Nevin Scott Barich,
writer and editor

Little informed Rowling that Bloomsbury had made an offer of $2,250 for the rights to publish the book, in addition to royalties. "I could not quite believe my ears," Rowling wrote. "'You mean it's going to be published?' I asked, rather stupidly. 'It's definitely going to be published?' After I had hung up, I screamed and jumped into the air. Jessica, who was sitting in her high-chair enjoying tea, looked thoroughly scared."

The years of hard work, the countless hours of thinking, planning, writing, and tweaking had paid off to meet Rowling's minimal goal of just having the book published. *Harry Potter and the Philosopher's Stone* hit the bookstores of Great Britain on June 26, 1997, and one of literature's great phenomena was born. Joanne Kathleen Rowling had become "J. K." because Cunningham was concerned that boys might not want to read books written by a woman.

In the United States, Arthur Levine, editorial director for Scholastic Press, read *Harry Potter and the Philosopher's Stone*. He liked it so much that he paid $105,000 for the rights to publish the book in the United States, retitling it *Harry Potter and the Sorcerer's Stone*. It was the largest amount ever paid to a first-time children's author and the largest amount Levine had ever paid for any book—period. He explained his reasoning this way: "In Harry Potter, the wand chooses the wizard; and when the wand chooses you, you take it."

Still not expecting lightning to strike, Rowling continued her teaching program while commencing work on her second book, *Harry Potter and the Chamber of Secrets*. To better fund her efforts, she applied to the Scottish Arts Council for a writer's grant. She submitted a proposal and writing samples and received a grant of $12,000.

Due in part to the publicity of winning the Smarties Book Prize, Rowlings first book began generating royalties—something she had never expected. She decided to devote herself to full-time writing. It was a risk, as she would give up her training to become a teacher, but she felt she was in a position to write full-time for two years. And the Smarties Prize turned out to be only the first in a very long line of awards her first book garnered.

Within those two years, the hardworking Rowling finished her second book, *Harry Potter and the Chamber of Secrets,* but even though she accomplished it within her publisher's timeline, the perfectionist in her asked the publisher to allow her another six weeks to add finishing touches because she wasn't satisfied with it. Rowling was worried she wouldn't meet the expectations of her readers. Her extra care and hard work paid off: the book skyrocketed to the top of many bestseller lists.

With the second novel, her fame started to grow, and after her third, *Harry Potter and the Prisoner of Azkaban,* her fortune also increased. She had 30 million books in print, but Rowling refused to rest on her laurels. The hunger to turn out great work still burned within her.

Rowlings became unhappy with the plot development of her fourth book, *Harry Potter and the Goblet of Fire.* While her first three books had followed the plots she'd planned years earlier, the

Rowling is an amazing author. She is able to capture every essence of people's emotions. She knows how to drag the reader into her magical world, and leave them begging for more. She is unique in that every book takes an exciting new twist on life, whether it be muggle or magical.

—Bailey Mintz, age 14

fourth one needed work. "I wrote what I thought was half the book, and 'Ack!' Huge gaping hole in the middle of the plot," Rowling said. She rewrote chapter nine thirteen times and spent ten hours a day on the book. She was already rich and famous and could have sold anything that had her name on it, but her love of writing and her perfectionism would not allow anything less than her best effort. *The Prisoner of Azkaban* was released in 2002 and was an immediate hit.

J. K. Rowling's books are a hit because her characters are believable and idealistic, and at the same time they all reflect Rowling's life values. Among the reasons the Harry Potter character resonates with the public is that Harry is a hero. He is courageous and loyal and shows talent in "the subject of Defense against the Dark Arts," something a true hero needs. Rowling admires these traits, just as she admired Jessica Mitford in part because of her courage. Harry's friend Hermione Granger is based on Mitford and even more so on Rowling herself. Hermione is kindhearted, and Rowling says the character is "near enough" her. She says that while she was never as clever as Hermione, "I was that annoying on occasion."

During the years before the birth of Harry Potter, Rowling worked to survive, but she lived to write. She often found herself bored at many of her jobs and carved out time during the workday to jot down ideas for her latest stories. It wasn't that she didn't care about these jobs, but rather that her creativity and passion for writing simply could not be contained. She knew what she wanted to do, and this is partly why she has achieved such staggering success on a global scale.

Rowling is drawn to causes and themes that matter. "If I wasn't just writing full-time—it was important that my time was being spent on something worthwhile," she said.

One of her favorite jobs was doing research for Amnesty International, an organization committed to protecting human rights around the world. Rowling's work involved researching cases of human rights abuse in Africa. No doubt, this research has inspired her telling depictions of the prejudices and politics certain wizards have toward muggles (human beings without magical powers), elves, giants, centaurs, and other enchanted creatures who populate Harry Potter's world.

Rowling's books inspire readers because of the timeless themes of heroism and the power of good over evil. Through the selfless and heroic actions of Harry, Ron, Hermione, Hagrid, Sirius Black, Dumbledore, and others, Rowling's books do more than encourage children to read; they encourage children to do the right thing. At the end of each school year (the end of each book), Professor Dumbledore speaks to the student body at Hogwarts and always leaves them with one principle to live by. As Rowling herself put it, "What's very important for me is when Dumbledore says [at the end of the first book] that you have to choose between what is right and what is easy." This is the setup for the next three novels. In each of them, Harry and his friends are going to have to choose, because what is easy is often not what is right.

I especially love the messages Professor Dumbledore leaves with the students at the end of each year. My favorite came at the end of Harry Potter and the Chamber of Secrets. *He said to Harry, "It is our choices, Harry, that show what we truly are far more than our abilities." WOW!! That's exactly what I teach my children and grandchildren!*

—RUTH WILLIAMS,
SPEAKER AND AUTHOR

When Hollywood came calling to put Harry Potter on the big screen, Rowling stuck to her vision and principles. She retained script approval and Warner Brothers gave her input on such things as the look of Hogwarts to keep the films as close to her vision as possible. "The vital thing for me was that it would be true to the book. . . . I didn't want the plot to change very much at all," she said. Because of the control Rowling retained in her dealings with Warner Brothers, all of the cast members in the movie series are British actors. And in an unprecedented decision in a town not known for honoring the vision of its writers, Warner Brothers announced that the final novel, *Harry Potter and the Deathly Hallows*, would be filmed in two feature-length parts to preserve the integrity of Rowling's plotline.

The first Harry Potter movie came out in 2001, and by September 2007, the first five movies had grossed $4.47 billion worldwide, making it the most successful movie franchise ever according to Warner Brothers. The Potter franchise has surpassed the six *Star Wars* and twenty-one James Bond movies and still has two more movies scheduled for release. Its success has put Rowling in the same enviable and rare position of creative control and box office clout enjoyed by two other stubborn visionaries who stayed true to their source material: George Lucas and Peter Jackson (who directed the *Lord of the Rings* trilogy).

Veronika Kwan-Rubinek, Warner Brothers Pictures president of international distribution, said in a 2007 press release, "This worldwide box office record once again proves that the appeal of the Harry Potter movies knows no border, no age limit, and no language barrier. Each of the five films has captured the hearts and sparked the imagination of audiences everywhere."

In late November of 2007, Rowling was featured on the cover of *Entertainment Weekly* and was named the magazine's Entertainer of the Year. "In this high-tech age," the article stated, "Rowling has turned back the clock." They lauded her as the force responsible for people toting around "her big, old-fashioned printed-on-paper books as if they were the hottest new entertainment devices on the planet."

Martha Stewart echoed similar sentiments when she wrote, "J. K. Rowling certainly made the world better with her Harry Potter series. She is a fabulous and gifted writer possessing a most fertile imagination, and she is most definitely a brilliant entrepreneur. Look at what she did: In an era

*What she does a lot of times
is multi-layered and there are so
many details. She might mention
something in passing in one book,
and then pick it up again two or
three books later. To me that's the
sign of a good writer. You know it's
a well-written book when they take
the time to do that. As far as I know,
she's researched the characters.*

*There's a lot of backstory
that doesn't appear in the book,
but she knows it.*

—CONNY ISRAELSON,
JOURNALIST

of television, video games and Internet distractions, she single-handedly enticed millions of children to read— children who might otherwise have never discovered what a fabulous world awaited them inside a book."

Rowling will not stop writing anytime soon. She has never done it for the money or the fame, so the fact that she has both of them now doesn't mean she'll stop touching the world with her words and imagination. Her reward, she insists, is the enthusiasm readers have for her work.

After finishing the first four Harry Potter books, she said, "I'm sure I'll always write, at least until I lose my marbles. I'm very, very lucky. Because of Harry's success, I don't need to do it financially, nobody's making me. I just need to do it for myself."

Lucky for us.

How to Be Like J. K. Rowling

1) **Invest time in what you believe in.** Rowling spent years writing the first Harry Potter book and plotting out the next six without any assurance that her untold hours of hard work would amount to anything. She followed her heart and her love of writing.

2) **Do what you love.** Rowling wrote her first story at age six. She never wavered in her commitment to write and make her living as a writer. She calls writing the work she loves best in all of the world. Even after she became rich and famous, she continued to write and perfect the Harry Potter book series until she completed her goal of seven books.

3) **Work hard.** There are no guarantees that hard work will pay off, but it's just about guaranteed that nothing substantial can be accomplished without it. Initially, Rowling carved out the time to write wherever she could between working and caring for her infant daughter. Even after she achieved financial independence several times over, her work ethic didn't change.

4) **Set goals.** Once Rowling conceived the Harry Potter idea, she set a goal of writing seven Potter books. She planned out all the plotlines and, early on, wrote the last chapter of the seventh book, before the first one was even finished. This was a show of commitment to and faith in herself that she was going to write all the books.

5) **Keep reading and writing.** Rowling's advice to young writers today is gold: "Read as much as you can. Keep writing and throwing it away until one day you do something that you don't think belongs in the [trash bin]. Stick to writing what you know about. Don't give up." Rowling started out as and remains a voracious reader. Many of the books she read shaped her talent

Cont'd

and craft and undoubtedly helped her in writing the Harry Potter series.

6) **Be detailed.** Rowling meticulously planned her books. Not only did she devise rich and elaborate wizardry histories and customs, she thought about all of her characters and their backstories so that she knew them as though they were living, breathing people. This meticulous detail is what caught the attention of Bloomsbury's children's division head, Barry Cunningham, and led to her first sale.

7) **Leave no stone unturned.** Walt Disney directed his employees to "plus" the experience of his movies and theme park attractions. Similarly, Rowling spent time even on little things—like folders—and it paid off. When she sent the first three chapters to the Christopher Little Literary Agency, office manager Bryony Evens took a second look at Rowling's submission because she was drawn to the interesting folder it came in. That one little detail got Evens to read the synopsis, and the rest is history.

8) **No laurel resting.** Rowling never became complacent. Even after achieving fame and fortune, when she became unhappy with the plot development of her fourth book, *Harry Potter and the Goblet of Fire*, Rowling spent countless hours on rewrites until she was satisfied with the results.

6

Lucille Ball
1911–1989

Perseverance

Luck? I don't know anything about luck.
I've never banked on it, and I'm afraid of people who do.
Luck to me is something else: hard work—and realizing
what is [an] opportunity and what isn't.

—LUCILLE BALL

One of the greatest tests of adversity is to persevere and succeed in spite of being told you can't do something. How many great achievements have been aborted because a naysayer told someone she was not good enough to accomplish her dreams?

The iconic Lucille Ball once heard that she didn't have what it takes to be an actress. Fortunately for American and even world culture, she didn't listen to critics. If she had, the face that has been seen by "more people, more often, than the face of any other person who ever lived," according to Ball's Jamestown Museum website, would have been a nonentity.

Born Lucille Ball on August 6, 1911, in Jamestown, New York, she was the first of two children born to Henry and Désirée "DeDe" Ball. As a child she faced her first adversity and monumental sadness in life when her father, a telephone lineman, died in 1915. Her mother, a pianist, encouraged young Lucy's acting aspirations. In addition, her grandfather took her to see vaudeville shows while she was growing up, and that further nurtured a love of performing. An expressive, exuberant teenager, Ball was also encouraged by her high school principal, Bernard Drake, to channel her energies into acting.

At first, she didn't see herself becoming an actress, but she did have a driving ambition to ease her mother's financial burdens. Ball's daughter, Lucie Arnaz, has written that her mother had an "I wanna make some noise" kind of ambition.

Today, of course, young women have multitudes of role models, such as Martha Stewart and Meg Whitman in business, Sandra Day O'Connor and Ruth Bader Ginsburg in law, Condoleezza Rice and Madeline Albright in government, to pattern themselves after to become successful. But in young Lucy's day, those kinds of role models were few and far between. So it was natural that eventually she'd see acting as her vehicle to success, because that's primarily where the female role models and examples of achievement were. She pursued acting by moving to New York City at age seventeen to enroll in the John Murray Anderson–Robert Milton Theater School, with the encouragement of her mother.

It was here Ball faced a choice when the school wrote to her mother saying it would be a waste of money for her to continue, because she "didn't have what it takes to be an actress." Rather than pack it in, Ball continued to persevere to make it in show business. She became a showgirl for the Ziegfeld Follies but was cut from the revue before ever getting beyond the rehearsal stage. She sensed that the follies were not her vehicle for success and agreed with the producers on their decision.

"But I didn't give up," Ball wrote in her book, *Love, Lucy*. "I wore out my soles trudging to casting offices and stuffed the holes with newspaper."

She was eventually picked for the chorus of a show called *Stepping Stones*. Ball was thrilled she lasted five weeks, but then the other shoe dropped. The show was revised to include dance numbers. Late one night after working on the show, the producer announced that anybody who couldn't do "toe work" was out. He told Ball, "You're a nice kid, but you just don't have it.

Why don't you go home to Montana and raise a big family?"

She left that night, dug her hands in her coat pockets, and walked home to her rooming house apartment. But as Ball recalled, "I can't say that I was discouraged. For some incomprehensible reason, I knew that someday I'd make it as an actress."

To say she did *make it* would be a monumental understatement. Her groundbreaking television show, *I Love Lucy*, which premiered in 1951 when she was forty years old, became and still is an American institution. In 1953, a staggering 67 percent of all homes in America tuned in every Monday night to watch it. *I Love Lucy* continues to be seen and enjoyed in more than seventy-seven countries while being dubbed in twenty-two different languages.

For over twenty years, television comedies starring Ball were an interwoven fabric of American society. When *TV Guide* picked its "50 Greatest TV Stars of All Time" in 1996, Ball was number one on their list.

She also broke ground by becoming the first female president of a major television production company when she bought out then ex-husband Desi Arnaz's share of Desilu Studios in 1962.

Ball's advice to struggling actors is suitable guidance to anyone who has a dream and has met with adversity: "You won't be happy, whatever you do, unless you're comfortable with your own conscience. Keep your head up, keep your shoulders back, keep your self-respect, be nice, be smart. And remember that there are practically no *overnight* successes. Before the brilliant hit performance comes [sometime there are] ten, fifteen, twenty years in the salt mines, sweating it out."

In Ball's case, while she had become "queen of the B movies," stardom eluded her until the age of forty. "It took her forty years to become an international star, and she became a star at an age when a lot of careers were in decline," said Kathleen Brady, author of *Lucille: The Life of Lucille Ball*. "She was a secondary Hollywood actress whose fame has outshone the greatest film stars of all time in my opinion. What made her successful was extraordinary perseverance. She persevered, she worked harder than anybody. Perseverance and hard work . . . that's really what her life was."

While still in New York, Ball began modeling to pay the bills after her initial career frustrations. Modeling also led to an opportunity to go to

Hollywood, where she was chosen to be a Goldwyn Girl. While she'd been shy and timid in New York, that wasn't the case once she reached Hollywood.

"She made sure she was not mousey, that she stood up for herself, that she didn't act afraid or intimidated, and she didn't. She made herself noticed," Brady wrote.

In 1933, Ball landed her first film role. In *Roman Scandals* she played a slave girl and was the only actress who volunteered to take a mud pie in the face that was intended for star Eddie Cantor. Rather than thinking it would hurt her fledgling career, she thought it might help her stand out and get noticed, which it did in a small way.

Her friends told her the audience wouldn't know who she was if she allowed her face to be obstructed. "They don't know who I am now anyway," Ball said.

"She would never turn down any work, because that would get you more work," said Michael Karol, author of *Lucy A to Z: The Lucille Ball Encyclopedia*.

Ball was put under contract to film studio RKO and by 1937 had graduated from several small roles to more substantial ones. It was also around this time she was tempted by expediency.

In theory, people shouldn't be applauded for doing the right, just, and moral thing. But in reality, people are human, and temptation takes many forms when you're struggling in life. Ball was presented with just such a temptation when she was still a struggling starlet.

Ball befriended an important producer—who fell in love with her. He was married and had small children, and Ball said their conversations started out about the challenges of raising a family. Then, before Ball really understood what was happening, the producer told her he wanted to divorce his wife and leave his children to marry her.

"I respected this producer's talent; he was attractive, young, and vital. But I couldn't allow myself to fall in love with him because of his wife and children," Ball wrote. "But, because I was ambitious, and because he was a great catch, I struggled with my conscience long and painfully. Friends told me, 'Why don't you marry him? He's a real talent and he'll make your career.' But in the end, I finally found the courage to turn him down."

Ball soon found out doing the right thing sometimes still has negative consequences. The producer lost interest in her career, but his wife didn't. She had enough influence beyond that of even her husband, due to some connected relatives, to make sure Ball would not appear in any A pictures at the RKO studio.

"My movie career just about ended then and there, but I never regretted that decision. I know what it was like to lose a beloved father early in life; no child was going to be put through that torture because of me," she said.

While filming *Too Many Girls* in 1940, she met a Cuban actor/musician named Desi Arnaz. The fateful pairing led to a romance and then marriage in late 1940. It was a case of opposites attracting, and in Ball's words, their differences give an insight into who she was.

"Friends kept pointing out that Desi was a romantic. He lived to enjoy life and never thought of tomorrow. I was a levelheaded realist who never lived beyond my means or went overboard drinking or gambling," Ball wrote.

Ball started getting better roles when she switched studios and worked for MGM, acquiring that "queen of the B movies" moniker mentioned earlier. But it was another medium—radio—that accelerated Ball's journey to stardom. In 1948, she became the star of the radio comedy *My Favorite Husband*. Ball played the scatterbrained wife of a banker.

The show was popular enough that in 1950 CBS proposed turning it into a television series. The network's plan hit a snag, however, when Ball insisted that the role of her husband be changed from a banker to a band-leader (Desi Arnaz). CBS balked at the idea. They felt their audience wouldn't accept the Cuban-born Arnaz and his thick accent as Ball's husband, even though they were actually married.

Rather than give in, Ball and Arnaz began a proof of concept that they funded out of their own pockets. They took their vision of what their show would look like on the road in the form of a nationwide vaudeville tour. Audiences loved it, and it convinced CBS to green-light the show. Ball and Arnaz insisted on having creative control and owning the rights to the show, which they received.

"She never took no for an answer, never ever. If things didn't work one way, she would find a way to make them work another way," Brady said.

Even though they now had a network behind them, Ball wrote that leaving her film career for the still-fledgling medium of television was still quite a gamble. "At that time, television was regarded as the enemy by Hollywood. So terrified was Hollywood of this medium, movie people were afraid to make even guest appearances. If I undertook a weekly television show and it flopped, I might never work in movies again," Ball wrote. "It would mean [Desi and I] would have to give up our respective radio programs, and Desi would have to cancel all his band engagements. It was a tremendous gamble; [but] it had to be an all-or-nothing commitment."

Going with her instincts and a premonition, Ball said she decided to press ahead with the show after having a dream in which her friend, the late comedic actress Carole Lombard, came to her and said, "Go on, kid. Give it a whirl."

The next day Ball called her agent, Don Sharpe. "We'll do it," she said. "Desi and I want to work together more than anything else in the world."

Through perseverance she'd become a sought-after and well-known movie actress, but stardom had eluded her. Ball was forty when *I Love Lucy* first aired. When she was at MGM from 1943 to 1946, she refined her comedic talents by learning from such comedy legends as Buster Keaton and Harold Lloyd. They emphasized to her that a performer has to work hard to make it look easy.

"When she was sitting around doing nothing at the studio, she was doing it with Buster Keaton and Harold Lloyd, who taught her how to use props, and what comedy timing is, and all that stuff. The point is even if you don't think something is working out, it can work out in a very different way," Karol said. "Lucy loved to learn from other people."

When I interviewed Lucy, she said, "They've made perfectionists and workaholics dirty words." She was a perfectionist, and a workaholic, and totally driven. It worked for her. She was totally devoted to her task.

—KATHLEEN BRADY,
LUCILLE: THE LIFE OF LUCILLE BALL

Ball categorized herself as a perfectionist and workaholic. Almost all of the scenes in *I Love Lucy* were the result of detailed rehearsals.

I Love Lucy premiered on August 15, 1951. By episode 20, the show was number one in the ratings and held that position for three years. In her book, Ball expanded on her penchant for perfection and hard work: "I wanted everything about the venture to be top-flight: the timing, the handling of props, the dialogue. We argued a good deal at first because we all cared so passionately; sometimes we'd discuss phrasing or word emphasis in a line of dialogue until past midnight."

Madelyn Pugh Davis was a lead writer on *I Love Lucy* with her writing partner, Bob Davis Jr. The two had also worked with Ball on the radio forerunner to *I Love Lucy, My Favorite Husband.*

"Lucy was a hard worker, and liked to get things right," Davis said. "Lucy would rehearse and rehearse, so that she was letter-perfect on all her lines and she wanted everyone else to be the same. As you know, we shot in front of an audience, and we seldom ever had to do retakes."

Karol said: "Lucy was always practicing her routines on the *I Love Lucy* show. For example, she and Vivian Vance were practicing them over and over again until they were absolutely perfect. That's why the Vitameatavegamin thing is such a work of art because she went over and over and over it until she had it totally down."

Desi Arnaz wrote in his autobiography, *A Book*, that when episodes called for Ball to satirize something she'd never done before, such as working in a pizzeria, "the comedic values depended on how well she satirized the way they twirl the dough around and flip it up in the air as they are molding it. She spent many hours at a pizza parlor after our rehearsals until she could handle that dough as well as the pizza maker. That, of course, is the only way. You have to know how to do it right before you can satirize it."

For other memorable episodes, Ball learned how to play the xylophone as a seal would play it, complete with the physical comedy of her mouth conforming to the different sizes of old-fashioned automobile horns. Arnaz said when their writers asked [Lucy] if she thought she could play *The Glow-Worm* on a saxophone, she told them to give her a week, and she met that commitment.

As most fans know, the plotlines of *I Love Lucy* episodes often dealt with some plan by Lucy to get into show business. Arnaz played Ricky Ricardo, a bandleader who rubbed elbows with movie stars. Lucy wanted to be more than just a housewife, and that was the source of the show's conflict and comedy.

I Love Lucy was so popular that major Hollywood stars of the day appeared on the show. Ball helped make television a respected medium.

As for the effect the show itself had on the American public, "Lucy brought a moving poignancy to even her most harebrained schemes. As Ricky's bored housewife, she always hoped for something more in life. That was a universal hook which touched everyone in her huge audience. We did not all want to make our mark in show business, her persistent goal, but who has not longed for something more?" wrote Wes Gehring in a 2001 *USA Today* article, "*I Love Lucy* Turns 50."

"Lucy Ricardo knows what she wants and tries to find a way to get it. I think that's something we can all enjoy," Brady said.

Ball and Arnaz struck such a chord with the American public that the birth of their son, Desi Arnaz Jr., became a major event of 1953. Ball's real-life pregnancy was written into the *I Love Lucy* show. She stopped working about seven weeks before her baby arrived, having already filmed the episodes about the birth of the Ricardo's baby. As it turned out, both the real baby and the fictional one made their debut on the same day, January 19. Thousands of letters and telegrams were waiting for Ball right after her baby was born. And forty-six million Americans watched *I Love Lucy* that same day to see Ricky Ricardo Jr.'s birth. Talk about cross-promoting!

"Among the things that make *I Love Lucy* endure is that the love between Lucy and Desi was genuine," said Coyne Steven Sanders, coauthor with Tom Gilbert of *Desilu: The Story of Lucille Ball and Desi Arnaz.*

The next day, January 20, former five-star general Dwight D. Eisenhower was sworn in as the nation's thirty-fourth president. Radio and news commentator Walter Winchell said the next Sunday, "This was a banner week: the nation got a man, and Lucy got a boy."

The innate honesty in Lucy's and the entire staff's performances, and the hard work they put into it, made *I Love Lucy* a cultural phenomenon.

It's first season, 1951–1952, changed the Monday night viewing habits of the nation long before Monday Night Football. The show was on from nine to nine-thirty, and Ball wrote that during that time taxis disappeared from the streets of New York. She said Marshall Field's department store in Chicago hung up a sign that said, "We Love Lucy, too, so from now on we will be open Thursday nights instead of Monday." Even the number of telephone calls across the nation dropped during that half hour.

At the height of the *I Love Lucy* craze, there was Lucy jewelry, Lucy dolls, and an extensive line of clothing that included sweaters, blouses, dresses, and pajamas, among other things. Ball and Arnaz became television's highest paid stars.

After the show ended in 1960, so did Ball and Arnaz's marriage. She said she always loved him but reached a point where she couldn't stay married to him.

Desi Arnaz said, "When I look back on our marriage now and ask myself what went wrong, I think that one of the problems was that we were both working too hard and were together too much—all day and all night. . . . There was really no chance to be away from each other and let things cool off."

In addition, Arnaz was a womanizer and developed a drinking problem. Ball had affairs in retaliation of his extramarital affairs. They both got angry and jealous. What made it especially sad is they were the great love of each other's life.

Even apart, the two had a healthy respect for the impact each had on the other's career. When the *New York Times Magazine* asked Arnaz why *I Love Lucy* was so successful and then asked him to divide the credit between the writers, the directors, and the cast, Arnaz said, "I would give Lucy 90 percent and divide the other 10 percent among the rest of us."

Madelyn Pugh Davis said Ball was a writer's dream. "She would do absolutely anything we wrote. If we had a crazy idea, we would check with Lucy to see if she minded doing it. She would say, 'Is it funny?' and we would say, 'We think so,' and she would say 'Sure, I'll do it.'"

"Red Skelton flatters me by saying I have the courage of a tiger," Ball wrote. "I don't think it's a matter of bravery; it's just doing what comes naturally. I do know that if an actress has the slightest aversion to pie in the face or pratfalls, the camera will pick it up instantly. The audience won't laugh; they'll suffer in sympathy."

Ball, for her part, said Arnaz was responsible for 90 percent of her business success due to his vision and acumen as a businessman.

"She was first to admit that Desi was the businessman. She would always give credit to people for their talent and skills. Even after she divorced Desi, and it was a bitter experience, she'd say 'Desi's the brains, Desi's the genius, Desi's the one.' She had that wonderful quality to give credit where credit was due," Stevens said. "For example, she never failed to give credit to her writers on the *I Love Lucy* show, Bob Carroll Jr. and Madelyn Pugh Davis, and the head writer and executive producer, Jess Oppenheimer, for their part in the success of the show. She always praised Vivian Vance as being the best comedy partner anyone could ever have."

Arnaz had run the studio he and Ball founded, *Desilu*, for eleven years. He eventually decided he wanted to retire, and Ball bought him out in 1962 and reluctantly, she said, she became the studio's president. She was the first female president of a major television production company.

While Ball didn't consider herself a businesswoman, she was smart enough to bring in good people to run certain aspects of the business where she lacked expertise.

"If she wasn't sure of anything, she would surround herself with the best people that she knew to teach her," Stevens said.

She always relied on her instincts. She personally gave the final go-aheads for the now classic television shows *Star Trek* and *Mission Impossible*. She especially believed in *Star Trek*.

One of the reasons Ball achieved immense popularity with the American public is that she never lost sight of the person she truly was. She had a down-to-earth quality and maintained humility within the context of being an iconic actress. She stayed true to her Jamestown, New York, roots, rather than "going Hollywood."

"Lucy had a great love of life, and an appreciation for ordinary life. I think that served her in good stead," Brady said. "Lucy is influential because she makes us laugh so hard and she makes us happy. That makes us love her. She makes the ordinary magical."

Later in life Ball came to embrace the teachings of Dr. Norman Vincent Peale, the author of *The Power of Positive Thinking*. She also got to know him personally. "Dr. Peale helped me realize that our professional achievements are secondary; the important thing in life is our relationship with other human beings. It's not what we set out to get, but how we go about the daily task of living," wrote Ball.

In addition, she said, "I believe that we're as happy in life as we make up our minds to be. All actors and actresses, no matter how talented or famous, have ups and downs in their careers. It's just the nature of the business. You have to learn to roll with the punches, and not take them personally."

The impact Ball had on American culture and women in particular was summed up beautifully by humorist writer Erma Bombeck. Bombeck wrote more than four thousand newspaper articles in over thirty years and was read by some thirty million readers in nine hundred newspapers. She also published fifteen books, most of which became bestsellers.

She learned from her mistakes. She wasn't introspective. Her philosophy in life was "get on with it." She didn't believe in getting caught up in her own problems. She believed there was always a way out, that there was always a solution.

—COYNE STEVEN SANDERS AND TOM GILBERT, *DESILU: THE STORY OF LUCILLE BALL AND DESI ARNAZ*

As Michael Karol tells us, Bombeck's tribute came in the mid-1980s on *Good Morning America*. The show did a weeklong series honoring Ball, and Karol transcribed Bombeck's words, which appear on his website (www.sitcom boy.com) and are reprinted here courtesy of Karol:

Dear Lucy Ricardo,

Remember me? I didn't think so. We never met, but for nearly a decade you dropped into my living room on a 10-inch black-and-white screen. I was the woman with the three kids under 5. I never told you what you, and Ricky, and Fred, and Ethel, did for me.

The fifties were tough times for housewives. The slick magazines were telling me I was a nurse, a mistress, a chauffeur, a chef, a financier, and a teacher. They forgot fireman—my oven caught fire three times a week. The suburbs pushed us out to a world of septic tanks and crab grass, where the second-highest spot in my week was visiting my meat in the frozen food locker.

Want to know what the highest spot in my week was? Monday nights, when my heroine, [the star of] I Love Lucy, came on the screen. You acted out every fantasy I could imagine. You did it all—you defied your husband by ordering furniture you couldn't afford, you eavesdropped on

Bill Holden in a restaurant and nearly fell in his lap, and there wasn't a week when you didn't try to leave the house and get a job. I remember the time you and Ethel got a job in the candy factory dipping chocolates. I had just been snowed in with three kids for 10 days, and the prognosis was, "She will never laugh again." But I did . . . you captured that free, independent spirit that is in every woman, and you did it all with style, femininity, intelligence, and good humor.

Bombeck ended her tribute with:

I've been sitting here trying to think what set you apart from the Harriet Nelsons, the Donna Stones, the June Cleavers, and Maude, Ann Romano, and Mother Walton, and you know what I decided? You were real. Yes, you were. With all the exaggeration, the clowning, and the contrivances, the best any of us could hope for was a bit of Lucy's perspective. I guess all I really wanted to say is that when the pages of women's history are being written, if the name Lucy Ricardo is not there, it will not reflect the heroine of 70 million housewives of the 1950s.

How to Be Like Lucille Ball

1) **Know when to trust your instincts.** Ball believed in herself even after the John Murray Anderson–Robert Milton Theater School told her she "didn't have what it takes to be an actress." She continued to believe in herself even after she was fired from the chorus of *Stepping Stones*. Study her words: "I can't say that I was discouraged. For some incomprehensible reason, I knew that someday I'd make it as an actress."

   She had no concrete reasons to believe she'd make it— nothing except her instincts, faith, and belief in herself. There's a fine line between a fantasy and a realistic dream. Ball's life serves as an illustration that bumps in a career path do not have to derail one's dreams. In Ball's case, she had confidence that was actualized.

2) **Persevere.** While Ball was a successful actress before *I Love Lucy*, it wasn't until that show, at age forty, when she took a chance in the new medium of television that she became a star.

   "Remember that there are practically no *overnight* successes. Before the brilliant hit performance comes [sometimes there are] ten, fifteen, sometimes twenty years in the salt mines, sweating it out," Ball wrote. While others might say Ball had already accomplished a lot before *I Love Lucy*, clearly Ball felt she hadn't achieved her full potential.

3) **Make adjustments.** Honest self-evaluation is important in life. In New York, Ball was shy and withdrawn as she pursued her career. When she arrived in Hollywood, she became more assertive, making sure to stand up for herself and make herself noticed.

Cont'd

4) **Never lose your moral compass.** Expediency hurts everyone, including the person employing it. Ball always followed her moral compass. "You won't be happy, whatever you do, unless you're comfortable with your own conscience . . . keep your self-respect, be nice, be smart," Ball said.

   When an influential producer wanted to marry her, and leave his wife and children, Ball struggled with her conscience. She found the strength to turn him down and never regretted her decision, even though it hurt her career.

5) **Prove your concept.** When Ball and Arnaz proposed that he play her husband on *I Love Lucy*, CBS didn't think the audience would buy the Cuban-born and heavily accented Arnaz as Ball's husband. So Ball and Arnaz funded a nationwide vaudeville tour featuring the two as husband and wife in a pre–*I Love Lucy* show. Audiences loved it, and the success of the tour convinced CBS to cast Arnaz.

6) **Know what you want.** Ball and Arnaz decided they wanted creative control of *I Love Lucy*, in addition to owning rights to it, and they received both. Some might have been happy just to have a show, but because Ball and Arnaz stuck to their convictions, they set the stage for their financial empire.

7) **Take calculated risks.** Ball had reached the level of a successful actress, even becoming known as the "queen of the B movies," but she wasn't a star and knew she hadn't yet reached her full potential. In addition, she and Arnaz wanted to work together. But television was a gamble because it was held in low esteem by the movie industry. If her show had flopped, Ball might never have worked in movies again. "It was a tremendous gamble," Ball wrote. "It had to be an all-or-nothing commitment." She'd clearly weighed both sides of the question and decided to forge ahead.

8) **Learn from mentors.** Ball loved to learn from other people. She took advantage of her downtime on the MGM studio lot

to learn comedy, especially physical comedy, from legends
Buster Keaton and Harold Lloyd. And when Ball became president of Desilu Studios, she surrounded herself with the best
people to compensate for what she didn't know about running
a studio.

9) **Work at your craft.** Buster Keaton reinforced in Ball the idea
that a performer has to work hard to make it look easy. Ball was
already an easy sell on that score. She called herself a perfectionist and a workaholic. She worked hard on the set, rehears-
ing endlessly to get everything just right.

10) **Give credit where it's due.** Humility keeps people grounded.
Ball was humble and down-to-earth despite being a huge star.
She always made it a point to give credit to Desi Arnaz and the
other people she worked with for her success and the success of
her show.

Madeleine Albright
1937–

Activism

I think of the blood that is in my family veins.
Does it matter what kind of blood it is? It shouldn't.
It is just blood that does its job. But it mattered to Hitler,
and that matters to us all, because that
is why six million Jews died.

—Madeleine Albright

A barrier for women came tumbling down in 1997, and history was made, when Madeleine Albright became the first female secretary of state of the United States.

"Set your sights as high as possible and pursue every opportunity," is Albright's advice to young people. She has also become a role model for women everywhere. The significance of being the first female secretary of state has never been lost on her. "I think I really am the embodiment of the turbulence of the twentieth century, as well as of the tolerance and optimism of the United States," Albright said in *Contemporary Heroes and Heroines Book III*.

The future secretary was born Maria Jana Korbel in Prague, Czechoslovakia, in 1937, against the backdrop of a Europe that had storm clouds of war brewing on the horizon. Her father, Josef, a member of the Czech diplomatic corps, was forced to flee to England with his wife and infant daughter when Hitler ruthlessly abrogated the Munich Agreement. The Nazis occupied the country in 1938 as the rest of the world stood by, watched, and did nothing.

In contrast to that world, and perhaps due to her life experiences, Albright's tenure as secretary of state was marked by activism. As a refugee from totalitarianism, Albright has called for American involvement abroad. Never one to coddle tyrants and dictators, in her diplomatic career she has always advocated a strong stand against them and their immoral persecution of those who are weaker, more vulnerable, and innocent.

She has never backed away from advocating the use of military force in places such as Bosnia and Haiti if such action could get the job done to protect people. "What's the point of having this great military you're always talking about if we can't use it?" Albright once asked former Joint Chiefs of Staff chair Colin Powell during a debate on U.S. policy in Bosnia, as quoted by Barbara Kramer in *Madeleine Albright: First Woman Secretary of State.*

"[Albright's] childhood taught her that freedom can never be taken for granted, and . . . American leadership is always critical to the defense of liberty," said Warren Christopher, her predecessor as secretary of state.

With respect to the six million Jewish people murdered in the Holocaust and the estimated fifty million killed in World War II, Albright spoke concerning the danger of appeasement and when intervention was warranted: "I am somebody that was liberated by Americans, but I think that if things had been done earlier, not so many lives would have been lost."

Young Madeleine was in England during "The Blitz" of 1940–1941. Her family spent many terror-filled nights in air-raid shelters, while German bombers roamed overhead raining down death and destruction. "I remember spending huge portions of my life in air-raid shelters singing 'A Hundred Green Bottles Hanging on the Wall,'" Albright said in *Madeleine Albright: Stateswoman.*

She still carries with her the chilling memory of coming out of those shelters in the morning and seeing the damage the bombs had done to the city, the result of unchallenged terrorism. Another memory from that time was the special steel table her family and others had that offered additional shelter for people in their homes. "They said if your house was bombed and you were under the table you would survive," Albright is quoted by Michael Dobbs in *Madeleine Albright: A Twentieth-Century Odyssey*.

Before becoming secretary of state, Albright made her reputation as a specialist in Russian and Eastern European studies and as a longtime foreign affairs adviser to top Democratic officials. She had displayed her considerable diplomatic skills as the United States ambassador to the United Nations under President Clinton.

During her time as ambassador she won over many of her colleagues with her straightforward, no-nonsense style, her iron will and her charm. When President Bill Clinton needed to appoint a new secretary of state during his second term in office, he turned to Albright, a person many believed was a natural for the job.

As a testament to her reputation and expertise, the United States Senate unanimously approved her nomination. She took over the reins at the State Department, where her hawkish outlook and penchant for ignoring bureaucratic protocol were almost guaranteed to shake up the often stodgy world of foreign affairs.

After World War II, the Korbel family had briefly returned to Prague and then moved to Yugoslavia when Josef was posted as an ambassador but fled in 1948 when the Communists took over the country. Granted political asylum in the United States, the family, which now included a son and another daughter, eventually settled in Colorado. Josef Korbel became a professor of international relations at the University of Denver. He was also the founding dean of its Graduate School of International Studies.

Her father was Albright's biggest influence by far. "A great deal of what I did, I did because I wanted to be like my father," Albright wrote. She emulated him in many ways. She wrote school papers on the same subjects as his books—foreign affairs and Eastern Europe. She worked hard in school because he believed in the value of a good education. She pushed herself to be the best she could be because he expected nothing less. He also instilled in her another valuable lesson: work hard and you can achieve your highest aspirations.

His passion for his work, Albright wrote in *Madam Secretary: A Memoir*, made "whatever period in history I was studying come alive with stories." He put any battle or diplomatic conference in context. "When he spoke of World War II," she said, "he never strayed far from the lessons of Munich: unspeakable tragedies ensue when great countries appease evil, make decisions over the heads of smaller powers, and do not pay attention to what is happening in faraway places."

She arrived in America at age eleven. "My family came here to escape communism and to find freedom. We did both," she wrote. Her ambition at that time was only to "speak English well, please my parents, study hard, and grow up to be an American," Albright said in *Madeleine Albright and the New American Diplomacy* by Thomas Lippman. "I spent a lot of time worrying, trying to make sure that I would fit in. . . . I wanted very much to be an American."

Growing up, Albright's education was anything but normal. Before settling in the United States, she was tutored at home in Yugoslavia because her father wanted no Communist influence from the country's school system seeping into the house. She was eventually sent to a Swiss boarding school. The teachers there were strict, and French was spoken exclusively. The lesson was simple and the incentive for it clear: learn to speak French or don't eat. Young Madeleine, who learned French quickly, advises others today on the value of learning another language.

Albright says of her high school years in Denver that she was a foreign policy wonk even then. "In my parents' home we talked about international relations all the time, the way some families talk about sports or other things around the dinner table."

She attended Wellesley College in Massachusetts and majored in political science. Never one to follow the crowd, Albright campaigned for Democratic presidential candidate Adlai Stevenson in 1956 on the predominantly Republican campus. As editor of the school newspaper, she also indulged her growing passion for journalism.

A few days after graduating with honors in 1959, she married Joseph Medill Patterson Albright, the heir to a newspaper fortune. She had met Joseph while working as a summer intern for the *Denver Post*.

At first, Albright's career ambitions were only focused on journalism.

Starting in Missouri with the *Rolla Daily News*, she then went to Chicago with her husband, who accepted a position with the *Sun-Times*. According to the *Los Angeles Times*, Albright's life as a journalist came to a screeching halt when an editor for another Chicago newspaper referred to her as "honey" and advised her to go find a career more suitable for a woman. "I listened to him and gave up the idea. I would fight it now, of course, but I think I'm better at what I do now than I would have been as a journalist," she said.

During the 1960s, Albright concentrated on raising her family consisting of three daughters (including a set of twins). When her husband's new job as city editor of *Newsday* necessitated a move to Long Island, New York, Albright resumed her education, this time at Columbia University.

Getting up every morning at 4:30 to study for a few hours before having to get her children ready for school, it took Albright the better part of a decade to complete her degree. But her determination paid off. Albright earned a doctorate in international studies in addition to a Russian studies certificate. Looking back on that time of her life, Albright said, "It was the hardest thing I ever did."

> *I do not believe that things happen accidentally.*
> *I believe you earn them.*
> —MADELEINE ALBRIGHT

In 1968, the Albrights moved to Washington, D.C. By standards of the day, Albright had an unorthodox mothering style to say the least. While most of the other mothers stayed home and concentrated only on the family, Albright had other ideas—ideas her daughter Anne supported. "I always thought my mother's work was very exciting, and my sisters and I never felt that she didn't have enough time for us."

By the mid-1970s, she had made the leap into Democratic politics, serving as chief legislative assistant to the late Democratic Senator Edmund S. Muskie of Maine. Muskie became not only a mentor to Albright, but one of her heroes. She says, "He gave me the confidence to know that no barrier or ceiling should stop me from serving freedom in my own life." She also admired Muskie's honesty and forthrightness.

Albright has had several other heroes in her life along with her father and Muskie, including Eleanor Roosevelt, Mahatma Gandhi, and Aung San Suu Kyi, the leader of the democratic forces of Burma, who was awarded the Nobel Peace Prize in 1991 for her nonviolent struggle for democracy and human rights.

Albright spoke out against the regime as the United Nations ambassador in Burma's capital of Rangoon in 1992. She had just completed an inspiring meeting with Mrs. Suu Kyi.

"As we talked," Albright said, "I was struck by the contrast between her ethereal beauty and steely resolve. Abroad, she could be leading an easy life. Silent, she could have a secure one. Instead she had chosen the hard road of principled and nonviolent opposition to an unprincipled and brutal regime."

I have been remarkably impressed by the fact that what you see [with Albright] is what you really get. I had been familiar with her tough talk, like everyone else, but it's a genuine reflection of what she believes in. She truly believes that the United States has to take a leadership position.

—A senior staff member to Secretary Albright, as quoted in Madeleine Albright and the New American Diplomacy by Thomas W. Lippman

After her meeting with Mrs. Suu Kyi, Albright then had a not-so-inspiring meeting with the military junta in power. At a press conference before departing, Albright recalled, "I said Burmese leaders could begin to move down the democratic path, and thereby reduce their isolation, or continue on the path of repression and ultimately ruin both themselves and their country." Albright said of her outspoken style: "I tell it like it is."

In 1977, Albright joined President Jimmy Carter's national security staff to act as a liaison with Congress. She had been handpicked for the job by Zbigniew Brzezinski, her former thesis adviser from Columbia, who became Carter's top national security adviser. Brzezinski and Albright felt they shared a common personal history. Both were from Eastern Europe. Both understood only too well the sacrifices made by their parents to provide them with lives free from oppression and tyranny. In this new role, Albright began exercising her legendary charm to smooth relations between the White House and Capitol Hill.

Albright says that her career plans were never that carefully thought out. "The best things that happened to me are the ones I haven't planned for," she explained. But she says, "I'm prepared for them. That's something different." Not only did her diligence, coupled with her persistence, impress her colleagues, but Albright's background and credentials in foreign policy studies helped advance her career. She not only handled every task given her but her work ethic opened doors that otherwise would have been closed. "Whatever job you have to do, do it well because people remember. Even if you're not making foreign policy, people remember the job you did," Albright said.

Slowly and methodically, Albright was establishing her credentials by building a network with the political "who's who" of Washington. She did it by inviting the crème de le crème of Democratic foreign policy makers to dinner parties at her home for free-form discussions and exchange of ideas. She made sure to use these one-night "think tanks" to forge relationships with the impressive group of politicians that was attracted to these gatherings.

Every Democrat who had aspirations for the Oval Office would at one time or another wind up at Albright's house for advice. Why wouldn't they? With twelve years of involvement in international affairs, as a legislative aide, congressional liaison, research professor, as well as foreign policy adviser, it was a no-brainer. She was the "go-to girl." Albright explains, "The people I work with appreciate the fact that I'm plugged into Washington. . . . I'm in the inner circle. I'm involved in everything."

While her professional life was gaining momentum, Albright's personal life was dealt a devastating blow in 1982 when her husband left her for another woman. The split, which she says took her totally by surprise, prompted her to reevaluate the direction of her life. At the time, she made it clear to anyone who would listen that she did not want a divorce. She did not want to be known as the ex-Mrs. "anything." She decided she needed to be proactive, take a few months, rethink, reevaluate, and come up with a plan of action.

The plan of action was to create a new focus, something to take her mind away from a failed marriage. Albright decided to join the faculty of Georgetown University that year as a professor of international affairs where she earned "teacher of the year" honors a record four times. She served as the director of the Women in Foreign Service program at the university's School of Foreign Service as well.

As usual, Albright was well prepared for her lectures. She was able to translate complicated curriculum into relevant, easy-to-understand information. She was respected as an outstanding, yet also demanding professor. Her outgoing, engaging, and enthusiastic approach was contagious. "Students flocked to her," said Peter Krough, the dean who hired Albright. "She was like a pied piper."

Like her father, Albright had a passion for her subject and she possessed the ability to make it come alive. The "pied piper" used role-playing to make things more interesting and to get her students involved. Having the young women take on roles of government officials in debates of foreign policy issues, she hoped it would get them involved in a field that up to that time was dominated by men. Albright was determined to change that.

One life lesson she relayed to students concerned meetings at the White House when she was on the National Security Council staff. She was often hesitant to offer her opinion, only to find one of the men would say exactly what she was thinking and then get the recognition for a good idea. The point she was trying to make to her students was that "there are lots of shy people in the world, and they don't go anywhere."

During this period, Albright continued to offer her home as a veritable foreign policy think tank, where she presided over the informal gatherings of intellectuals and politicians discussing current events and issues. She also became even more involved in Democratic politics, serving as an adviser to presidential candidate Walter Mondale and his running mate, Geraldine Ferraro, during the 1984 campaign, and to Michael Dukakis in the 1988 race. According to the *Los Angeles Times*, it was widely believed that Albright would have been offered a top job if Dukakis had won the election. Instead, after his defeat, she took the position of president of the Center for National Policy, a Democratic think tank. By this time, she was a well-known figure in Washington and a standout in a field long dominated by men.

Following Bill Clinton's election to the presidency in 1992, Albright was named the U.S. representative to the United Nations. She was the lone woman on the fifteen-member Security Council and only the second woman to serve in that capacity for her country, Jeanne Kirkpatrick being the first. "It's a great thrill to represent the United States," Albright told a reporter for the *Los Angeles Times*. "And I'm sure that whether you're male or female, you have the same feeling when you are representing the most powerful country in the world." Furthermore, she remarked in *Time*, "At this stage in world history, practically every foreign-policy issue has something to do with the UN. It puts me in the wonderful position of being there at the takeoff, during flight and at the landing."

One particular flight landed her center stage when two small planes operated by a Cuban exile group called Brothers to the Rescue flew close to Cuban airspace. Cuban fighter jets intercepted and shot them down, killing the pilots. On tapes of the Cuban fighter pilots' conversations, recorded by U.S. intelligence, one was heard exulting about their feat, using the vulgar Spanish term for testicles.

In typical Albright fashion, turning their own language against them, she denounced the Cubans in front of the whole United Nations by saying, "Frankly, this is not *cojones*; this is cowardice," a line that ruffled a lot of feathers, particularly those of diplomats from Spanish-speaking countries.

However, it did delight many Cuban Americans as well as President Clinton. Albright's statement was "probably the most effective one-liner in the whole administration's foreign policy," Clinton said. "The Cuban Americans loved it so much they had bumper stickers made up. I have a bumper sticker with Madeleine's quote on it."

> *I don't always agree with her . . . but she is not [politically correct]. She is just honest; that goes a long way with me.*
>
> —Senator Jesse Helms

Albright, in her position, understood the power of the one-liner in relation to the media and how to use it to full advantage when pressing an important point for world consumption. A December 1996 *Time* magazine article described her as "the master of the sound bite, explaining complex issues in ten-second phrases that lunch-pail Americans can understand."

When President Clinton was considering the composition of his second-term foreign policy team, memories of how he carried Florida in November 1996, of sixty thousand Cuban Americans packed into Miami's Orange Bowl cheering "Madeleine, Libertad!" for Albright, weighed heavily in her favor.

Albright's position on the crisis in the former Yugoslavia also served to raise her stock. She consistently argued for a diplomatic approach, coupled with military intervention by the United States and its NATO allies to stem the tide of Bosnian Serb territorial expansion and "ethnic cleansing." Clinton's cabinet was divided on what course to pursue. Clinton finally sided with Albright and authorized U.S. and NATO air strikes against Bosnian Serb positions, which stopped them in their tracks and led to the Dayton Accords and the end of the war in Bosnia.

"I would rather be out front and criticized for saving lives than sitting back and waiting for somebody else to state the case," Albright said.

One of Albright's friends told a reporter that Bosnia was a turning point in her career. "Until then, she still thought of herself—at least, a little bit—as a divorced housewife. But on the most important foreign-policy question of the first term, she was right and the guys were wrong."

When President Clinton nominated her for the job of secretary of state, Albright gained an unexpected understanding of her personal background. While doing research for a piece in the *Washington Post*'s Sunday magazine, reporter Michael Dobbs had learned from Albright's cousin in Czechoslovakia that the Korbels were actually of Jewish origin. They chose to raise their children in the Roman Catholic faith, perhaps for career reasons on Josef's part or maybe to shield the family from anti-Semitism as Nazi Germany swept across the continent of Europe. Dobbs also learned that three of Albright's grandparents as well as more than a dozen other relatives had been victims of the Holocaust.

These revelations surprised Albright, who recalled that her parents had simply said that some family members had died during the war, an explanation she didn't think of challenging then and refuses to criticize now. As she remarked in a *Newsweek* interview: "My parents did everything in their power to make a good life for their children. They were very protective of us. . . . What they gave us children was the gift of life, literally. Twice, once by giving us birth and the other by bringing us to America to escape what, clearly now, would have been a certain death. So I am not going to question their motives. . . . I have been and am very proud to be an American. . . . I have been proud of the heritage that I have known about and I will be equally proud of the heritage that I have just been given."

As one of the most outspoken and effective members of President

Clinton's foreign policy team, Albright was the natural choice to replace Warren Christopher as secretary of state when he announced his intention to resign after the 1996 election. Albright immediately faced a wide variety of pressing issues, including disagreements with China over human rights abuses and trade issues, the expansion of NATO to include several Central European nations formerly within the Russian/Soviet Union sphere of influence, and the need to fill key vacancies at several U.S. embassies around the world. The ongoing conflict in the former Yugoslavia also demanded attention, as did the precarious peace in the Middle East between the Israelis and the Palestinians.

One of Albright's first endeavors in her new role was to set off on a whirlwind, ten-day tour abroad that saw her visit nine major world capitals, including Rome, Moscow, and Beijing. Her goal was to establish her presence on the world stage, and that she did exceedingly well. The tour was a resounding success; the dignitaries she met were greatly impressed by what a *U.S. News and World Report* article described as her ability to "balance consideration for foreign sensibilities and unapologetic advocacy of U.S. policies."

> *[Albright] has been an extraordinarily visible and outspoken secretary of state.*
>
> —Thomas W. Lippman,
> MADELEINE ALBRIGHT AND THE NEW AMERICAN DIPLOMACY

Albright has poured much of her energy into efforts to convince the American people as well as their elected representatives in Washington that foreign policy does matter. "What I'm trying to do," she explained in the *New York Times*, "is to connect with the American people in order to get support for foreign policy so we can get money for foreign policy so we can do foreign policy."

Albright continued to travel overseas a great deal, visiting a number of countries, among them China, Korea, Russia, the Czech Republic, and even Vietnam, where she was the first U.S. secretary of state to set foot in Ho Chi Minh City since South Vietnam fell to the communist North in 1975. While she generally received high marks, especially for pushing through NATO enlargement, securing Senate ratification of the Chemical Weapons Convention, and gaining Senate approval for administration nominees to more than a dozen key State Department posts, she also encountered some criticism.

Some would accuse her of favoring style over substance, claiming that she ignored hot spots such as Zaire, China, and the Middle East if there was no good news to report.

In September 1997, Albright made her first official trip to the Middle East on a quest to mend a deadly rift in Arab-Israeli relations. Albright says of those trips, "I am often asked whether I was condescended to by men as I traveled around the world to Arab countries and other places with highly traditional cultures. I replied, 'No,' because when I arrived somewhere, it was in a large plane with 'United States of America' emblazoned on the side."

> *We have consistent principles and flexible tactics. We will continue to speak out about human rights violations.*
>
> —MADELEINE ALBRIGHT

Her message to both sides was characteristically tough. She said each side had a mutual responsibility to honor the 1995 peace agreement reached by the late Israeli Prime Minister Yitzhak Rabin and PLO leader Yasser Arafat and to move the peace process forward. But Albright had left Jerusalem after only three frustrating days, characterizing her visit as a failure because she could not convince the Israelis and Palestinians to resume talks. Declaring that "I will not come back to tread water," she vowed to stay away until Israeli Prime Minister Benjamin Netanyahu and Arafat had made some "hard decisions." Shortly after her visit, Netanyahu and Arafat agreed to meet face-to-face for the first time in eight months for the purpose of reestablishing a dialogue between them, a move Albright hailed as "a step forward."

Despite the uphill struggles she had faced on many fronts, Albright considered her job "a great privilege," as she remarked in the *New York Times*. Former Secretary of State George C. Marshall, the architect of the massive post-World War II economic plan that bears his name, is the person Albright often looked to for inspiration as she went about her work. She credits the Marshall Plan with building a bulwark against communist inroads in at least half of Europe during the Cold War.

"I truly do believe in the goodness of American power," Albright said to Nancy Gibbs of *Time*. "I don't just mean military force. I mean the role the U.S. can have in the world when it's properly used." As she remarked in the *New York Times*, "We are in one of those phases of history where we are the creators. So getting it right is really important."

During a commencement speech at Mt. Holyoke College in Massachusetts, Albright offered some valuable insights to its graduating class:

Madeleine Albright, a secretary of state like no other, has tried to renovate diplomacy in theory and practice to reflect—and to promote— the inevitable evolution of her adopted country's global role.

—THOMAS W. LIPPMAN,
MADELEINE ALBRIGHT AND THE NEW AMERICAN DIPLOMACY

Hitler is dead. Stalin is dead. Lenin is dead. And the only Marx that still matters is on late night television shooting elephants in their pajamas. The temptation is to coast. To sit back, avert our eyes and assume that what does not affect us immediately will not affect us ever. But then we have to ask, what if half a century ago, Secretary of State George Marshall had decided that America had done enough in helping to win the second world war; and that we could let a Europe in ruins fend for itself?

What if President Truman had decided that the surrounded city of Berlin was too remote, and that Americans were too weary of conflict and too wary of new commitments to mount an airlift on its behalf? What if Eleanor Roosevelt had decided that it was enough for Americans to worry about the rights of our own citizens and that we did not need to lead in forging the Universal Declaration of Human Rights? . . . It is certain, if you aim high enough, that you will find your strongest beliefs ridiculed and challenged—that principles that you cherish may be derisively dismissed by those claiming to be more practical or realistic than you. But no matter how weary you may become in persuading others to see the value in what you value, have courage still, and persevere.

How to Be Like Madeleine Albright

1) **Reach for the stars.** Albright did, and made history as the first female secretary of state in the United States. "Set your sights as high as possible and pursue every opportunity," she said.

2) **Stand up for those in need.** An activist secretary of state shaped by her life experiences early on, Albright believed in American involvement abroad when necessary. In her diplomatic career, Albright always advocated a strong stand against tyrants and dictators.

3) **Learn from role models.** Albright's father, Josef Korbel, a professor of International Relations and a diplomat, took time to nurture his daughter, a future secretary of state. He fed her intellectually by taking an interest in her studies. "In my parents' home," Albright said, "we talked about international relations all the time, the way some families talk about sports or other things around the dinner table."

   Josef preached the values of a good education and the virtue of hard work. Albright pushed herself to be the best she could be because of those high expectations, and she embraced a valuable lesson: work hard and you can achieve your highest aspirations.

4) **Sacrifice for your goals.** To continue her education after marriage and motherhood, Albright juggled school around her other responsibilities. In pursuit of her doctorate in international studies, she got up in the early hours of the morning to study. While it took her almost ten years to complete her degree, she did it without neglecting her family. One of her daughters remembers fondly, "We used to do our homework together." Albright recalls that time as "the hardest thing I ever did."

5) **Speak your mind.** A central theme in Albright's life is the lessons

Cont'd

learned from the appeasement of Germany in World War II. In office, she was not one to hold her tongue. "I tell it like it is," she said. She was known for her honest, outspoken manner, and she wasn't afraid of ruffling feathers, as she demonstrated when she told Burmese leaders in 1992 that their path of repression would "ultimately ruin both themselves and their country."

6) **Nurture contacts.** Albright applied her work ethic to every task she with given, leaving lasting impressions on her colleagues. "Whatever job you have to do, do it well, because people remember. Even if you're not making foreign policy, people remember the job you did," Albright said.

7) **Network.** Albright was proactive in developing her connections in Washington, inviting top Democratic foreign policy makers to dinner parties at her home and using these one-night "think tanks" to forge relationships. "The people I work with appreciate the fact that I'm plugged into Washington . . . I'm in the inner circle. I'm involved in everything," she said at the time.

8) **Develop confidence.** It is a matter of doing one's homework and being prepared. If you are prepared, there is no reason to lack confidence. Albright learned to speak up when she had an educated opinion. While on President Carter's National Security Council staff, she was often hesitant to offer her opinion, only to find someone else would say what she was thinking. "There are lots of shy people in the world, and they don't go anywhere," Albright said.

8

Estée Lauder
1906–2004

Quality

I've always believed that success comes
from not letting your eyes stray from that target.
Anyone who wants to achieve a dream must
stay strong, focused, and steady.

—ESTÉE LAUDER

stée Lauder's cosmetics company didn't just have her name. In many ways it bared her soul. It was a personal extension of her values about beauty, customers, and her love for her work.

Lauder didn't learn business from a book or a school, but through her own drive and instincts, in addition to trial and error. In the process, she became the richest self-made woman in the world. Her business achievements landed her on *Time* magazine's 1998 list of the twenty most influential "builders and titans" of the twentieth century.

She had been making and selling her own cosmetics since she was a teenager and founded the Estée Lauder Company in 1946 when she was almost forty. At first, she and her husband, Joe, manufactured their four initial skin-care products on their kitchen stove. By the time Lauder died in 2004 at age ninety-seven, Estée Lauder Companies, Inc., was an international beauty business empire that in 2003 had posted sales of $5.1 billion. It had some two thousand products and twenty-one thousand employees. As of 2006, that figure grew to twenty-eight thousand employees, and the corporation ranked 340th on the 2006 Fortune 500 list. The company currently earns over $6.4 billion in revenues and controls 45 percent of the cosmetics market in United States department stores.

To build her empire, Lauder minded her p's and q's: *persistence* and *quality*.

"What makes a successful businesswoman?" Lauder wrote in *Estée: A Success Story*. "It's persistence. It's that certain little spirit that compels you to stick it out just when you're at your most tired. It's that quality that forces you to persevere, find the route around the stone wall. It's the immovable stubbornness that will not allow you to cave in when everyone says to give up."

Lauder's son Leonard, who helped the company reach even greater heights when he succeeded his mother as president, told *Time* magazine that "ambition" was the defining word he would use about her.

Lauder was just a very ambitious and driven person. I don't think that's something that came out of her journey. I think it was just what she was born with.

—Nancy F. Koehn, professor of business administration, Harvard Business School

Her mission was to help women look their best and draw confidence from that. Her message was one of taking care of and enhancing the gifts each woman has. "Glow is the essence of beauty, and it's the absence of radiance that diminishes beauty—at any age," Lauder said.

As the years went on, Lauder never let her own age, which she called "the best kept secret since D-day," hold her back or define her. For example, after turning day-to-day operations of her company over to her sons, Leonard and Ronald, in the early 1970s, Lauder stayed active as chairman of the board until her mideighties. She committed herself for forty-plus years to being present at every new Estée Lauder cosmetics counter opening anywhere in the country, and eventually outside of it, including Moscow and other eastern European cities.

"It wasn't youth that made me so energetic, it was enthusiasm. That's why I know a woman of any age has it within her to begin a business or a life's work of any sort. It's a fresh outlook that makes youth so attractive anyway, that quality of *anything's possible*. That spirit is not owned only by those under thirty," she said.

By never compromising on quality, she ensured that the proof of success was getting her products in people's hands. From the time she started making and selling cosmetics, the power of a free sample and a free gift with purchase was always part of her marketing strategy. By the early 1950s, the Estée Lauder Company was doing well enough to allocate $50,000 for advertising, but she was told that still wasn't enough to launch a proper campaign. So she plowed that money into even more free samples and the marketing of them. She called free samples the most honest way to do business.

"You give people a product to try. If they like its quality, they buy it. They haven't been lured by an advertisement, but convinced by the product itself," Lauder wrote.

Other companies followed Lauder's example, but they missed her point. While Lauder was giving away her best, they were giving away their failures in the form of colors and creams that didn't sell. "They tried to unload their lemons on customers; many still do. Bad business, I say. How can you expect a customer to return for more if you've given her your worst, even for free?" Lauder wrote.

"The giveaways and the later gift-with-purchase that Estée pioneered created an opportunity to exercise her sales approach, encourage spontaneous buying, and increase customer loyalty," wrote Nancy F. Koehn in *Beauty and Business: Commerce, Gender, and Culture in Modern America*.

Born Josephine Esther Mentzer on July 1, 1906, in Corona, located in Queens, New York, she was the youngest child of her Hungarian-Jewish immigrant parents. Her mother, Rose, had been married previously, and that union produced six children. Then she had Grace, Estée's older sister by two years, and Estée with Max

Business is a magnificent obsession. I've never been bored a day in my life, partly because as a true business addict it's never been enough to have steady work; I had to love what I was doing. Love your career or else find another.

—ESTÉE LAUDER

Mentzer, a tailor by trade, who opened a hardware store. The store gave young Estée, as she was nicknamed, her first experience as a saleswoman and a merchandiser, two skills that would eventually be part of what informed her unerring business sense.

As a child, Estée was introduced to the importance of skin care through her mother's example. Rose taught her daughter about the harmful effects of the sun's rays on the skin and protected hers by wearing gloves and using a parasol. Thus began young Estée's passion and interest in skin care.

Her career began with what she called her "shining moment." Her mother's brother, John Schotz, emigrated from Hungary at the outbreak of World War I. Schotz was a chemist and skin-care specialist who warned her about the dangers of using harsh detergent soaps on the face. Lauder became his apprentice and he her mentor in the making of cosmetics. The importance of this relationship was never lost on Lauder.

"Do you know what it means for a young girl to suddenly have someone take her dreams quite seriously? Teach her secrets?" she wrote. She said that it was through her uncle's influence that she recognized her true path in life. She watched and learned from him.

Lauder's parents also were supportive of the two's interest and helped build them a laboratory in a stable behind their house, where Estée and her uncle refined their cosmetic formulas. "I could think of nothing else," Lauder wrote. "After school, I'd run home to practice being a scientist." At sixteen, Lauder was spending all of her free time learning from Schotz as he worked.

"She took careful note of how her uncle prepared each product, learning how to combine oils, wax, borax, lanolin, and other ingredients," Koehn wrote.

In high school, Lauder, who was known for her beautiful complexion, tried out her newest skin-care formulas on her classmates, just as she had been doing with her family. "I didn't have a single friend who wasn't slathered in our creams," she said. It made her very popular, but that wasn't important to her. What was important, she said, was that her passion for her work was further nurtured. She discovered she felt most alive by not simply making cosmetics, but by applying them to people's faces. The latter, which she learned from Schotz, would become one of her business signatures and a literal example of hands-on selling.

In 1924, Schotz started a company called New Way Laboratories, and Lauder sold their skin creams to beauty shops, beach clubs, and resorts.

Her next step after high school was taking her own products to the beauty salons of New York City and the surrounding areas. It was here she employed her philosophy of giving away something free as women waited under hair dryers. She'd learned the promotional value of the free sample from her father, who used it in his hardware store.

While Lauder had a passion for cosmetics themselves, her ambition to succeed was fanned, and maybe even ignited, by an offense that she never forgot. Lauder had complimented a customer in the Florence Morris Beauty Salon on the blouse the woman was wearing and asked her where she bought it. Lauder said the woman smiled, looked straight into her eyes, and said, "What difference could it possibly make? You could never afford it."

Lauder considered the woman thoughtless and cruel but thought that "maybe she was a catalyst for good in the end; maybe I wouldn't have become Estée Lauder if it hadn't been for her." Lauder vowed that no one would ever say that to her again. "I promised myself. Someday I will have whatever I want: jewels, exquisite art, gracious homes—everything."

While building her career, Lauder married garment businessman Joseph H. Lauter in 1930 (they changed the spelling of their last name a few years later). Their son Leonard was born in 1933, but the couple divorced in 1939. Estée Lauder's ambition had driven a wedge between them. She had begun to experience success for herself and said she didn't know how to be both a wife and businesswoman.

"I was also mothering my zeal for experimenting with my uncle's creams, improving on them, adding to them. I was forever experimenting on myself and on anyone else who came within range," Lauder recalled, alluding to her hands-on approach of not just presenting her products, but applying them to the faces of her customers. "Good was not good enough—I could always make it better. I know now that *obsession* is the word for my zeal. I was obsessed with clear, glowing skin, shining eyes, beautiful mouths."

Lauder listed her home-based business as *Lauter Chemists* in the New York telephone directory. Koehn writes that most of Lauder's income came from her All-Purpose Crème, lipsticks, and eye shadows that she sold, with the help of her free samples, in Manhattan beauty parlors. She later split her time personally and professionally between New York and Miami. Lauder improved her products by listening to customers and incorporating what they wanted into her formulas.

Lauder said years later that one factor in her divorce from Joe was that, having married so young, she thought perhaps she was missing out on some things in life. The time apart, though, made the heart grow fonder in their case. Lauder said she discovered that she had "the sweetest husband in the world." The two remarried in December 1942. From that life experience came her advice on choosing a spouse: "Look for a sweet person. Forget rich."

They went into business together as they welcomed their second son, Ronald, into the world in 1944. The structure of the Estée Lauder Company they founded in 1946 placed Estée, of course, in charge of product development, marketing, and sales. Joe had experience in manufacturing and finance. For capital, Estée's father loaned them money, and the couple used their savings.

Lauder concentrated on selling her products to higher-end department stores instead of beauty salons. She put more emphasis on packaging. While her uncle had used medicinal jars and tin lids, Lauder chose opal-white jars with black lids. From the outset, she was sharply focused on how she wanted to position her company.

She wanted the name Estée Lauder to not only stand for quality but also prestige—the best of the best. She courted the rich and famous as customers for publicity. Princess Grace of Monaco, the former actress Grace Kelly, said of Lauder: "I don't know her very well, but she keeps sending me all these things." In time, Princess Grace became a customer and Lauder's friend.

One story says Lauder orchestrated a purported "chance meeting" with the Duchess of Windsor while making sure the press happened to be there to witness it. Princess Diana asked that Lauder be invited to a White House dinner in the princess's honor in 1985. Lauder became friends with the Reagans, and Raisa Gorbachev sought Lauder out in New York in 1989.

"Whether your target is big or small, grand or simple, ambitious or personal, I've always believed that success comes from not letting your eyes stray from that target. Anyone who wants to achieve a dream must stay strong, focused and steady," Lauder wrote.

"From the beginning, I knew I wanted to sell the top-of-the-line, finest-quality products through the best outlets rather than through drugstores and discount stores," she wrote. "Our credibility would be harmed if we cheapened our image."

"To exploit the new possibilities [post–World War II], [Lauder] constructed a meaningful identity for her products, one that women associated with quality, self-expression, reinvention, [and] elegance," Koehn wrote.

> *[Lauder] would give her famous friends and acquaintances small samples of her products for their handbags; she wanted her brand in the hands of people who were known for having "the best."*
>
> —GRACE MIRABELLA, *TIME* MAGAZINE

Todd G. Buchholz, a former director of economic policy for the White House, wrote in his book *New Ideas from Dead CEOs*, that Lauder was "a marketing genius who was tirelessly ambitious, determined, and elegant. Lauder's positioning of her brand and company, in high-end department stores and with high-end celebrity clientele, is called *signaling* by economists." Lauder called it "keeping your image straight in your mind."

Buchholz further called Lauder relentless on quality control. She never cut corners when it came to quality.

While Lauder did want her brand name associated with elegance and her products sold only in exclusive department stores, she never saw herself as catering only to women of means. Rather, she saw every woman as her customer. "People, no matter where they live or what their finances, will spend if they're convinced of worth," she said.

She had a special understanding of her customers, the women who bought her products. "The most beautiful face in the world? It's not Elizabeth Taylor's, not Christie Brinkley's, not Brooke Shields's—it's yours. This is not advertising copy—it's what I truly believe. The reason why your face is so beautiful is that it's unique. It has your incredible depth and personality written all over it. It has your creativity and radiance," Lauder wrote.

When she approached the Saks Fifth Avenue's buyer for cosmetics, Robert Fiske, he wasn't initially interested in Lauder's products. Undaunted, she went to her old standby to demonstrate their worth. While speaking at a charity luncheon at the Waldorf-Astoria Hotel that included Saks customers, she donated over eighty of her lipsticks as gifts. They and their distinctive metallic packaging were such a hit that women started asking for them at Saks, which prompted Fiske to place an initial order for $800 worth of Estée Lauder cosmetics.

"There formed a line of people across Park Avenue and across 50th Street into Saks asking for these lipsticks, one after another," Fiske said.

Lauder worked with Saks to send out stylish cards to their customers that announced in gold lettering: "Saks Fifth Avenue is proud to present the Estée Lauder line of cosmetics: now available at our cosmetics department." The products sold out in just two days, and Saks Fifth Avenue became a regular customer. Reaching customers that way became something Lauder did at the other high-end department stores that retailed her products.

The Lauders were creating their creams and lotions in a converted restaurant that became their laboratory, and improvement remained always uppermost in Lauder's mind. "I learned early that being a perfectionist and providing quality was the only way to do business," Lauder wrote. "Anyone who wants to achieve a dream must stay strong, focused and steady. She must expect and demand perfection and never settle for mediocrity."

Lauder was equally relentless in lobbying department stores to give her products counter space in their already competitive cosmetic departments. Upon meeting female buyers, she'd offer to demonstrate her products on them. She invited store buyers to lunch, eventually on her New York City office terrace. Lauder designed this elegant space to create the right mood for discussing products associated with beauty and elegance.

"She was determined and gracious," said former Nieman Marcus chief Stanley Marcus. "It was easier to say yes to Estée than to say no."

Lauder said of her proactive approach that, regardless of what the product was—whether it was lipstick, dry goods, fragrances, or doorknobs—just about everything had to be sold aggressively. "I have never worked a day in my life without selling. If I believe in something, I sell it, and I sell it hard. I was unstoppable, so great was my faith in what I sold," she related.

At every new Estée Lauder cosmetics counter opening, she would stay at least one week to train the saleswomen, whom she called her "most important asset, the link to my customer." This training included everything from merchandising to proper personal presentation, to how to approach customers, to having the confidence to touch their faces and apply her products.

"I'd stop to make up every woman who stopped to look," Lauder said, as quoted by Koehn. "I would show her that a three-minute makeup could change her life."

"Estée Lauder's personal appearances at her cosmetics counters drew large crowds of shoppers who came to see the entrepreneur, have a makeover, and sample her products. She had learned early on that touching her customers was a very effective way of establishing a connection with them," wrote Nancy F. Koehn in the *Harvard Business School's Working Knowledge Pages*.

Taking nothing for granted, Lauder stood at the main entrances of the department stores that agreed to carry her products to track customer movements. At Saks, she discovered that nine out of ten women would wander to the right upon entering the store. Wherever the traffic was, that was where she would press to secure her space on the cosmetics sales floor.

Lauder also put a premium on the merchandising of her sales counters. She wanted the counters to give the effect of being "tiny, shining" spas. She often got accessories from other departments in the store that complemented her presentation to draw attention to it. She also changed her packaging, discarding the opal glass containers for a pale, cool turquoise color for her jars. This shade became known as "Estée Lauder blue." This signature color was everywhere. The new coloring reflected the elegant, glamorous image she pursued, and it proved appealing to consumers.

"I knew," Lauder said, "that women would not buy cosmetics in garish containers that offended their bathroom décor. I wanted them to be proud to display my products."

"By the late 1950s . . . thousands of women understood the appeal of the Estée Lauder brand—its combination of tangible products and intangible associations such as elegance and consumer control. Estée now had momentum toward building one of America's leading beauty companies," Koehn wrote.

During the week she was opening a sales counter, Lauder would try to see every beauty editor of every magazine and newspaper in that city. She brought them her signature samples and applied them on their faces. Her natural warmth was evident. "Everywhere, I made friends," Lauder said.

"[Lauder] simply outworked everyone else in the cosmetics industry," wrote Grace Mirabella in *Time* magazine.

Another part of her personal and business philosophy, which she dubbed *Lauderisms*, was to not burn bridges, even if someone had instigated an offense. This meant never reporting her displeasure in writing to a person who had upset her. She felt that if she did this, the object of her anger would have a permanent reminder of it. Lauder called it *carving anger in stone*. If, on the other hand, you tell a person face-to-face why you're angry, you get the same satisfaction as a letter, but without the permanent record of it. It also allows for give and take in the moment, followed by a cooling-off period. "You can then always smooth things over, and the relationship is not lost forever," Lauder wrote.

Another downside to severing business relationships, Lauder said, were the untruths that could follow, which could hurt business or damage reputations. "If I had a disagreement with an owner or a manager and decided to leave, do you think that the word in the industry would have it that I decided to pull out? It would not. Rumors would spread that my products were inferior or not selling, even if that was not the truth," Lauder wrote.

Lauder insisted saleswomen use her products, so they could see their benefits. This way they'd sell them honestly, tapping product knowledge from their own results. Lauder stressed that they be honest with customers and never sell them things they did not need. "The customer can always tell when you're being less than candid," she said.

Lauder set an example for her sales force with her positive attitude. All her life, she followed the Mark Twain dictum to steer clear of petty people who belittle ambition and advised others to do the same. Like Twain, she believed great leaders are upbeat and, most important, inspire those they lead to feel they can become great also.

Knowing that she was literally the face of her company to buyers, salespeople, and customers, Lauder put a premium on always looking her best and expected the same of her sales staff. "I'd always be immaculate. If [I] looked shabby or tired or messy, no one in the world would be interested in [my] opinion on what sells in the beauty field," she wrote.

Lauder also expanded her company by developing and introducing new products and introducing them in new venues. In 1953, she introduced her company's first fragrance, called Youth-Dew. It was a bath oil and perfume that retailed for $8.50 a bottle and raised the company's sales volume from $400 a week to $5,000 by 1955. Youth-Dew grew in sales from $50,000 to $150 million by 1984. Lauder knew the profit margin was far greater for fragrances than skin creams. Youth-Dew was followed by some of the best-known fragrances, such as Aliage, Private Collection, JHL, Beautiful, Pleasure, and Beyond Paradise.

In 1964 and 1965, Lauder added a fragrance and grooming product for men called Aramis. Clinique followed in 1968—the first allergy-tested, fragrance-free cosmetic brand. This new skin-care and makeup line was aimed squarely at a younger generation of health-conscious women. Sales of the line's lipsticks alone numbered more than $17 million by the late 1990s. Prescriptives, introduced in 1979, was a collection of highly individualized products.

For a business to grow in the face of both competition and an economy in a down cycle, Lauder believed, "You take a share away from someone else by coming up with a better product."

Another of her *Lauderisms* was to keep an eye on the competition. She never wanted to copy them, but to outdo them by being better. "Innovation doesn't mean inventing the wheel each time; innovation can mean a whole new way of looking at old things," she wrote. The Lauder company had a room set aside for closely studying competitive products. "It would be foolish to wear blinders," Lauder wrote of understanding the competition.

When Lauder and her husband decided to risk investing their life savings to give the company a chance to expand, their lawyer and accountant begged the two not to do so. They predicted financial ruin. Lauder went ahead anyway and was successful. "Accountants and lawyers make great accountants and lawyers," she said. "We need them, but we make the business decisions."

Lauder had a great belief in the power of trusting herself. "I act on instinct, quickly, without pondering possible disaster and without indulging in deep introspection," Lauder wrote. "Trust your instincts. I've discovered that pondering 'facts' and other people's judgments usually leads me down the wrong path."

She said her first instinct was usually the right one. "My body, my mind, my heart tell me yes or no, and I've learned to act on my visceral reaction." She did not feel instinct, or common sense, was mystical or mysterious. Lauder saw a more practical reason for it. "Our brains are really tiny computers that register millions of impressions, every day, and store them away for future use. When it's time to compile the impressions, we do so instinctively—and that's called common sense. Common sense, instinct—trust that part of yourself, whatever you call it."

Lauder's passion was to help women look their best. She believed when a woman felt beautiful, she was more confident, and the world responded to her better in her pursuit of her goals and aspirations.

"Why are all brides beautiful?" Lauder asked. "Because on their wedding day they care about how they look. There are no ugly women—only women who don't care or who don't believe they're attractive."

Lauder enjoyed living well and had a Manhattan mansion and homes in the south of France and Palm Beach, Florida. After Joseph Lauder died in 1984, she cut back her day-to-day work with her company. Among the things she put effort into were her philanthropic ventures. Lauder continued to be involved with new launches until she fell and broke her hip in 1994.

The legacy Lauder left was that of a very warm, kind person who built a great company out of her passion for her work. Professor Nancy F. Koehn tackled the question of what exactly put Lauder on *Time* magazine's list of the twenty most influential builders and titans of the twentieth century. Koehn pointed to Lauder being a trailblazer and an example for women, noting that when she was building her company, there were very few women in big business.

"Women didn't create global corporations. She used to say she wanted a national brand. That's just not what women did then. It's why she's considered a builder, because she built something really important. Not just the company, but the market. Lauder created the market for prestige cosmetics. She did it. She's the most important actor on that stage. There's no question that she deserves to be in *Time's* list."

Lauder said, "If you have a goal, if you want to be successful, if you really want to do it and become another Estée Lauder, you've got to work hard, you've got to stick to it and you've got to believe in what you're doing."

How to Be Like Estée Lauder

1) **Practice persistence.** Lauder wrote that persistence is what makes a successful businesswoman. In her own life, she had patiently learned her craft by the time she started her company, nearing the age of forty. In her role as the head saleswoman of Estée Lauder, she heard the word *no* quite a bit, but it never stopped her.

   She wrote that persistence is "that certain little spirit that compels you to stick it out just when you're at your most tired. It's that quality that forces you to persevere, find the route around the stone wall. It's the immovable stubbornness that will not allow you to cave in when everyone says to give up."

2) **Know when to be hands-on.** There is a gap between micromanaging and delegating. That said, Lauder believed it was important for her to be at every Estée Lauder department store counter opening, and she acted on this belief for more than forty years. She trained saleswoman, helped merchandise the counters, and did her own public relations in every city she visited.

3) **Ignite enthusiasm.** Now, as a general rule, you can only be enthusiastic about things you are personally excited about and that you love to do. For Lauder, she loved being in the cosmetics business. It was her calling. "It wasn't youth that made me so energetic, it was enthusiasm," she wrote.

4) **Embrace mentors.** When one shows up in your life, recognize that individual and take advantage of the opportunity to learn from someone who takes an interest in you. For Lauder, it was her uncle, John Schotz, who introduced her to understanding and making cosmetics. "Do you know what it means for a young girl to suddenly have someone take her dreams quite seriously? Teach her secrets?" she wrote.

Cont'd

5) **Find "encouragers."** Parents or spouses have to be careful not
to squelch someone's dream, but if they do, find someone who
won't. There are too many negative and cynical naysayers.
Lauder's parents were supportive of her and her uncle's interests and built a laboratory behind their house in a stable. "I
could think of nothing else," Lauder wrote. "After school, I'd
run home to practice being a scientist." Everyone needs
"encouragers."

6) **Turn negative experiences into motivational ones.** Lauder
never forgot the woman who insulted her when she was just
starting out in the cosmetic industry. Lauder vowed that no
one would ever tell her she "could never afford it" again,
because she would have the rewards of wealth. "Maybe she was
a catalyst for good in the end; maybe I wouldn't have become
Estée Lauder if it hadn't been for her," she wrote.

7) **Always work to improve.** It took a lot for Lauder to be satisfied with her products. "Good was not good enough—I could
always make it better. I know now that obsession is the word
for my zeal. I was obsessed with clear, glowing skin, shining
eyes, beautiful mouths."

8) **Know your focus.** Lauder knew how she wanted to position
her company, and she never strayed from that vision. She
wanted the Estée Lauder brand to be associated with the highest quality through not only the product itself but through
where it was sold and by whom it was used. Lauder worked to
place her products in high-end department stores and in the
hands of suitable celebrities. "Our credibility would be harmed
if we cheapened our image," Lauder said.

9) **Think outside the box.** At the time Lauder was developing her
business, the use of free samples and gifts with purchases were
not the norm in the cosmetics industry. But Lauder made

Cont'd

them her signature. Anyone in business can have their own signature marketing, if they simply make the effort to think about it and to learn from others.

10) **Cover every detail.** From noting the direction customers walked when first entering a store, to incorporating accessories from other departments and creating "tiny, shining" spas at her cosmetic counters, Lauder took nothing for granted. She put a premium on the merchandising of her sales counters. Her signature color for her bottles was blue, and she ensured that it was everywhere.

11) **Don't burn bridges.** Lauder advised never sending a note or letter to someone when angry. Communicating displeasure in writing creates a permanent record that can prolong the aggravation. Lauder felt it was better to talk to the offending individual and to allow for a cooling off period. She also believed that a burned bridge could result in the dissemination of falsehoods and rumors concerning her products.

12) **Set a positive example.** Lauder personally embodied a positive attitude and conveyed it consistently and successfully. She steered clear of petty people who belittled her ambition and believed that leaders must remain upbeat and inspire those they lead to feel that they, too, can become great.

13) **Look the part.** Lauder accepted the responsibility of being the face of her company. She put a premium on always looking her best and expected the same of her sales staff. Pride in your appearance, Lauder said, makes a difference in your confidence and can enhance how effective you are in business situations and with others.

14) **Know your business.** This sounds like a no-brainer, but sometimes the simplest essentials are overlooked. Lauder knew there was a greater profit margin in fragrances than in cosmetics, so

Cont'd

she expanded into that area and reaped huge financial rewards with products like Youth-Dew.

15) **Know your competition.** Some in business subscribe to the belief that you should only worry about your own corporation. Lauder did that but made the added effort to know what her competitors were doing. One of her *Lauderisms* was to keep an eye on the competition. "It would be foolish to wear blinders," she said.

16) **Trust your instincts.** Lauder believed in the power of trusting herself. She said she acted on instinct "without pondering possible disaster and without indulging in deep introspection." She felt there was good reason for people to trust their instincts. She wrote: "Our brains are really tiny computers that register millions of impressions, every day, and store them away for future use. When it's time to compile the impressions, we do so instinctively—and that's called common sense."

9

Jane Addams
1860–1935

Compassion

*What after all has maintained the human race
on this old globe despite all the calamities of nature and
all the tragic failings of mankind, if not faith in new
possibilities and courage to advocate them.*

—Jane Addams

These words, displayed as a part of the American Adventure within Walt Disney's Epcot Center, are seen and remembered by thousands every day. Because Addams's life was a uniquely American experience, as well as the epitome of generosity, it is especially appropriate for her thoughts about making the world a better place for all to be incorporated in this particular setting.

Addams's establishment of Hull House in Chicago in 1889 as a settlement center for the poor cemented her reputation as a founder of social work. It was the first settlement house established in the United States and provided a variety of much-needed social services for the large population of urban poor of turn-of-the-century Chicago. Hull House still serves the

She is the foremost woman of the nation, not far from being its greatest citizen.

—PROFESSOR HALVDAN KOHT, ON AWARDING ADDAMS THE NOBEL PEACE PRIZE

city of Chicago's underprivileged to this day.

However, Addams focused on many other causes that equally reflected her kindness and empathy. She was a pacifist who campaigned against World War I, not because of any political ideology, but out of humanitarian compassion: she didn't want to see young men killed and maimed. She was a proponent for the women's suffrage movement to give them the right to vote during an era when both of these causes were extremely unpopular.

She was a remarkably compassionate individual who became the first American woman to earn the Nobel Peace Prize in 1931. Her accomplishments were especially notable given the limited opportunities afforded to women during this era.

Her path in life in many ways parallels that of the Good Samaritan who could not pass by the injured man by the side of the road. Instead, she chose to care in an active way for those who were suffering. Addams reached out to others across socioeconomic and racial lines to provide compassion in action, just as the Samaritan did in bandaging the wounds of the afflicted traveler and providing for his physical needs.

Addams's strong and abiding sense of responsibility toward others was clearly evident from her early childhood. Her goal in life was to care for the underprivileged and to advocate for their rights.

When she was only six years old, Addams experienced a recurring dream in which she found herself in a deserted village, standing alone in a blacksmith's shop. The task had fallen to her to make a wagon wheel that would save humanity, but she did not know how to do it. She would find the local blacksmith, hoping he would show her how to forge the wagon wheel,

She believed in God and talked a great deal about Him. But she felt the best way to practice her religion was to live it.

—LOUISE DEKOVEN BOWEN

but the daunting task would remain hers alone to bear. She was, as author Barbara Garland Polikoff described her in *With One Bold Act: The Story of Jane Addams*, "a child who dreamed repeatedly of her duty to make a wagon wheel on which the affairs of the world depended."

The message was that she needed to learn to help people. She had developed a profound sense of duty to others by an early age, and no doubt her father was a big reason why. The eighth daughter of John Addams and his wife, Sarah Weber Addams, Jane Addams was born in Cedarville, Illinois, on September 6, 1860. Her mother died before she was three, which left her father as the central figure in her life.

He was a prosperous banker and Illinois state senator who was a close friend and political ally of Abraham Lincoln. Senator Addams was a staunch abolitionist who, as his daughter would discover years later, used their family home as a stop on the Underground Railroad, sheltering escaped slaves at a time when such assistance, if discovered, could end in prison time and huge fines.

Although she described herself as "an ugly, pigeon-toed little girl" due to childhood curvature of her spine, she learned at an early age to put aside her self-centeredness and to focus on the example being set by her father.

Jane Addams believed that her father possessed an "inner light" that informed his actions. With Lincoln, he helped found the Republican Party. As a Quaker, he helped establish a local congregation where he later taught Bible class.

Her father's overall example was especially critical to her formation. As noted in *Trailblazing American Women: First in Their Fields*, by Barbara Kramer, Addams remarked, "I centered upon him all that careful imitation which a little girl ordinarily gives to her mother's ways and habits."

During Jane's formative years, John Addams's courage and compassion shaped her to consider the plight of those around her. In one instance, she was excited about wearing a new coat to a worship service. Her father gently reproved her, pointing out to her that many children did not come from families that could afford nice clothes. She quickly put on her old coat instead, as she wanted to avoid causing pain to these less fortunate children. As Bonnie C. Harvey describes in her biography *Jane Addams: Nobel Prize Winner and Founder of Hull House*: "She asked her father, 'Why don't the

She had compassion without condescension. She had pity without retreat into vulgarity. She had infinite sympathy for common things without forgetfulness of those that are uncommon.

—WALTER LIPPMAN

other children have good new coats like mine?' Her father explained that some families do not have enough money for things they need and want. Jane responded, 'Then what can be done about it?' Her father failed to give her an answer. She spent the rest of her life seeking one."

The Quaker faith ingrained in her called for socially useful work and action to rectify social wrongs. With its emphasis on peace in its services, the Quaker tradition, which was the great guiding force in John Addams's life, was a profound influence in the formation of Jane's character. Quakerism taught her to accept the biblical admonition to "love one's neighbor as oneself" as central to her life.

Her father valued truth as an important foundation in their lives. As Polikoff recounts, he told his then eight-year-old daughter: "It is very important not to pretend to understand what you don't understand. . . . You must always be honest with yourself inside, whatever happens."

Her emphasis on truth allowed her to truly see the needy in her own state of Illinois. Rather than ignoring the difficulties these people faced, her honest evaluation gave her the ability to later turn her empathy into action. Her ability to see the world for what it was would also put her on the path to her destiny.

Addams recalled in her memoir *Twenty Years at Hull-House* that an important idea came to her one day while she and her father were driving their buggy through a run-down neighborhood filled with shabby little shanties crammed onto wood pilings to protect the shacks in case the river flooded. Stunned by the squalor, Jane wanted to know why anyone would live under such conditions.

When her father explained to her that many people were so poor that these were their living conditions, Jane responded, "When I grow up, I will have a large house, but it will not be built among the other large houses, but right in the midst of horrid little houses like those."

While Addams's father had instilled in her the desire to do something meaningful for others with her life, she lived in a society where the traditional role of women was almost entirely limited to home, family, and hearth.

Even a thinker as progressive as Addams's beloved father was enough of a product of his time that he felt his daughter's primary role in life would be as a wife and mother, even though—thanks to his example—Jane Addams wanted to dedicate her life to helping others. Conflict arose when John Addams insisted that his daughter attend Rockford Female Seminary despite her desire to attend medical school.

It may be difficult today to understand the many societal and legal restrictions on women's lives at the time when Addams was a young woman. Women had no right to vote under the United States Constitution. Society placed severe limitations on a woman's ability to express opinions or enter into public debate. As for education, in 1880, when Addams was a college student, only 1.9 percent of American women were enrolled in college. She had already entered a highly select group due to her advanced studies, but she began to experience pressure from her beloved father and stepmother to return to the family.

Life would take a sorrowful turn for Addams when her father died abruptly from acute appendicitis in 1881.

In 1882, Addams dutifully earned her A.B. degree at Rockford. She also studied for a short while at the Women's Medical College in Philadelphia. Yet, her stepmother pressed Addams to resume her place in the family, hoping that she would marry her son. The societal norm at the time, if she was not to marry, would have been for Addams to retire to her home as a spinster daughter. Addams knew that this path was not the right approach for her to attain the goals she had set for herself.

As family demands intruded too much upon her studies, Addams's health deteriorated, forcing her to abandon her education. She underwent surgery to correct her spine and subsequently endured many months of bed rest and, eventually, terrible depression exacerbated by her grief over the loss of her father. In retrospect, Addams remarked that "during most of that time I was absolutely at sea."

In time, Addams began to emerge from her poor health and state of depression as she worked at a nursing home several days a week. Her volunteerism was a critical factor in her healing process. In Addams's day, chronic illness could have been diagnosed under the fashionable term "neurasthenia," which male physicians patronizingly treated as a form of hysteria. She took a different view.

"I have seen young girls suffer and grow sensibly lowered in vitality in the first years after they leave school. . . . There is a heritage of noble obligation which young people accept and long to perpetuate. The desire for action, the wish to right wrong and alleviate suffering haunted them daily. Society smiles at it indulgently instead of making it of value to itself," Addams said.

She would later express in *Twenty Years at Hull-House*, "We have in America a fast-growing number of cultivated young people who have no recognized outlet for their active faculties. They hear constantly of the great social maladjustment, but no way is provided for them to change it, and their uselessness hangs about them heavily."

In her book *Jane Addams: Champion of Democracy*, author Judith Bloom Fradin provides this insight: "As she knew from personal experience, young women who repressed these demands on their intellects and consciences endured a psychic strain that endangered their health."

Eventually, Addams was sent abroad for a rest cure in Europe. Little did she know that the trip would set her back on course with her life's mission.

As she and a friend visited London in 1883, she observed tremendous poverty, which had a profound effect on her. She vividly recorded an encounter with the abject misery of impoverished Londoners in her journal, as quoted by Fradin:

> *On a Saturday night, I saw for the first time the overcrowded quarters of a great city at midnight. From the top of an omnibus which paused at the end of a dingy street lighted by occasional flares of gas, we saw two huge masses of ill-clad people clamoring around two hucksters' carts. They were bidding their farthings and ha-pennies for a vegetable held up by the auctioneer, which he at last scornfully flung to the successful bidder. One man had bid on a cabbage, and when it struck his hand, he instantly sat down on the curb, tore it with his teeth, and devoured it, unwashed and uncooked as it was . . . food which was already unfit to eat.*

After this experience, Addams began an obsessive hunt to observe as much of the living conditions of London's underbelly as she could—certainly not what her family had in mind for her "grand tour" of Europe. But her sense of purpose was finally coming together, taking hold at last when she and her close college friend Ellen Gates Starr visited Toynbee Hall.

Toynbee Hall was a settlement house, an experimental center for social services located in the very worst of London's bleak East End neighborhoods: Whitechapel was a district teeming with poor immigrants, prostitution, homelessness, and appalling crime. (Mere months after Addams's visit, Whitechapel would become the stalking and murdering grounds of Jack the Ripper.)

Manned largely by male college graduates, Toynbee Hall provided badly needed social services for Whitechapel residents while providing training for those who hoped to enter the field of social work. Fradin notes that Addams also found kindred souls among its volunteers: "Several of the residents confessed to feeling lost after college graduation—a feeling that lasted until they came to work at Toynbee Hall."

Addams was so impressed and inspired by Toynbee Hall's mission and its fulfillment of it that her childhood vision of owning a large house among the shanty shacks of Chicago began to take sharper focus. Upon her return to Chicago, Addams resolved to find her ideal house where the need was greatest. Unlike Toynbee Hall, which focused on the needs of young men, Addams envisioned that her settlement house would primarily serve young women in need and that women would provide the services. She sought to capture the unused skills of many women who were also of upper-class background, encouraging them to contribute time and money to the emergence of the project.

The Chicago where Addams and Starr sought to establish their settlement house was a burgeoning city of many cultures whose poorer neighborhoods were aptly and colorfully described by the great American muckraker Lincoln Steffans as "loud, lawless, unlovely, ill-smelling, new; an overgrown gawk of a village, the teeming tough among cities." The levels of poverty, violence, and desperation of the Nineteenth Ward of Chicago, where Addams would set down her roots, were not far removed from those of Whitechapel. Would a determined team of women be able to rise to the challenge?

In 1889, Addams acquired a vacant mansion built in an especially "unlovely" neighborhood by Charles Hull in 1856. Addams and Ellen Starr moved in, set up housekeeping, and opened Hull House to serve the public on September 18, 1889.

Addams's creativity in searching for ways to serve the underprivileged was unparalleled at this time. She personally resided in Hull House from the time it was first established until she passed away. According to Kramer, she wrote later that when she first moved into the impoverished area, "We had no definite idea what we were there to do. But we hoped, by living among the people, to learn what was needed and to help out."

To build up Hull House, Addams persuaded many upper-class men and women to contribute time, energy, and money to her courageous efforts in the impoverished area of Chicago where she served the community.

One of the helpers at Hull House, philanthropist Louise deKoven Bowen, worked there during the Great Depression. As recounted by Judith Bloom Fradin, Bowen talked about some of the difficulties they faced during that challenging time: "There were times at Hull House when Miss Addams and I did not know what to do with the crowds of unemployed. They came to us to ask for help. A woman was to have a baby—where should she go? A man who had lost his leg—what could he do? A woman who had lost her breadwinner and was helpless. Hull House tried then, as it has always tried, to give help to all these people."

Addams was not trained to administer a large organization such as Hull House, but she was persistent and hardworking in setting up this complex and bustling center. She vigorously raised funds for the organization and negotiated shrewdly with contractors to obtain the best possible services for the community. Although at times the work must have seemed overwhelming, she was always willing to keep going, despite her own concerns about her qualifications for leadership.

One important key to Hull House's success was Addams's patience and willingness to listen to the needs of the people she served, rather than to impose her own ideas of what they needed upon them. One Christmas, she observed that the children attending a Hull House party were avoiding the lovely ribbon candy that she had put out for them. She wondered why they would shun such a treat.

According to Addams biographer Bonnie C. Harvey, "When they told Addams they worked fourteen hours a day in a candy factory, she was appalled. No wonder the sight of candy made them ill. . . . She had not been aware that many immigrant families counted on the money their children earned. Addams understood for the first time that she had known nothing of real poverty before she came to Hull House. She had wanted to provide art and beauty for the people. Now she realized that their need for simple sustenance was far greater."

Hull House served the needs of thousands of immigrants. Its constituency ran the ethnic gamut: German, Irish, African-American, Greek, Italian, Eastern European, Russian, Jewish, British, Native American, and more. No one was turned away. Addams's ability to appreciate the diversity of the many immigrants who came to this special community for help was strikingly ahead of its time.

One person who had relied on the services at Hull House later explained, "Hull House was American because it was international and because it was perceived that the nationalism of each immigrant was a treasure, a talent, which gave him a special value for the United States."

Another critical attribute was Addams's inherent kindness, which she frequently displayed. On one occasion, she woke up to find a thief searching her room. The man raced toward the window, but she called out to him that he would be hurt if he went that way. She instructed him to take the stairs instead and let himself out of the front door. The thief complied, leaving empty-handed but hopefully learning from her impulsive concern despite his actions.

Addams was well known for giving away virtually all of her possessions. At Christmas, she would graciously accept her gifts, and then proceed to give them away as quickly as she received them.

"Action indeed is the sole medium of expression for ethics," Addams noted on one occasion. Her gentle heart required that she take steps to lessen the suffering of others, rather than simply observing the needy and feeling sorrow at their situation.

> *I was constantly shadowed by a certain sense of shame that I should be comfortable in the midst of such distress.*
>
> —JANE ADDAMS

Addams was also a strong believer in democracy. *Feminist Writers* author Michelle A. Spinelli describes Hull House as a manifestation of that ideal: "Hull House was the physical embodiment of the spirit of democracy that Addams envisioned. Settlement workers—mostly white, middle-class women who rejected geographic and social boundaries

based on class, gender, and ethnicity—moved into immigrant neighborhoods and organized social programs for industrial workers and their
families."

Addams clearly envisioned a future where democracy would expand to
new horizons: "Unless our conception of patriotism is progressive, it cannot hope to embody the real affection and the real interest of the nation."

Another area where Addams exerted her influence was in pursuing
equality for women. Her activism for women's suffrage and other issues of
concern to working women, mothers, and girls caught up in the vicious
cycles of poverty demonstrated her desire for the democratic process to free
women from their previous oppression. Polikoff notes that, even during
Addams's junior year at school, she wrote about the improvements being
made in women's education and explained that, "She wishes not to be a
man; not like a man, but she claims the same right to independent thought
and action."

Addams believed that democracy would ultimately lead to more rights
for women. She also felt that if the poor women in the Nineteenth Ward
were finally allowed to vote, their sense of compassion and desire to nurture their own children would result in more participation in the civic
process.

Certainly Addams's own example as an activist and leader helped to
change the perceptions of women's ability to
participate in the American democracy. No
less an American man's man than former
President Theodore Roosevelt, he called
Addams "the best argument for women's
suffrage."

*We stand united today
in a belief in beauty, genius,
and courage, and that these
can transform the world!*

—Jane Addams

Another underpinning in Addams's life
was her emphasis on the importance of friendship. One example of her loyalty was shown toward a close friend, Flora Guiteau. Flora had a mentally
unstable half brother, Charles, who had often been a visitor at Addams's
home, along with the rest of his family. Charles shot President James
Garfield on July 2, 1881. The president lingered for seventy-eight days and
then died from the injuries.

Fradin records: "At this point, almost all of Flora's friends abandoned her. However, Jane Addams remained a friend to her throughout this difficult ordeal and, in fact, sat with her when Charles was hanged in order to give her what comfort she could."

In terms of her personal life, Addams appears to have not been interested in marriage. About 50 percent of the first-generation female college graduates did not marry, and many educated women who opted out of marriage during the turn of the century settled down with other unmarried women to live their lives as they wished without economic dependence on men. Addams's first close friendship of this nature was with Ellen Gates Starr, but eventually she developed a relationship with another social reformer at Hull House, Mary Rozet Smith. Strong friendships were critical to Addams's ability to maintain the emotional strength she needed to carry on her challenging mission.

Addams's opposition to World War I as a result of her pacifism was another area where her empathy in action was evident. Her earlier pleas for a "moral substitute" for war during 1906 set the stage for her later resistance.

She cofounded the Women's Peace Party, which advocated that women "demand that war be abolished. As women, we are particularly charged with the future of childhood and with the care of the helpless and the unfortunate."

Because she had personally lived in a multicultural society in Hull House, Addams firmly believed that unity across different nationalities was a real possibility. When she described her beliefs in a speech at Carnegie Hall, she was attacked in the press as unpatriotic. The more she tried to clarify her earlier statements, the more the press demeaned her efforts. Addams later lamented, in her book *Peace and Bread in Time of War*, published in 1922, that during wartime it was "impossible for the pacifist to obtain an open hearing."

One statement she made following World War I reflects her desire that war as a practice come to an end: "Although we are so near to the great War with its millions of dead, we assert that war is not a natural activity for mankind, that it is very abnormal that large masses of mankind should fight against other large masses. We claim that mankind's natural tendency is to come into friendly relationship with ever larger groups." Such statements got her expelled from the Daughters of the American Revolution, who

Her life has been a beacon in the dark periods of our history, and she has been the center of some of the finest activities of the human spirit.

—LABOR LEADER SIDNEY HILLMAN

ridiculously branded her "the most dangerous woman in America today."

A primary tenet of the Quaker belief system was the doctrine of nonresistance and peace, which must have been an important factor in Addams's decision to speak out against the war. The conviction was that a Friend, or Quaker, could not fight or support the war in a direct manner. Perhaps Addams, with her tremendous influence through her many writings, speeches, and organization, felt compelled to express her beliefs, even though she knew it would lead to controversy.

Addams received an important measure of vindication for her beliefs in 1931, when she was awarded the Nobel Peace Prize. In presenting the prize to her, Professor Halvdan Koht declared: "Carrying on this social work amongst people of widely different nationalities, it was natural that she should take up the cause of peace. . . . She is the foremost woman of the nation."

Addams died four years later, in 1935, having accomplished in her single lifetime more than she ever could have imagined to ease the suffering of untold thousands. More importantly, Hull House survived and remains in existence today. Jane Addams's greatest legacy currently serves sixty thousand people a year. Hull House provides family services, literacy training, senior services, foster care, child care, and domestic violence training—programs whose ancestry rests in the innovative programs Addams envisioned for the original community where she lived for most of her life.

Deeds make habits, habits make character, character makes destiny!

—JANE ADDAMS

How enormous is the impact of a single woman whose work to better the lives of others remains as vigorous in the age of the Internet as it did in the age of the horse and buggy.

How to Be Like Jane Addams

1) **Give back.** Addams came from a privileged background. Her father was a successful banker before becoming an Illinois state senator. She was left an inheritance and did not have to work. She could have lived her life as a woman of leisure, but she chose to contribute something important to society and to those less fortunate.

2) **Don't limit your caring.** Addams's establishment of Hull House in Chicago as a settlement center for the poor cemented her reputation as a founder of social services, but she also worked for women's suffrage and in the peace movement. Addams did all of these well. She was the first American woman to win the Noble Peace Prize, and former President Theodore Roosevelt called Addams "the best argument for women's suffrage."

3) **Be a Good Samaritan.** Addams committed her life to social responsibility. She couldn't turn a blind eye to another's suffering. She didn't look down at the disadvantaged and think they were less than anyone else. For Addams, "Love one's neighbor as oneself" was central to her life. Her Quaker faith also called for socially useful work and action to rectify social wrongs.

4) **Learn from role models.** Addams had an exceptional role model in her own father. John Addams set an example of selflessness and compassion. He was a prosperous banker and state senator who taught Jane compassion for those less fortunate. He put himself in danger to help runaway slaves. He taught Bible school. He valued honesty. Among his friends was another man of great compassion and integrity, Abraham Lincoln.

5) **Have empathy for others.** Even as a young child, Addams demonstrated concern and caring for those less fortunate. She avoided wearing her new coat to worship services when she

Cont'd

realized that many children who would be there came from poor families and couldn't afford such nice things. And when she saw the squalid conditions people were living in when riding through a poor neighborhood with her father, she made the determined announcement that one day, when she grew up, she would live in a large house "right in the midst of horrid little houses like those."

6) **Take action.** Addams's gentle heart required that she take steps to lessen the suffering of others, rather than simply observing the needy and feeling sorrow at their situation. She acted on her concern for others, devoting her life to helping the poor of Chicago.

7) **Be honest with yourself as well as others.** Addams embraced her father's belief that truth was an important foundation of life. "It is very important not to pretend to understand what you don't understand. . . . You must always be honest with yourself inside, whatever happens," he told Jane. Jane Addams's ability to see the world for what it was would put her on the path to her destiny.

8) **Challenge society's norms.** While Addams's father had instilled in her the desire to do something meaningful for others with her life, she still lived in a society where the traditional role of women was almost entirely limited to home and family. Even her father felt that his daughter's primary role in life would be as a wife and mother. But Addams didn't allow societal norms to alter her path in life or define her. Addams thought for herself and lived her life the way she wanted to—for the benefit of the less fortunate.

9) **Be hands-on.** Addams personally resided in Hull House from the time it was first developed until she passed away. By living among the impoverished, she learned what they most needed.

Cont'd

As Mother Teresa said, "If we really want to know the poor, we must know what poverty is." Addams realized that she had known nothing of real poverty before she moved to Hull House.

10) **Ask for help.** Believing that it was the responsibility of the rich to help the poor, Addams persuaded many upper-class men and women to contribute time, energy, and money to her courageous efforts in the impoverished area of Chicago where she served the community.

11) **Be a true friend.** Addams was a kind person and a true friend. She remained loyal to her close friend, Flora Guiteau, even after others abandoned her. When Flora's mentally unstable half brother was hanged for shooting President James Garfield, Addams stayed by her side, providing what comfort she could.

Civil rights leader Martin Luther King Jr. said, "The ultimate measure of a man is not where he stands in moments of comfort and convenience, but where he stands at times of challenge and controversy."

10

Meg Whitman
1957–

Collaboration

I learned early on in my career that you could
be just as effective if not more so . . . talking to people
about what you were trying to accomplish
and enlisting them in the decision.

—Meg Whitman

It was a fortuitous contact for Margaret Cushing Whitman in 1998. The general manager of Hasbro Inc.'s Playskool Division and a young, rising corporate star who had produced impressive results for such established companies as Procter & Gamble, Disney, and Florists' Transworld Delivery (FTD), Whitman was being asked if she would be interested in running a fledgling Internet company.

At first, Whitman had no interest in taking the top spot at eBay when David Beirne of Ramsey Beirne Associates, an executive search firm, approached her about becoming their chief executive in 1998. She had been recommended by Bob Kagle, a partner at the venture capital firm Benchmark Capital, whose aim was to have her reshape founder Pierre

Omidyar's little-known auction site into a more profitable performer. She was skeptical that that could happen.

She reluctantly agreed to take the interview as a courtesy to Ramsey Beirne, to maintain her professional relationship with them. "I remember sitting at my computer saying, 'I can't believe I'm about to fly across the country to look at a black-and-white auction classified section," Whitman said to FastCompany.com. But then Whitman took a second look. She clicked her way around eBay's site. She saw possibilities in what she found: through Internet sales, stay-at-home moms could make extra money, and retired people could supplement pensions. People could even make full-time livings. Buyers could purchase items from the comfort of their home, often for less money than in a retail store. They also had easy, twenty-four-hour access to a marketplace that featured almost any item anyone could want. With the success of Amazon.com, Whitman knew the potential of the Internet. Then she discovered that eBay, called Auction Web at that time, was growing at a staggering rate of 40 percent per month.

After spending two hours researching the site, Whitman recognized a groundbreaking opportunity. "I just had a feeling this thing was going to be huge," she said. Whitman later put it like this: "You can buy a book on Amazon and it's a great experience, but if all else fails, you can, in fact, go to Barnes & Noble. There's no ability to do what you do on eBay in any other venue."

After about a month of soul searching and meetings, she took the job, and did she ever deliver! To say she increased revenue would be a massive understatement; eBay exploded from around $5.7 million in annual revenue to over $4 billion by 2005. In her first two years on the job, the company went from registering 34 million auctions to 265 million.

During her tenure at eBay, which began in 1998 and ended in 2008, Whitman not only became the world's first female Internet billionaire but also showed up regularly on different respected magazine's lists of the nation's best CEOs. In 2002, *Worth* magazine ranked Whitman number one on their list. At one point, *Fortune* magazine ranked her the second most powerful woman in business.

Whitman helped change the way the world buys and sells. Her focus, drive, and forthright determination helped make eBay a household name for nearly every Internet user on the planet. It has been called the world's online marketplace. With 105 million registered customers by mid-2004, eBay was equivalent to the eleventh most populous nation in the world, wrote Leslie Alan Horvitz in *Meg Whitman: President and CEO of eBay.*

Whitman started out in college figuring she would spend her eventual career trying to help patients as a doctor rather than working to attract customers as a business-woman. When the then seventeen-year-old Whitman enrolled as a pre-med major at Princeton University, she had every inten-tion of making medicine her future. But after selling advertising for a university magazine, she was thrilled by her sense of

Customers really matter, the financial discipline of the bottom line really matters, having a return-based investment philosophy [matters]—I'm spending a dollar on something so what am I going to get back for that?

—MEG WHITMAN

achievement. She decided that business "was more fun than physics" and retooled her ambitions. The business world was where she wanted to be.

Realizing that she needed as much education as possible before setting out to conquer that world, she finished her bachelor's degree in economics at Princeton in 1977 and went on to Harvard University, where she gradu-ated in 1979 with a master's degree in business administration.

Whitman then looked for places to learn the ins and outs of the market-place. Each step provided her with new experiences and new mentors to learn from. Her first job was in brand management at Procter & Gamble, and she learned an invaluable lesson there. Great brand names, she said, have two com-ponents, "features and functionality." People have to not only want it but also must have a practical need for it.

After Procter & Gamble, Whitman became vice president at Bain & Co., a consulting firm, in 1982. When she went to work at Walt Disney Co. in 1989, she had worked her way up the chain of command to become senior vice president of marketing

My view is that, just as in many businesses, brands really matter. There will always be a role for destination sites. Eighty million users come to our destination. I think that will be the vast majority of our future business.

—MEG WHITMAN

in the consumer products unit. After a stint at Stride Rite Division, she became president and CEO of Florists Transworld Delivery (FTD), the world's largest floral products company, before moving on to her position at Hasbro in 1997.

In every job, she built a reputation as a woman of action who made quick decisions, and she became a "go to" person for ailing companies.

Whitman puts her energies into learning about her companies' customers. She studies customers by learning their buying patterns and paying attention to their feedback. She listens thoughtfully to customer complaints and notes their preferences. That is a Whitman hands-on trademark.

A business leader has to keep their organization focused on the mission. That sounds easy, but it can be tremendously challenging in today's competitive and ever-changing business environment.
A leader also has to motivate potential partners to join.

—MEG WHITMAN

Many executives spend the bulk of their hours trying to persuade the world of their products' superiority. That isn't how Whitman works. Instead, she credits customers for showing her how to build a superior product and keeping it that way. "When you are trained in MBA School or in most other businesses, you use the words, 'Drive, push, go after' and it's not that way here. [At eBay], you have to use the community of users to chart the course of the company," Whitman said to the Benchmark Press in 2003.

Whitman built on her passion and love for business to develop her leadership skills. She felt that customers were the foundation, bricks, and mortar, of a healthy business. At eBay, Whitman relied on that belief to help build the nascent firm into "a model organization in which the collective intelligence and enthusiasm of its 157 million customers determine and drive the daily actions of its 9,300 employees," wrote William Meyers in a 2005 *U.S. News and World Report* article.

Born in 1957 in Cold Spring Harbor, Long Island, Whitman was the youngest of three children. Her father was a businessman and her mother a homemaker.

But Whitman's mother, also named Meg, was no shy, retiring lady of leisure. She was adventurous and took her children on long trips, one to

Canada and Alaska, for example. When actress Shirley MacLaine was invited to China in 1973 in the wake of a normalizing of relations between the United States and China, she was asked to assemble a women's delegation to accompany her. One of the people she wanted to bring was a "conservative Republican housewife." Whitman's mother was suggested. She met with the actress and confidently told MacLaine she was what she was looking for. MacLaine agreed, and Whitman's mother made the trip to China. She subsequently went on to lead multiple delegations to China.

Whitman's mother's action gave credence to her words. She told her daughter she could do anything she wanted to do and not to be bound by people's expectations. Whitman internalized that message and took it further, trying to learn something from every situation. As a competitive swimmer in high school, for instance, Whitman had to balance schoolwork, chores at home, and her swimming practice. The experience taught her, she said, to not only be a strong swimmer but also how to manage her time.

When she was running eBay, she'd be up at 6 AM during the work week. Whitman would exercise for thirty minutes, drive her two sons to school, and be at her desk by 8:30 to begin her day at the company's San Jose, California, offices.

Her father, Hendricks Hallet Whitman, was a Harvard University graduate and a successful businessman. He expected his children to take their studies seriously and produce good grades. "He encouraged his children to strive for a high level of achievement but never at the expense of their ethical values. He stressed that it was possible to get ahead in life without walking over other people," Horvitz wrote.

Whitman has carried her father's edicts with her throughout her career. When CBS *MarketWatch* named Whitman their CEO of the Year in 2003, their editor-in-chief David Callaway said, "At a time when corporate corruption and executive greed is making headlines on a daily basis, CBS *MarketWatch* wanted to recognize leaders who have excelled in building value for customers, employees, and shareholders."

Whitman has a thorough, detailed approach to business. She is especially skilled at noting trends and figuring out a way to fit them into a company's marketing plan. When she joined Florists' Transworld Delivery in 1995, for instance, FTD was floundering. The company's rivals—1-800-Flowers and

Florist.com—were wiping the floor with the once-proud FTD service through their websites. Whitman had studied the numbers and knew the online marketplace represented vast opportunity. "To turn FTD around, Meg oversaw its planned conversion from a cooperative, owned by an association of florists, into a privately held company," wrote Horvitz.

This allowed her to act on her discovery that the company hadn't yet jumped on the Information Highway because they hadn't reached consensus about how to do so. She went to work winning over the florists by meeting with them in person to describe her plan. "Meg was willing to mix it up with florists all over the world. . . . She would shake their hands and kiss their babies," said an FTD executive quoted in Horvitz's book. Persuaded by her confidence and knowledge, the florists agreed to the conversion.

In short order, Whitman retooled FTD and launched it on the Internet. By 1997, FTD was on top again as the largest floral products company in the world.

One attribute that defines Whitman's business approach is keeping an open mind. Although she had put FTD online, she wasn't steeped in the actual workings of the website. When approached for the eBay spot, she wasn't really very Internet savvy, but she saw the situation as an opportunity to learn. Whitman decided to move from the East Coast to San Francisco to work for the small start-up company. The decision—which uprooted her neurosurgeon husband and two children—shocked her friends. Yet Whitman refused to second-guess herself, even as her friends criticized her choice. She stuck to her path, confident that this was now the chance of a lifetime.

That confidence enabled her to turn the small Internet site into the powerhouse that eBay is today. Her attitude coming in made an indelible impression on her future team. Bob Kagle, the partner at venture capitalist Benchmark Capital of Menlo Park, California, and an eBay board member, remembers Whitman's "quick wit, a tendency to speak in a burst of single-clause sentences and no shortage of self-confidence."

Yet, it took more than just a good first impression to improve a company. As a frontier business, eBay needed a new kind of corporate leader. Meyers described Whitman as one who leads by not leading, is in charge but not controlling, and who has a hands-off management approach.

Whitman was aware of her strong points and what she had to offer at eBay: "My job was to uncover what was going well," she said, and build on that, as opposed to immediately looking for what is wrong. "That [approach] doesn't actually work very well. . . . people are very proud of what they've created, and it just feels like you are second-guessing them all the time."

Upon taking over the position at eBay, Whitman learned there was no marketing plan in place. To put one together, she employed her customary detail-oriented approach. Her background wasn't in high tech, but she applied basic business principles. For example, Whitman wanted to learn about the people who visited the site and how many became registered users. She wanted information on how long each user stayed online, how long pages took to load, and which days were the busiest traffic days. With that kind of detailed data, Whitman could make decisions, with her team and the expert consultants she brought in, on how best to allocate the company's financial resources.

Still, Whitman put data into its proper perspective. "You have to be careful because you could measure too much," she said

To fend off impending competition, including Amazon.com, Whitman focused on developing a loyal customer base for eBay. She wasn't worried about short-term profits; she just wanted to get people to the site and make it easy for them to use it. She wanted to make eBay "the place to go." Whitman was building the brand's name and identity.

Whitman read eBay message boards to learn what customers liked about the eBay experience and what they didn't like. Customers were encouraged to express their opinions on changes eBay was contemplating.

Whitman also takes her cues from her team. Unlike many American corporate leaders, she listens carefully to advice and then works to build bridges until she has

> *Sometimes it's a little bit like being a politician. . . . We have work to do in understanding our users' sentiments.*
>
> —MEG WHITMAN

consensus. Backed by the agreement of her team, Whitman then puts an action plan into play. She works extra hard at making customers part of the plan as well.

While many executives sit in a big corner office, dictating to employees and likely never understanding customers' needs and concerns, Whitman dumped that stereotype to fit eBay's infant corporate culture. She worked in a cubicle next to other employees rather than in a closed office.

"I [hadn't] been in a cubicle since 1985 because my other jobs have been at more traditional companies, but we wanted to reflect our trading community by having offices that are open and allow for free communication and sharing of ideas. . . . Being accessible is really important in our business where information is so valuable," Whitman said.

She asked questions and then shared the answers with everyone at the company. "It's different from traditional leadership," Whitman said. "It's usually: What does the center want to do? It is command and control. At eBay, it's a collaborative network. You are truly in partnership with the community of users. The key is connecting employees and customers in two-way communication. We call it, 'The Power of All of Us.'"

Open, two-way communication has been a consistent tenet in every executive position Whitman has held. "I learned early on in my career that you could be just as effective if not more so [by] talking to people about what you were trying to accomplish and enlisting them in the decision," she said.

Never one to surround herself with "yes men" and "yes women," Whitman seeks constructive criticism in her constant bid for improvement. In that vein, she usually seeks the direction for her next change from customers. "Whenever she's out traveling, she's talking to people who use eBay, Starbucks coffee cup in hand," said Jeetil Patel, analyst with Deutsche Bank Securities, to the Benchmark Press.

Whitman, unlike those who live by a long-entrenched corporate manual, operates as an entrepreneur. She believes the online marketplace knows no borders and can "empower people to make a living in ways that they could not before eBay. Our best ideas are our customers' ideas." Her customer focus makes her stance—and that of eBay—loud and clear to competitors.

Whitman said that at Hasbro, for example, she and the other executives tried to pick out the next hot toy, but "at eBay, we don't worry about that. Our army of users figures out what's hot before we even know."

In 2000, Whitman rejected rival Yahoo's $30 billion buyout offer. She felt certain that Yahoo's leadership wouldn't give the attention and care the customers at eBay needed and were accustomed to. "We didn't just want to be an auction functionality for Yahoo's shopping channel," Whitman said.

Whitman knew the importance of community among eBay customers. She initiated face-to-face meetings with customers to get their views directly and, as a result, the Voice of the Customer program was born. Every few months or so, returning customers are flown to San Jose to share their ideas about what they feel is working and what isn't. "Meg has a heartfelt understanding of real people," said eBay board member Scott Cook. "She's an odd combination of homespun and corporate executive."

Whitman not only led eBay but partook in its service: she's talked about trading Beanie Babies and Pokémon cards with her children on eBay and has even named her most treasured collectible: Burger King Mr. Potato Head.

Whitman has a keen sense of supply and demand. When people wanted to start auctioning their cars through eBay, she thought "there were a hundred reasons not to do it," but she listened to customers and gave them what they asked for. It has proven to be one of the site's more popular services. Also, she encouraged major companies such as IBM, Sun, Dell, Iomega, Acer, and Xerox to create a presence on eBay.

Whitman credits three key elements that have contributed to her eBay success. First, she doesn't try to control her buyers and sellers. They do not report to her, and the items going up for sale are not hers. Whitman sees that her job is to provide the best and safest forum for customers to practice free enterprise.

Second, Whitman never assumes to know more than the marketplace or its consumers. She won't try to outsmart the buyer like a trader on Wall Street but rather listens and influences her team, so they can come up with the right decisions. Third, Whitman is not afraid to take risks, but only because she listens to customers to better serve them.

One of the biggest crises Whitman faced at eBay was when the company's servers went down late in the day on June 10, 1999. As the outage went on, Whitman recognized this was a major problem. If eBay wasn't online, it wasn't in business.

With impending competition, the public relations fallout from people making a daily living on the site was significant. Horvitz wrote that Whitman set an example by vowing to remain in the office, no matter how long it took, until eBay was back online. Others in important management and technical positions followed suit. The company's survival was at stake.

While engineers worked to restore the site, Whitman called an emergency Friday morning meeting. With the customer service department being bombarded by frustrated and angry customers, Whitman directed her staff to do whatever was necessary to show eBay customers how much they were valued. Millions of dollars in fees were refunded in addition to customer complaints being handled by e-mail and personal phone calls.

After twenty hours, eBay was back online. For Whitman, though, the crisis wasn't over. She reportedly spent the next month working nonstop to restore customer confidence and to ensure the infrastructure was in place so there wouldn't ever be a repeat of the problem.

Whitman's plan of building loyalty proved itself effective—one week after the twenty-hour blackout, auction listings on eBay reached 2.2 million, which was close to the preblackout levels. The company reached 4.1 million listings per week within three months.

Whitman called missteps "learning experiences" and says, "Most of the time we've made the right decisions and when we haven't, we've fixed them."

Right after September 11, 2001, Whitman started the Auction for America to raise $100 million in 100 days. It was met with great enthusiasm, with people donating even rare items such as memorabilia belonging to New York Governor Pataki and baseball legend Joe DiMaggio. "A mom has started a virtual lemonade stand on Auction for America, auctioning off virtual cups of lemonade and her daughter's artwork," Whitman said of the effort to FoxNews.com. She saw the potential for connection and community and raised it up high for everyone to see.

Whitman has become a role model, not only in the Internet market, but for every facet of life—leading people by example, following her own path, and listening carefully to others' opinions to find the best answers. "Our company is built and managed on validation," Whitman said about eBay. Traffic and registered users told her how well the company was doing and progressing. "Where else can you wake up and see how much you are liked each day?"

How to Be Like Meg Whitman

1) **Research every opportunity.** Even someone as experienced and savvy as Whitman almost missed her eBay opportunity. She had worked for major companies like Disney, and working for a small Internet start-up didn't seem to be a good career move. But after researching eBay, she discovered it was growing by a staggering 40 percent per month and that it was a one-of-a-kind service. Whitman put it like this: "You can buy a book on Amazon and it's a great experience, but if all else fails, you can, in fact, go to Barnes & Noble. There's no ability to do what you do on eBay in any other venue."

2) **Recognize your passion.** Whitman was enrolled as a premed major at Princeton University, but after selling advertising for a Princeton magazine, she discovered a new passion. She decided that business "was more fun than physics" and changed her major.

3) **Educate yourself.** Whitman earned a bachelor's degree in economics from Princeton and a master's degree in business administration from Harvard. While many successful business executives and others succeed without Whitman's level of education, having it is still preferable and leads to better opportunities upon graduation.

4) **Accept no limitations.** Whitman's mother gave her the mind-set that she could do anything she wanted to do and not be bound by other people's expectations. Whitman's mother demonstrated this in her own life by, among other things, leading cultural delegations to China.

5) **Practice time management.** As a competitive swimmer in high school, Whitman balanced schoolwork, chores at home, and her swimming practice. The experience taught her how to manage her time.

Cont'd

When she was running eBay, she got up at 6 AM to exercise for thirty minutes before driving her two sons to school, and arriving at her desk by 8:30.

6) **Be ethical.** Whitman's father was a successful businessman who encouraged his children to achieve, but never at the expense of their values. He believed that success was possible "without walking over other people."

Whitman employed her father's edicts throughout her career, and in 2003, was named CEO of the Year by CBS *MarketWatch*. "At a time when corporate corruption and executive greed is making headlines on a daily basis, CBS *MarketWatch* wanted to recognize leaders who have excelled in building value for customers, employees, and shareholders," said *MarketWatch* editor-in-chief David Callaway.

7) **Listen.** Whitman, unlike many American corporate leaders, listens carefully to advice and then works to build consensus among her employees. She also makes it a point to reach out to customers to hear what they have to say about her company's business. She considered eBay a collaborative network. "The key is connecting employees and customers in two-way communication. We call it, 'The Power of All of Us.'"

8) **Be unorthodox when necessary.** While she hadn't been in a cubicle since 1985 because her other jobs were at more traditional companies, Whitman felt the corporate culture of eBay in 1998 lent itself to the CEO being accessible in that manner. "We wanted to reflect our trading community by having offices that are open and allow for free communication and sharing of ideas. . . . Being accessible is really important in our business where information is so valuable."

9) **Be detailed.** Whitman has always been extremely hands-on with her employees and customers, knowing the ins and outs

Cont'd

of every portion of her company. She brought her customary detail-oriented approach to eBay, gathering extensive data on the people who visited the site. She wanted to know how many became registered users, how long each user stayed online, how long pages took to load, and which were the busiest traffic days. But Whitman kept this information in perspective: "You have to be careful because you could measure too much."

10) **Know your customers—literally.** Whitman got out among her customers frequently. Before launching a website for FTD, she met with florists all over the world to personally describe her plans. At eBay, she and her team began the company's Voice of the Customer program, bringing customers in to headquarters to share their ideas in face-to-face meetings. And whenever she traveled, Whitman sought out eBay users and asked about their experiences with the site.

11) **Seek diverse opinions.** Whitman doesn't surround herself with "yes men" and "yes women." Rather, she seeks constructive criticism from those she works with and seeks the input of her customers before determining her next direction for change.

12) **Act in a crisis.** There's a fine line between panicking and acting, between being paralyzed by fear and doing something decisive about the problem. During eBay's twenty-hour blackout in June 1999, Whitman set the example by staying at the company's headquarters until she resolved the crisis. She took decisive action to ensure eBay's customer base knew how much they were valued, refunding millions of dollars in fees. She then worked tirelessly to restore customer confidence and ensure that there would never be a repeat of the problem.

Whitman calls missteps "learning experiences" and says "most of the time we've made the right decisions and when we haven't, we've fixed them."

11

Shirley Chisholm
1924-2005

Maverick

*I was the first American citizen to be elected to
Congress in spite of the double drawbacks of being female
and having skin darkened by melanin. When you put
it that way, it sounds like a foolish reason for fame.
In a just and free society it would be foolish. That I am a
national figure because I was the first person in 192 years to
be at once a congressman, Black and a woman proves,
I think, that our society is not yet either just or free.*

—Shirley Chisholm

The first African-American woman ever to sit in the U.S. Congress, "fighting Shirley Chisholm," as she liked to be called, established herself as a vocal defender of women and the poor. Articulate and energetic, she gained national recognition for her efforts, and in 1972 she launched a groundbreaking campaign for the Democratic nomination for president, the first black woman to seek the nomination from a major party. Chisholm's extraordinary life and career was made possible by the strong determination she mustered to achieve her goals in the face of the tremendous obstacles that she faced as a black woman living in mid-twentieth century America.

Chisholm was a woman of many singular achievements, among which, most notably, are her two autobiographical works. The first, *Unbought and Unbossed*, written in 1970, details her early life and her rise in politics, culminating in her election to the House of Representatives. The second book, *The Good Fight*, details her hard-fought run for the 1972 Democratic Party nomination. Both works express her self-confidence in her ability and her beliefs and hopes for the future of blacks and women. "Shirley Chisholm is true grit," Susan Brownmiller writes in *Shirley Chisholm*. "Her cometlike rise from clubhouse worker to Representative in the United States Congress was no accident of the political heavens. It was accomplished by the wiles of a steely politician with a belief in her own abilities which at times approaches an almost Messianic fervor."

> *I am, was, and always will be a catalyst for change.*
> —SHIRLEY CHISHOLM

Chisholm was a maverick her entire life, never accepting the role society created for her. By virtue of her strong determination, she achieved many things in the political arena. She was elected to political office at the state and federal level and honored with awards and degrees. "I do not want to be remembered as the first Black woman to be elected to the United States Congress, even though I am. I do not want to be remembered as the first woman who happened to be Black to make a serious bid for the presidency. I'd like to be known as a catalyst for change, a woman who had the determination and a woman who had the perseverance to fight on behalf of the female population and the Black population, because I'm a product of both, being Black and a woman."

Shirley Chisholm was born Shirley Anita St. Hill in Brooklyn's Bedford-Stuyvesant neighborhood, one familiar to contemporary moviegoers from the films of Spike Lee. Shirley's father, Charles St. Hill, a native of British Guiana (now the nation of Guyana), grew up in Cuba and in Barbados before coming to the United States, where he worked at a bag factory. Her mother, Ruby (Seale) St. Hill, also emigrated from Barbados and worked as a seamstress. From 1928 to 1934 Shirley and her younger sisters Odessa and Muriel (a third sister, Selma, was born later) lived with their maternal grandmother in Barbados. Her parents remained in Brooklyn struggling to save money during the Great Depression.

Young Shirley excelled in the British-style school system and developed a Caribbean accent that she retained for life. "Years later I would know what an important gift my parents had given me by seeing to it that I had my early education in the strict, traditional, British-style schools of Barbados," Chisholm wrote in *Unbought and Unbossed*. "If I speak and write easily now, that early education is the main reason."

Chisholm's father was an avid reader who introduced his daughter to the teachings of the Black Nationalist leader Marcus Garvey, while her mother emphasized the importance to her children of receiving a quality education. Chisholm adored this man who made it a point to read at least two newspapers a day and followed his lead to improve her mind. An excellent student in high school (with an IQ of 170), Chisholm received scholarship offers to Vassar and Oberlin colleges but enrolled in the more financially accessible Brooklyn College. At Brooklyn College, Shirley developed the strong debating skills that were to serve her well when she entered politics. A colleague once observed that while Chisholm enjoyed debating and weighed issues judiciously, once she took a position, "You couldn't blast her out of it."

During her sophomore year, she also discovered a wellspring of new people who shared the political passions her father had inspired in her. She joined the school's Harriet Tubman Society. In *Unbought and Unbossed*, she wrote, "There I first heard people other than my father talk about white oppression, Black racial consciousness, and Black pride."

Chisholm was superbly adept at oratory and possessed an outstanding ability to construct logical arguments, talents that might suggest a career in law. While in college, her favorite instructor, a blind, white political science professor named Louis Warsoff, suggested she ought to go into politics. She deeply respected Professor Warsoff, whom she described as "one of the first white men whom I ever really knew and trusted" and as the man who taught her "that white people were not really different from me." To his suggestion that she pursue public service, she responded, "You forget two things. I'm Black—and I'm a woman."

Instead, Chisholm became a nursery-school teacher when she graduated. In her autobiography she notes, "There was no other road open to a young Black woman. Law, medicine, even nursing were too expensive, and few schools would admit Black men, much less a woman." She went on to receive a master's degree from Columbia University and spent her prepolitical career as a teacher, early-education expert, and employee of the child welfare bureau in New York City.

By the late 1950s, Shirley had become active in Democratic Party politics in her local Bedford-Stuyvesant neighborhood. She worked her way into the male-dominated New York political clubs and refused to submit to the long-established hierarchies and power systems that dominated politics in the city. Chisholm learned from bitter experience that the New York City political machine used women to raise money, but refused to allow them any real power. As she struggled against the prejudices of politically powerful men, Chisholm was to remark that throughout her career, "Of my two 'handicaps,' being female put many more obstacles in my path than being Black."

By the 1960s, the American civil rights movement had brought about significant changes in state and national laws regarding discrimination against African-Americans. The movement had also greatly affected the consciousness of many American citizens, both white and black, making the very idea of racial equality a national issue. At the same time, the women's movement was gaining momentum, though not as quickly as the civil rights movement.

Chisholm and six others founded the Unity Democratic Club and managed to do what other clubs had failed to do: "take over the entire Seventeenth Assembly District political organization and boot out the failing but still potent white machine." She ran for the New York State Assembly in 1964 and won, waging an old-fashioned street corner campaign, speaking fluent Spanish in Puerto Rican neighborhoods, and winning especially the trust of women voters in the district.

Reelected twice, Chisholm spent a total of four years in Albany, declining to play the role of the quiet freshman lawmaker, but instead pressing for legislation that directly benefited her poor constituents. Her achievements in Albany included legislation providing for publicly supported day care centers, unemployment insurance for domestic workers, and reversal of a law that caused female teachers in New York to lose their tenure while they were out on maternity leave. She was largely responsible for the passage of a bill creating the program known as SEEK (Search for Elevation, Education, and Knowledge), which assisted black and Puerto Rican students in pursuing higher education. Chisholm served in the state assembly until 1968.

When the Supreme Court mandated the redistricting of Brooklyn to give minority areas an equal voice, Chisholm was the choice of a citizens committee that had interviewed many candidates. She was chosen for her independent and indomitable spirit and her strong determination to win. While there were already ten or so black United States congressmen, a black *female* member of Congress was still unheard of. But Chisholm was not easily daunted by the prospect of setting new precedents. Because of her outspokenness and her refusal to cooperate with the schemes of the New York political machine, she was forced to fight her way to victory the hard way, earning her the nickname "Fighting Shirley Chisholm."

I know that as a freshman in Congress, I'm supposed to be seen and not heard. But my voice will be heard. I have no intention of being quiet.

—Shirley Chisholm

Labeled a maverick throughout her political career, she learned quickly that "if you decide to operate on the basis of your conscience, rather than your political advantage, you must be ready for the consequences and not complain when you suffer them. There is little place in the political scheme of things for an independent, creative personality, for a fighter. Anyone who takes that role must pay a price."

Running against nationally known black civil rights leader James Farmer, she found herself up against a well-funded machine candidate. "I didn't have the money for a conventional congressional campaign; I had to make up for it with hard work." About the time her nomination was

I told them that no one has a right to call himself a leader unless he dares to lead. That means standing up to be counted on the side of his people, even at the risk of his political security. It means giving clear direction, so the people do not have to guess where you stand.

—Shirley Chisholm

announced, Chisholm became seriously ill. She was diagnosed with a massive tumor; it was benign but required surgery. In late July, she underwent surgery for removal of the tumor.

Convalescing did not sit well with Chisholm. She complained to her husband, Conrad, "I've got to get out and speak to the people." Both Conrad and her physician wanted her to stay home, but she responded, "The stitches aren't in my mouth. I'm going out."

Soon, Chisholm mounted a vigorous campaign and astonished her supporters with her strong determination. Again depending on grassroots support, and especially on the support of women voters, she campaigned under the slogan, "Fighting Shirley Chisholm: Unbought and Unbossed." Chisholm won the election by a margin of 2.5 to 1, making her the first black woman member of Congress in history.

Thus began her tenure in the U.S. House of Representatives from the 91st through the 97th Congress (1969–1982). Chisholm made a point of hiring women for her staff and devoted much of her time to aiding individual constituents through her influence as a representative. She served on several House committees: Agriculture, Veterans' Affairs, Rules and Education, and Labor. During the 91st Congress, when she was assigned to the Forestry Committee, she protested, insisting that she wanted to work on committees that could deal with the "critical problems of racism, deprivation and urban decay." (There are no forests in Bedford-Stuyvesant.)

Viewing herself primarily as a spokesperson for the disadvantaged, Chisholm was often criticized for her refusal to forge firm political alliances and to take part in the practical, day-to-day bargaining of political life. The Washington Congresswoman Catherine May said, "The arrival of personalities like Shirley Chisholm . . . shook our august body to its foundation." May further noted that Chisholm was "not what the male members of Congress had come to expect from a female colleague" because she "got just as demanding and as noisy and as difficult as the men did!"

I have no intention of just sitting quietly and observing. I intend to speak out immediately in order to focus attention on the nation's problems.

—Shirley Chisholm

Chisholm has said of herself, "I do not see myself as a lawmaker, an innovator in the field of legislation. America has the laws and the material resources it takes to insure justice for all its people. What it lacks is the heart, the humanity, the Christian love that it would take. It is perhaps unrealistic to hope that I can help give this nation any of those things, but that is what I believe I have to try to do."

In her first speech on the House floor she spoke out against the Vietnam War, announcing her plans to vote against any and every military appropriations bill while in Congress. She began to protest the amount of money being expended for the defense budget while social programs suffered. She argued that she would not agree that money should be spent for war while Americans were hungry, ill-housed, and poorly educated.

Chisholm protested the traditional roles for women professionals—secretaries, teachers, and librarians. She argued that women were capable of entering many other professions and they should be encouraged to do so. Black women, too, she felt, had been shunted into stereotypical maid and nanny roles from which they needed to escape both by legislation and by self-effort. Her antiwar and women's liberation views made her a popular figure among college students, and she was besieged with invitations to speak at college campuses.

In 1972, Chisholm waged an unprecedented campaign for the Democratic presidential nomination, gaining the support of many disadvantaged groups. She was the first black and the first woman to seek a major party nomination for president. Of the daunting task she had chosen with this campaign, she explained, "The United States was said not to be ready to elect a Catholic to the presidency when Al Smith ran in the 1920s. But Smith's nomination may have helped pave the way for the successful campaign John F. Kennedy waged in 1960. Who can tell? What I hope most is that now there will be others who will feel themselves as capable of running for high political office as any wealthy, good-looking white male."

Chisholm began the race like all her previous political ventures, as a poorly funded and hardworking underdog. This time, however, her work ethic and drive were not enough to succeed. She attempted to put together a coalition of blacks, feminists, and other minority groups. In addition to her interest in civil rights for blacks, women, and the poor, she spoke out about the judicial system in the United States, police brutality, prison reform, gun control, political dissent, drug abuse, and numerous other topics. She appeared on the television show *Face the Nation* with three other Democratic presidential candidates—George McGovern, Henry Jackson, and Edmund Muskie—and emerged as the most progressive contender, more so than George McGovern, who won the presidential nomination at the Democratic National Convention.

The next time a woman runs, or a Black, a Jew or anyone from a group that the country is "not ready" to elect to its highest office, I believe he or she will be taken seriously from the start. The door is not open yet, but it is ajar.

—SHIRLEY CHISHOLM

Chisholm only captured 10 percent of the delegates' votes. Even so, her campaign cannot be deemed a failure because of the groundbreaking nature of the endeavor. "In terms of Black politics, I think an effect of my campaign has been to increase the independence and self-reliance of many local elected Black officials and Black political activists from the domination of the political 'superstars.'" As a result of her candidacy, Chisholm was voted one of the ten most admired women in the world. In her account of her presidential campaign in *The Good Fight* she wrote, "The mere fact that a Black woman dared to run for President, *seriously*, not expecting to win but sincerely trying to, is what it was all about. 'It can be done'; that was what I was trying to say, by doing it."

"We Americans," she added, "have a chance to become someday a nation in which all racial stocks and classes can exist in their own selfhoods, but meet on a basis of respect and equality and live together, socially, economically, and politically. . . . I hope I did a little to make it happen. I am going to keep trying to make it happen as long as I am able. I will not run for President again, but in a broad sense my campaign will continue. In fact, it is just beginning."

An interesting sidebar to her presidential run, and a strong example of her compassionate spirit, was Chisholm's unlikely visit to her rival, Democratic candidate and Alabama Governor George Wallace. Wallace, an avowed segregationist during the early years of the civil rights movement, had made a notorious stand against school desegregation in 1963 by physically attempting to block black students from enrolling at the University of Alabama and four elementary schools in Huntsville. By 1972, he was still actively campaigning against busing as part of his presidential bid. While campaigning in Maryland, he was shot five times by Arthur Bremer, a lone gunman looking for a quick claim to fame. One bullet that lodged in Wallace's spine left him paralyzed from the waist down for the rest of his life.

No one running against Wallace in 1972 could have been more diametrically opposed to everything he stood for than Chisholm. Yet, she looked in on him while he was recuperating from his injuries in the hospital. As Chisholm later recalled to the *New York Times*, Wallace wondered if her visiting would not bother her supporters. She replied, "I know what they're going to say. But I wouldn't want what happened to you to happen to anyone." Of Wallace's response, she said, "He cried and cried and cried."

Before the decade was out, Wallace became a born-again Christian and apologized and sought forgiveness from black civil rights leaders for his segregationist stance. During his final term as governor (1983–1987), to which he was elected with the support of a majority of black voters, he made a record number of black appointments to government positions in Alabama.

As for Chisholm, when she fought for a bill to give domestic workers the right to a minimum wage, her former White House rival George Wallace wielded his influence among Southern congressmen to help push the legislation through the House.

In the wake of her presidential bid, Chisholm established and chaired the National Political Congress of Black Women and wrote *The Good Fight*. In 1977 she was appointed to the House Rules Committee and elected secretary of the Democratic Caucus. She also served as vice chairman of the Congressional Black Caucus. That same year she divorced her first husband and later married businessman Arthur Hardwick.

After her unsuccessful presidential campaign, Chisholm continued to serve in the U.S. House of Representatives for another decade. As a member of the Black Caucus she was able to watch black representation in the Congress grow and to welcome other black female congresswomen. Finally, in 1982, she announced her retirement from public service, bringing an end to a political career that made her as well-known nationally as she was in her home district.

From 1983 to 1987, Chisholm served as Purington Professor at Mt.

Holyoke College in Massachusetts where she taught politics and women's studies. In 1985 she was the visiting scholar at Spelman College, and in 1987 Chisholm retired from teaching altogether. She continued to be involved in politics by cofounding the National Political Congress of Black Women in 1984.

Chisholm also worked vigorously for the presidential campaign of Jesse Jackson in 1984 and 1988. "Jackson is the voice of the poor, the disenchanted, the disillusioned," she was quoted as saying in *Newsweek*, "and that is exactly what I was."

When Jesse Jackson started his campaign for the presidency in 1984, Chisholm began working for him. With more time available, her support increased for his 1988 campaign. In the eyes of many, his campaigns were a direct result of her earlier attempt. Jackson's New Jersey chairman, Newark mayor Sharpe James, credited Shirley for paving the way. "If there had been no Shirley Chisholm, there would have been no 'Run, Jesse, run,' in 1984 and no 'Win, Jesse, win' in 1988," said James In 2008, Barack Obama would follow more successfully in Chisholm's footsteps, becoming the first black candidate to win the Democratic nomination for president.

Working for the Jackson campaign was not the extent of Chisholm's political activities. Following several disappointments at the 1984 Democratic Convention, Chisholm was determined to continue the struggle. She gathered nine black women together. This then led to a major four-day convention of five hundred black women. They created a new organization, the National Political Congress of Black Women (NPCBW). Chisholm was chosen as its first leader. The group grew fast, with eighty-five hundred members in thirty-six states by 1988. By this point, it was beginning to wield some real political power. The group sent a delegation of one hundred women to the 1988 Democratic National Convention to present demands for promoting civil rights and social programs. Thus, Chisholm remained a potent force in politics.

Though petite, standing just five feet,

> *The Constitution they wrote was designed to protect the rights of white, male citizens. As there were no Black Founding Fathers, there were no founding mothers— a great pity, on both counts. It is not too late to complete the work they left undone.*
>
> —SHIRLEY CHISHOLM

four inches tall, Chisholm earned a reputation as a powerful presence in Washington. A remarkable woman whose historic presidential campaign paved the way for others, she was a pioneer who refused to accept the status quo that society had set for women. Throughout her public life, Chisholm was the voice of the poor, the disenfranchised, and the powerless. She brought significant changes in the 1960s in both state and national laws regarding discrimination against minorities, and her involvement in politics greatly affected the consciousness of many Americans, making racial equality a national issue. Chisholm's refusal to cooperate with political machines at the local, state, or national level forced her to fight her way to victory the hard way. She followed the dictates of her conscience, often prompting her opponents to declare that she was on the verge of committing political suicide.

Whenever she heard it, Chisholm knew she must be doing something right. "That phrase sort of made me feel at home," she said.

Ending a lifetime of distinguished and courageous public service during a period of dramatic social changes in the United States, Shirley Chisholm died in 2005.

How to Be Like Shirley Chisholm

1) **Make your own path.** Chisholm was a maverick her entire life. She never accepted the role society tried to confine her to. As such, Chisholm became the first African-American woman ever to sit in the U.S. Congress, and the first black woman to seek the presidential nomination from a major party.

2) **Seek education.** Both of Chisholm's parents were instrumental in her education. Her mother emphasized the importance of receiving a quality education. Her father was an avid reader, reading two newspapers daily, which inspired young Shirley to improve her own mind. Chisholm benefited from the strict British-style schooling she received in her early years in Barbados. She graduated from Brooklyn College and then went on to earn a master's degree from Columbia University.

3) **Follow your conscience and do what's right.** Upon her election to the New York State Assembly in 1964, Chisholm declined to play the role of the quiet freshman lawmaker expected of her by her party's political leadership. She opted instead to work directly for her constituents, many of whom were poor, to improve their lives. She successfully supported legislation to provide publicly funded day care centers, unemployment insurance for domestic workers, and job protection for female teachers on maternity leave.

   Following the dictates of her conscience often prompted her political opponents to declare that she was on the verge of committing "political suicide"—music to Chisholm's ears: "That phrase sort of made me feel at home."

4) **Overcome obstacles by outworking people.** Running against a nationally known black civil rights leader during Chisholm's first run for the U.S. Congress, she found herself up against a

Cont'd

well-funded machine candidate. "I didn't have the money for a conventional congressional campaign; I had to make up for it with hard work." She campaigned under the slogan, "Fighting Shirley Chisholm: Unbought and Unbossed" and won the race.

5) **Know your purpose.** While a new U.S. Representative, Chisholm served on several House committees: Agriculture, Veterans' Affairs, Rules and Education, and Labor. However, when she was assigned to the Forestry Committee, she protested, insisting that she wanted to work on committees that could deal with the "critical problems of racism, deprivation and urban decay."

6) **Be compassionate.** A moving example of Chisholm's compassionate spirit is her hospital visit with segregationist George Wallace after the shooting that left him paralyzed. When Wallace wondered what her supporters would say, Chisholm told him that she "wouldn't want what happened to you to happen to anyone," a statement that moved Wallace to tears. Perhaps that measure of compassion was among the things that led Wallace to become a born-again Christian and to seek forgiveness from black civil rights leaders for his segregationist stance. During his final term as governor, Wallace made a record number of black appointments to government positions in Alabama.

7) **See the big picture.** Chisholm recognized she had no chance to win the 1972 Democratic nomination for president, but in light of Jesse Jackson's subsequent attempt and then Senator Barack Obama's successful bid to win the nomination in 2008, Chisholm's words seem especially prophetic: "The United States was said not to be ready to elect a Catholic to the presidency when Al Smith ran in the 1920s. But Smith's nomination may

Cont'd

have helped pave the way for the successful campaign John F. Kennedy waged in 1960. Who can tell? What I hope most is that now there will be others who will feel themselves as capable of running for high political office as any wealthy, good-looking white male."

Martha Stewart
1941–

Perfectionist

I am a perfectionist, and especially when
you're doing the kind of thing that people are looking
at and trying to learn from, it's terribly important
to do it in the finest fashion possible.

—MARTHA STEWART

artha Stewart seemingly has it all, but the self-made business-woman is still willing to do whatever it takes to see her vision become reality.

Seeing a grand design through from beginning to end is what great innovators and business leaders have always done. It's the difference between making only a buck, or making a mark. And Martha Stewart has certainly made her mark.

By 1997 Stewart, through her focused work ethic, had made herself into a household brand name in the field of homemaking. Beginning with a small catering business in the mid-1970s, she first gained the larger public's attention in 1983 through her bestselling books about home decorating and food preparation. Then a merchandising agreement with Kmart came in 1987. Over the next six years, Martha launched a magazine and then her television show. She had the makings of a multimedia company and decided to create one.

There was one major obstacle, however. She did not own what would be the foundation of her business, her magazine, *Martha Stewart Living*. To foster her vision, she put everything on the line and borrowed $85 million, signed for personally, to buy the rights to her magazine from Time Warner. Stewart's lawyers, advisors, and friends cautioned her against doing this. They questioned if the magazine's focus on better living and homemaking might go out of style. Stewart felt she understood her customers and market so well that she knew interest in her talent was here to stay. "People are always looking for new ways to decorate and embellish their surroundings," she said. Nobody could argue with that.

She wasn't motivated solely by money, however (if you are able to borrow $85 million, you are already doing pretty well). She said she was motivated by her vision of all that she could bring to her customers and felt limited by Time Warner's ownership. She saw Time Warner as a "wonderful corporate parent," but essentially a magazine and book publisher. She said at the time, "They are not a television company or an online service or merchandising company, and those are areas where I foresee tremendous growth [for my company]."

Stewart's big-picture plan was more than just owning her magazine; her magazine was the foundation from which her company could grow in many different directions to provide "useful and necessary information and wonderful products to our valued customers," she wrote.

While borrowing $85 million was seemingly risky, Stewart distinguished between calculated risk and taking a chance. She called herself a risk taker and wrote in her 2005 book, *The Martha Rules*, "The natural question to ask yourself is whether what you are considering doing is a well-calculated risk or whether you are poised to take what I would call a chance—a long shot that depends largely on luck. I dislike taking chances, but I think taking a well-calculated risk is the cornerstone of entrepreneurship."

In full control as chairperson and chief executive officer, Stewart founded Martha Stewart Living Omnimedia, Inc., in 1997. The company went public in 1999, and on its first day of trading, the stock opened at $18 a share, hit a high of $52, and ended the day at $36. Before trading that day, Stewart's worth was estimated at $250 million. At the end of that day, she was worth more than $1 billion on paper.

The $85 million proved to be a good investment. She joined a select few women such as Mary Kay Ash, Oprah Winfrey, Estée Lauder, and J. K. Rowling in building a financial empire from scratch. By 2000, Martha Stewart Living Omnimedia had profits of over $21 million and annual sales of over $285 million.

Right from the start, Stewart knew what she wanted in her business and had the drive and determination to make it happen. But take it from her, building a multibillion-dollar brand and company from scratch wasn't a piece of cake, even if she made it look that way.

"To many onlookers, what I have accomplished may appear easy, but it was all done with hard work, old-fashioned elbow grease and a certain amount of emotional pain and suffering," Stewart said, as quoted by Bill Adler in *The World According to Martha*.

"Stewart's mantra," wrote Joann F. Price in *Martha Stewart: A Biography*, is "stay focused and work to the max!"

Susan Wyland, former editor of *Martha Stewart Living* magazine, said in 1996, "Not only does Stewart work exceptionally hard, but she also had a dream and she was clear about it from the beginning."

By 2002, that dream made Stewart the richest self-made businesswoman in America and a cultural icon readily identifiable by her first name, like Oprah and Madonna.

Iconic status doesn't mean she hasn't stumbled along the way. She spent five months incarcerated in a federal prison after being found guilty of making false statements to the government about a questionable stock sale. Yet she handled that ordeal with grace, dignity, and strength. She took her sentence standing up, friend Donald Trump said to *Newsweek*. "There were no tears. No dropping to the ground. I've seen very strong men who can't handle that."

As with many successful public figures, Stewart is not without her detractors. She was blasted by the media and scorned by hardworking people in middle-class America. However, on balance, there are far more positives to take and learn from Stewart's life than negatives. To dismiss her because of a mistake or because of the things said about her personally that may not be accurate would be to cheat ourselves of the life lessons of this remarkable businesswoman.

It is easier to pursue perfection and put in untold hours when it's a labor of love, and that's what Stewart's work is to her. She has always loved cooking, gardening, and homemaking. Even with her fortune made, Martha says she still loves getting up in the morning, which for her is anywhere from 4 to 6 AM, to get to work after her morning exercise routine, which consists of activities such as hiking and yoga.

I think you have to be really intensely serious about your work, but not so serious that you can't see the lightness that may also involve your life. You have to have that lightness too. You have to not be so heavy-handed and so ostentatious. It's very important not to be.

—MARTHA STEWART TO THE ACADEMY OF ACHIEVEMENT, 1995

"Build your business success around something that you love—something that is inherently and endlessly interesting to you," Stewart said in her 2005 book, *The Martha Rules*. "Doing the work you love gives you boundless energy. You are imbued with enthusiasm. Your senses seem sharper. You wake up with new ideas every day and with solutions to conquer the challenges that cropped up the day before. You are always confident that goals are attainable, that creativity and ingenuity and hard work and passion for the work will make 'it' all come together."

In 1996 she broke her business down to the basics: write cookbooks and teach people how to do creative things. In an article written for *Cosmopolitan* in 1997 entitled "The Importance of Being Myself," Stewart listed the twelve golden rules by which she lives her professional and personal life. Number five is to "make everything as simple as possible, but not simpleminded. This is a rule I've borrowed from Einstein, and my television segments illustrate his directive: I try to reduce the number and complexity of the steps in a project to the bare minimum without harming either the efficacy or beauty of the result."

When asked by *Business Week* editor-in-chief Stephen B. Shepard in 2002 to name the number one attribute that has made her so successful, Stewart said, "It's my curiosity and that I want to learn something new every day." When asked about the most important characteristics for success by the Academy of Achievement in 1995, Stewart said, "It's a commitment to a person's interests and the ability to be open-minded, which encompasses curiosity."

Clues to some of the things that drive Stewart might be found in her childhood. She was born Martha Helen Kostyra on August 12, 1941, in Jersey City, New Jersey. The second of six children raised in Nutley, New Jersey, near New York City, she certainly did not start out with financial advantages. She has referred to her family's financial situation back then as "meager." Other biographers have termed it working-class poor. Whatever you call it, six children to care for is a financial challenge for any average-income family.

Stewart credits her father, Edward, a pharmaceutical salesman, with teaching her about gardening and decorating in addition to setting the example of being a "total perfectionist." It's a trait Stewart embraced naturally and has made the cornerstone of her business life.

"I continue to be as picky and as impossible as ever. I am a perfectionist, and especially when you're doing the kind of thing that people are looking at and trying to learn from, it's terribly important to do it in the finest fashion possible," Stewart said in 1996.

From both her father and mother, also named Martha and a sixth-grade teacher, Stewart says she and her siblings had a "you-can-do-anything-you-want" attitude impressed upon them. Her parents assured her that she could accomplish whatever she desired if she tried and worked hard enough. She says she and her siblings were also brought up unpretentiously.

Stewart credits her mother with giving her the foundation to become successful because of the stability she brought as a stay-at-home-mom until all her children were in school. Stewart's mother then went back to her profession of teaching, so she was leaving the house and coming home at the same time as her children.

The Stewart children were expected to work and start saving for college early on. Stewart describes herself as a "very proper, very busy, very driven" child who earned money babysitting and had fun organizing birthday parties for neighborhood children. It was her household duties that introduced young Martha to cooking, sewing, and gardening, things she found weren't chores at all, but rather things she enjoyed doing.

While in high school she earned money from modeling in department stores and in fashion magazines. She even landed television commercials with Clairol and Lifebuoy soap among others.

A straight-A student, Stewart attended Barnard College in New York City and earned a bachelor's degree in history and architectural history, graduating in 1963. While in her sophomore year in 1961 she married Yale law student Andrew Stewart. That year her sense of style brought her to the attention of *Glamour* magazine, who named her as one of America's ten best-dressed college students. In 1965 Stewart gave birth to daughter Alexis.

She continued to earn money modeling until 1965 when she went to work on Wall Street as one of the few female stockbrokers. Her time at the small firm of Monness, Williams, and Sidel taught her some fundamental and harsh truths that she brought into her own business years later. One was that good intentions count for very little on Wall Street, and that if a public company doesn't make money, it is not a success. She said she saw companies fail because they took on too much debt and tried to expand too rapidly. Stewart vowed never to run a business that way.

She also took notice of the key difference dynamic leaders made. They "inspired employees to attain impressive goals—and so I've worked hard to motivate people and hire the right executives," Stewart wrote.

Although she'd managed to earn a six-figure income, Stewart left Wall Street in 1973 amid an economic downturn. She wanted to be home more with her daughter. The family had moved from their New York City apartment into a large fixer-upper house in Westport, Connecticut, in 1972. The Stewarts began renovating the house, which had been built in 1805. It was at this point in her life that she saw that fixing up her home, cooking, working in her garden, and little beautification projects like painting shutters had value beyond her family. It had value to everyone. She had discovered what would become her life's work.

"Focus your attention and creativity on basic things, things that people need and want. Then look for ways to enlarge, improve, and enhance your big idea," Stewart wrote in *The Martha Rules*. This is the essence of her business success.

Her love of gourmet cooking led her to start a catering business. She began with an ad in a local newspaper in 1976, and Martha Stewart Inc.

was launched in her basement kitchen. One of her first catering jobs was a wedding for three hundred people. Her reputation grew, and she began serving corporate clients as well as celebrities.

Always looking for ways to get her catering business publicity and exposure, Stewart began selling her homemade bakery items and freshly prepared dinners at The Common Market, a small food court in Westport, situated among high-end retail shops. She eventually managed The Common Market and opened her own store there, The Market Basket.

Within ten years Martha Stewart Inc. had become a $1 million a year business. She began to establish her brand by writing articles for the *New York Times* and becoming the food and entertainment editor and cooking columnist for *House Beautiful*.

Her famous perfectionist streak and work ethic was evident from the start of her business. Before Stewart would write a catering proposal for a perspective client, she might stay up all night reading cookbooks. Information was currency to her then, as it is now.

"There was no amount of research into any aspect of what I was doing that I considered excessive or not worth the effort," Stewart wrote of her catering days. "Good information always provides a return on investment whether it's used immediately or filed away for when it's needed."

Stewart maintains, with the help of assistants, more than a thousand folders to catalog ideas. When ideas come into her mind, she captures them. She uses e-mail to log them or writes them in a notebook. Stewart tears pages from magazines she subscribes to that might be used for decorating or gardening ideas. She captures ideas with a camera also. "Big ideas are everywhere. They are swirling all around us," Stewart wrote. This database of ideas forms much of the basis of the content for her many projects.

It's been said that the reward of doing great work is more work, and Stewart's catering business began to grow by referrals along with her reputation. Even then she was creating her brand: *Martha Stewart* stood for quality and excellence.

"Quality should be placed at the top of your list of priorities, and it should remain there. Quality is something you should strive for in every decision, every day," Stewart wrote of her business philosophy.

Her success in the catering business led to Stewart's first big idea. She saw that her clients wanted a resource where they could find everything they would likely need in one place when entertaining. Stewart conceived the idea of a book that combined cooking, decorating, flower arranging, and etiquette.

She wasn't worried that a book might lessen her demand as a caterer, because Stewart was already thinking of the bigger picture. She was moving from catering to positioning herself as an expert on entertaining. "This was a far more interesting, expansive, and exciting notion—one that filled me with so many ideas I could barely sleep," Stewart wrote. "I discovered that I loved teaching people to do the things that I enjoyed doing, and I loved encouraging people to do them well."

Martha believes in leading by example. The fourth of her golden rules is to "live as you teach others to live. My own homes and gardens are evidence that I do as I preach. My surroundings are no different from the environments pictured in my books and on the pages of my magazine."

Making connections are as important in success as taking advantage of opportunities. Stewart was presented with one when she catered a launch party for a book by Abrams Publishing, where her husband, Andy, was president and chief executive officer. The president of Crown Publishing Group, Alan Mirken, was there and was impressed with the food and the entire party. He asked Andy who was responsible and was introduced to Martha. She'd been thinking about writing a cookbook, and Mirken encouraged her to do so when ready.

This eventually led to a book contract with Crown and a healthy $25,000 advance for the prospective author. Stewart's first book was called simply *Entertaining*. It was published in 1982 and became a bestseller. It has had over thirty printings since. In addition to employing Stewart's concept of being a primary resource for anything and everything to do with entertaining, it was enhanced with 450 photographs that struck a chord with readers due to the genteel country lifestyle they presented.

Striking while the iron was hot, Stewart followed up *Entertaining* with a succession of books; *Martha Stewart's Quick Cook* in 1983, *Martha Stewart's Hors d'Oeuvres* in 1984, *Martha Stewart's Pies & Tarts* in 1985, and *Weddings* in 1987.

These books helped establish Stewart as an author and authority on the subjects of cooking and entertaining. Today she has close to thirty books on cooking, gardening, home decor, and business that have sold more than 9.5 million copies. Her advice on being a successful author is to write the book you would want to read.

By 1987 her name and credibility led the way to a merchandising deal with Kmart to serve as their lifestyle expert while also marketing a line of products. The exposure from Kmart's advertising further helped to make her a household name. (Today Kmart sells over $1 billion a year of Stewart's branded products.)

Her initial book success led Stewart to approach Time Warner about publishing a magazine that would be an extension of her work. They agreed, and in 1990, her magazine, *Martha Stewart Living*, was born. Stewart's personal touch was evident. The magazine boasted beautiful photographs of decorated rooms that told a visual story. There were articles about the best way to perform household tasks, and, of course, there were recipes. Subjects like dating, dieting, and fixing hair were left to other magazines. By 1995 the magazine was providing customers for Stewart's mail-order business. *Martha Stewart Living* boasted 2.1 million subscribers by 2001.

Martha Stewart Living Omnimedia, Inc. (MSLO), has market penetration in publishing, television, merchandising, and Internet/direct commerce. Stewart thinks of it as a content company, and MSLO provides information and products in eight content areas: home, cooking and entertaining, gardening, crafts, holidays, housekeeping, weddings, and child care. Stewart publishes four magazines: *Martha Stewart Living, Everyday Food, Weddings*, and *Body+Soul*.

"I think Martha Stewart has proven that each of the different genres—magazine, Internet, radio, newspaper, television, and cable on television—all complement each other and feed off of each other. . . . Martha is someone who understands her audience and her brand better than almost anyone," said Ed Wilson, president of CBS-affiliated syndicator Eyemark Entertaiment, which distributes *Martha Stewart Living*, in 2000. Stewart believes her crossover into different media venues helped her connect with customers.

Evolving from a base, as opposed to radical change, is part of Stewart's business philosophy. For example, she said in 1998 that the reason she allocates so much money for the production of her TV show is because she's compiling a library of correct procedures for gardening and home projects that can be available through the Internet. In 2005, she signed a deal with Warner Home Video to produce how-to DVDs that utilized sixteen hundred hours of her backlogged television shows.

Stewart says being an entrepreneur requires a person to do more than just "go to work," much more than just "do a job." It bears repeating that the only way most people reach that level of commitment is to love what they do the way Stewart does.

Martha is a unique combination of the beauty of the orchid and the efficiency of a computer.

—MORT ZUCKERMAN, CHAIRMAN,
U.S. NEWS & WORLD REPORT

"Entrepreneurs," Stewart wrote, "must be curious and always learning." When she's not seeking information, she's absorbing it: "I listen and listen. One of my best qualities is that I listen and I make judgments on what I hear. And I have done that since the beginning of this business. To me, the most important people to listen to are my readers, my viewers, my listeners, and my Internet users. I read every letter. I think about what they say." She says her company focus comes from her customers' needs and wants. If her company receives thousands of inquiries about knives, it means that they will make knives.

"Entrepreneurs also need," Stewart continued, "unflagging energy . . . and even the strength and desire to put up with sleep deprivation and long hours of intense concentration. To many, these characteristics might sound rather daunting, but among successful entrepreneurs, these are common traits."

Stewart's conviction on federal charges of conspiracy, obstruction of justice, and making false statements in March 2004 stemmed from a stock sale. She was originally also accused of insider trading, but that charge was later dropped. In December 2000 Stewart sold four thousand shares of drugmaker ImClone's stock, the day before it dropped dramatically on news that the FDA would not review the company's application for its cancer drug Erbitux. Stewart avoided a $46,000 loss, and the timing of the sale raised suspicions. The founder of ImClone, Sam Waksal, was a friend of Stewart's, and that caught the eye of the Securities and Exchange Commission.

Rather than draw out the appeals process and continue the erosion of her name and that of her company, whose stock dropped considerably during the allegations and subsequent trial and conviction, Stewart served a five-month sentence at the federal prison camp in Alderson, West Virginia.

All reports are that Stewart got along well with fellow inmates and was a model inmate herself. She taught a daily yoga class to other prisoners during her incarceration. Upon her release on March 4, 2005, Stewart set out to rebuild her brand and company.

Of her prison stay and ordeal, she said to Larry King in March 2005, "I tried to represent the values of dignity and grace that I cherish so deeply, even when it was really difficult. I hope I succeeded."

Securities regulators stripped Stewart of her positions of chairman and CEO of her company and denied her a seat on her own board. While extremely pained by this, Stewart got back to work once she was released from prison. She's written more books, helped design Martha Stewart–branded homes for builder KB Homes, and launched a twenty-four-hour radio channel.

Her company struggled during the time of the allegations against her and subsequent incarceration because of the relationship of her name to her brand. But that has only made Stewart work harder to help restore her company to profitability.

"It's not like I'm an absentee founder, holed up in my chateau in France," she told *People Magazine* in November 2006. "I'm working every day."

Stewart continues to evoke strong opinions from both her fans and critics. Her fans speak with their pocketbooks. The critics of her business see fault in what they perceive is promotion of a lifestyle and level of perfection that most woman can't attain. Stewart stated many years ago what continues to be her philosophy regarding what her customers want: "Having something to dream about is very important to most people."

She says her books and magazines are dream publications to look at, but they're also practical. "Women can take the recipes, the ideas, and use them every day, because what I'm really giving them is not a fantasy but a reality

Life is too complicated not to be orderly.

—MARTHA STEWART,
HARPER'S BAZAAR

that looks like a fantasy."

Some critics also say she promotes style over substance and the pursuit of material possessions. Stewart says in answer to them, "They make me sound like I'm such a materialist. . . . In fact, I'm an idealist. What do I write about and promote? Good things. Simple ideas. Making your home more beautiful, making your family happy. Is that so wrong? You don't have to have a lot of money to enjoy your friends, your life."

With all that she's achieved, with her legions of customers and fans, the proof is in the pudding. Stewart is giving people what she loves and they want. And that's a winning business recipe.

"My life is my business. My business is my life," she says.

How to Be Like Martha Stewart

1) **Understand calculated risks.** When Stewart borrowed $85 million to buy her magazine from Time Warner, she distinguished between taking a calculated risk and taking a chance. She wrote "a chance [is] a long shot that depends largely on luck," but a "well-calculated risk is the cornerstone of entrepreneurship."

2) **Embrace your curiosity.** Follow your instincts and probe for answers in your given calling. Stewart has said her number one attribute for success is her curiosity: "It's energy; it's wanting to learn something new every day."

3) **Work hard.** As Stewart has said, to many onlookers, what she has accomplished may appear easy, but it was all done with hard work, old-fashioned elbow grease.

4) **Work at what you love.** It is easier to pursue perfection and put in untold hours when it's a labor of love. "Build your business success around something that you love—something that is inherently and endlessly interesting to you," Stewart said.

5) **Understand your business basics.** Stewart said she primarily writes cookbooks and teaches people how to do good and useful things. The formula that has worked for Stewart was to focus her attention and creativity on the basics, things that people need. She then looked for ways to improve and enhance her "big idea."

6) **Keep things simple.** Stewart distinguishes between "simple" and "simpleminded." Her approach has been to reduce the steps in a project to the bare minimum, while always maintaining the quality of the end result.

7) **Strive for perfection.** You may not always attain it, but in the spirit of an old expression, if you shoot for the stars and don't

Cont'd

make it, you may still reach the moon. Stewart is proud of her perfectionism and remains "as picky and as impossible as ever."

8) **Exercise detailed preparation.** Understand thoroughly what you need to do to succeed. There was no amount of research Stewart considered excessive.

9) **Generate ideas through awareness.** Not many people succeed in a vacuum. For Stewart, idea generation is the currency of her company. "Big ideas are everywhere. They are swirling all around us."

10) **Set an example.** Don't just talk, act. It gives you credibility both internally and externally. As Stewart says, "Live as you teach others to live."

11) **Be a good listener.** It's becoming a lost art. Stewart considers her willingness to listen to be one of her best qualities And she believes her customers are the most important people to listen to. She reads every customer letter.

13

Mary McLeod Bethune
1875–1955

Education

*Our aim must be to create a world of fellowship
and justice where no man's skin color or religion is held
against him. "Love thy neighbor" is a precept that could
transform the world if it were universally practiced.*

—MARY MCLEOD BETHUNE

Very early on in life, Mary Jane McLeod learned the value of an education when she accompanied her father, farmer Samuel McLeod, to the local cotton mill to sell the cotton they grew on their family farm. Mary's father could not read a scale, so he had to rely on the integrity of the mill's white owner to receive a fair price for his cotton. When the owner weighed Samuel McLeod's cotton and announced that it was about 250 pounds, Mary wondered how he came to that conclusion.

She realized that if she had an education, she could understand how the mill owner came up with those numbers. She began to pray for the opportunity to attend school. It became the thing she wanted most of all.

Eventually, she did go to school. Then, on an ensuing trip to the mill, she brought with her the newfound ability to read the numbers on the mill owner's scales. The owner said that her father's cotton came in at 280 pounds. But Mary studied the scales and countered, "Isn't it 480 pounds?" The owner conceded that she was right. Soon, other farmers, white as well as black, who couldn't do math asked the bright little girl to calculate the weight of their payloads.

"From the first, I made my learning, what little it was, useful every way I could," Bethune would later recall. This would be a recurring theme throughout her life—when she pursued education, many others would benefit.

That precocious little girl grew up to become Mary McLeod Bethune, who from the 1920s to the mid-1950s would be hailed as the most influential black woman in the United States. Energetic, strong-willed, and hardworking, this devoutly religious daughter of former slaves wisely intuited that only education could tap into the potential of black children to expand their horizons and leave behind lives of poverty and thwarted hopes. She devoted her life to being an educator, activist, and public servant to open up opportunities to all black Americans. Starting with $1.50 and a strange dream of a visit from the legendary Booker T. Washington, she would found Cookman-Bethune College. She would establish influential black women's clubs and consolidate their power on the national level, become an adviser or representative of every United States president from Calvin Coolidge to Harry S. Truman, and use her unique abilities to knock down barriers for black Americans to take part in government, the military, job training, employment opportunities, and higher education.

Born on July 19, 1875 in Mayesville, South Carolina, Bethune was born a free person as opposed to most of her siblings, who were born into slavery and later emancipated at the end of the Civil War. Her mother, Patsy, continued to work for her former owner, and eventually she and Samuel purchased thirty-five acres of land from him to start the rice and cotton farm that would sustain their large family. Like the rest of her brothers and sisters, young Mary helped her parents work the land and learned to pick cotton at a very early age, developing both a strong work ethic and a great appreciation of the value of manual labor.

Legend has it that the midwife who delivered Mary told her mother that her new daughter's eyes were wide open, which meant that the baby would see things before they happened. Imagine, some twelve years later, what the sale price of that extra two hundred pounds of cotton would mean to Mary's family—which included sixteen brothers and sisters, her parents, and her grandmother. Clearly, Mary's early intuition that her lack of education was something she had to change meant that her powers of observation were keen indeed. She understood that education was the only way out of poverty.

Devoutly Methodist, the McLeods managed to build a cabin large enough to house the family, calling it "The Homestead." At night, Mary would gather with her family to listen to her grandmother Sophia, who spoke often to the children of her gratitude for what little they had. As Andrea Broadwater recounts in her book *Mary McLeod Bethune: Educator and Activist*, Sophia would declare to the family, "Dear God, I am so happy to be living in this loving family circle . . . having good things without having to count the lashes that bring blood trickling down your back."

Early on, Bethune exhibited the concern for others and unselfishness that would characterize her choices for the rest of her life. Her mother observed that Mary always wanted to share the few things she had with other children. According to *Ebony* magazine, Bethune said later, "I knew then, as I stood in the cotton field helping with the farm work that I was called to a task which I could not name or explain."

Faith, selflessness, gratitude for the simple things they had, hard work, and making do with what was at hand were values Bethune would put to use later as an educator struggling to build a school from the ground up.

The McLeod family was well liked in their local community, and they were known for helping their neighbors in need. But Bethune's childhood during Reconstruction was not without its dangers. One day during a visit into town, her wide-open eyes watched as some white men shoved a lit match under a black man's nose. When the black man flung his arms in surprise and accidentally knocked down one of his white tormentors, Samuel McLeod seized his daughter and warned her not to look back. As they fled, she heard the white men calling to lynch the unfortunate black man, whose only crime had been an understandable reflex to their nasty prank. The horror and immorality of that episode never left her, and later she would become a resolute advocate to end the horror of lynching.

Although blacks were the majority population in Sumter County, a black child had little access to public schools. There were none in the immediate area that accepted black students. But when a small Presbyterian mission school opened five miles from the Bethune family farm, nine-year-old Mary was more than willing to walk the five miles each way to learn to read and write. Her parents recognized her gifts and allowed her to attend.

"It was a humble one-room school," she later recalled of the Trinity Mission School in Mayesville, South Carolina. "The blackboard was only painted cardboard. But that didn't matter. For there I saw letters make words. I was reading! At home, I gathered the other children around me to teach them what I knew." A natural educator was born!

What the "humble one-room school" lacked in amenities, it more than made up for with its teacher Emma Jane Wilson. Miss Wilson soon recognized in Mary an extraordinary drive to learn. She became her mentor. When the little girl quickly absorbed all that could be taught to her at Trinity Mission School, Miss Wilson found a white patron to fund Mary's continuing education at a new school, the Scotia Seminary for Negro Girls in Concord, North Carolina.

Her education carried with it not only Bethune's future, but the hopes and expectations of her entire rural community. As Andrea Broadwater described it, "When Mary Jane McLeod left for Scotia Seminary in 1887, everyone in the community stopped work. They walked or rode on oxcarts to the Mayesville train station and watched their Mary Jane board the train for a brand-new world."

And a brand-new world it was indeed. The Scotia Seminary's faculty was racially mixed, granting Mary her first exposure to whites who did not subscribe to the Reconstruction era racism she knew at home. The teachers taught that skin color had no bearing on a person's intelligence. As Bethune biographer Malu Halasa wrote, "The white teachers taught that the color of a person's skin has nothing to do with his brains, and that color, caste, or class distinctions are an evil thing."

Six years of exposure to such then radical notions as cooperation and equality between the races would help shape Bethune's approach to reaching across the color line to achieve her goals.

The seminary also emphasized two disciplines near and dear to Mary's heart: religion and industrial education. The tiny child who knew the value of hard work from picking her father's cotton fields embraced what the school offered. In addition to core academics, she learned cooking, sewing, laundering, and cleaning. Inspired by her religious instruction, she hoped one day to become a missionary who could teach people in Africa.

Without faith, nothing is possible. With it, nothing is impossible.

—MARY McLEOD BETHUNE

Another scholarship sent Bethune on the next step toward her goal of missionary work, allowing her to enroll in the interdenominational Moody Bible Institute for Home and Foreign Missions in Chicago. But after completing a year of preparation for missionary work, Bethune, then twenty-two, was informed by the Presbyterian Mission Board that it had no openings in Africa for black missionaries. The news was quite a blow. She would refer to it as the greatest disappointment of her life.

Although deeply discouraged by this reversal, she headed home to find a way to be of service to others. If nothing else, she was certainly qualified to teach. She joined the staff of the Haines Institute in Augusta, Georgia, where fate would provide her with another mentor.

Haines's founder, Lucy Craft Laney, was a former slave and the only black woman educator in charge of a school that compared favorably with the best southern secondary institutions for blacks, which were run by men. Laney's passion for serving others struck a profound chord for Bethune, who said, "I was impressed with her fearlessness, her amazing touch in every respect, an energy that seemed inexhaustible and her mighty power to command respect and admiration from her students and all who knew her. She handled her domain with the art of a master."

Laney modeled for her the way to teach primary, grammar, normal, and industrial courses, as well as the nuts and bolts of school administration. Bethune grew to believe that one of the best ways to improve the living conditions of black people was to educate black women. In the one year that she developed under Laney's wing, Bethune found her life's mission: she began to dream of one day founding her own school. Bethune realized that blacks in America needed Christ and school just as much as blacks in Africa did. "My life work lay not in Africa but in my own country," she said.

Her next teaching job was at the Kindell Institute in Sumter, South Carolina. There, she met Albertus Bethune, a tall, handsome fellow teacher five years her senior. They married in 1898 and moved to Savannah, Georgia, where Albertus pusued a career as a menswear salesman. There, Bethune gave birth to their only child, son Albert McLeod Bethune, in 1899. She quit teaching for a time, but not even marriage and a baby could quell her ambition to establish her own school. While Bethune loved little Albert "with a devotion that can never die," she insisted, as quoted by Andrea Broadwater, "This married life was not intended to impede things I had in mind to do. The birth of my baby boy had no tendency whatever to dim my ardor and determination." Soon, Bethune grew restless to take up her life's work, and her retirement was short-lived.

Albertus Bethune did not share either his wife's commitment to missionary work nor her vision of a new school. Mary supplemented their income by selling insurance, and he wanted her to continue with this job, but when she was invited to run a mission school in Palatka, Florida, it was an offer she could not turn down.

Her vision was a grand one: education would be the primary means for her people to advance and prosper. When her efforts in Palatka did not produce the educational institution of her dreams, she sought opportunity in a new town—Daytona Beach. Initially attracted to the area by a highway construction project, she hoped to educate the children of the black highway workers. She found these workers, who struggled against squalid living and working conditions, uninterested in educating their children. Years later, Bethune told *Reader's Digest* she found "ignorance and meager educational facilities, social prejudice and crime. This was the place to plant my seed."

As Bethune took the first steps to build her school, her marriage soured, and eventually Albertus abandoned his wife and son altogether. She never saw him again, although they remained legally married until his death in 1918. At this point in her life, she could not have been more disadvantaged: a single mother, a black

If our people are to fight their way up out of bondage we must arm them with the sword and the shield and buckler of pride—belief in themselves and their possibilities, based upon a sure knowledge of the achievements of the past.

—MARY McLEOD BETHUNE

woman living in the Deep South—where education for blacks was frowned upon—hoping to build her dream with a less-than-whopping investment capital of $1.50.

But Bethune was a woman with a vision—a vision that came to her one night in the form of a dream. In it, a big man on a horse appeared to her near the Halifax River. Bethune spoke to him about her desire to build a school. The man introduced himself as one of her lifelong heroes: the black educator and activist Booker T. Washington. He handed her a dirty handkerchief, from which he plucked a large diamond. Washington told her, "Here, take this and build your school." Then, he rode off.

According to Broadwater, Bethune would later tell potential supporters, "Invest in a human soul. Who knows? It might be a diamond in the rough." No diamond could have been rougher than the tract of land she settled on in 1904 to build her school: a former landfill that was largely overgrown swampland. With a promise to pay the owner $5 down and $5 a month, she began to cobble together her own little cabin school out of a two-story frame building on the property. She enrolled five girls ages six to twelve and her son Albert as her first students. Her primary goal was to make the school, which she eventually called the Daytona Normal and Industrial Institute, financially self-sufficient.

To run the school, she had to be more than resourceful. Crates she scrounged from the local dump became her students' desks. Pieces of wood burned at the top became pencils. Pens were filled with mashed elderberries for ink. Bethune made the most of secondhand and discarded desks, chairs, and dishes she retrieved from hotel trash bins, which she then had her students repair and refurbish. Per Broadwater, McLeod recalled, "I haunted the city dump and the trash piles behind hotels, retrieving discarded linen and kitchenware, cracked dishes, broken chairs, pieces of old lumber. Everything was scoured and mended. This was part of the training to salvage, to reconstruct, to make bricks without straw."

To purchase land and put up more buildings, Bethune tapped parents and local black churches to help her make sweet potato pies, fried fish, and ice cream to sell to local construction workers. According to Halasa, she solicited local businesses for furniture, and then for money. "I rang doorbells and tackled cold prospects without a lead. I wrote articles for whoever

Once inside the walls of the college there are neither blacks nor whites, only ladies and gentlemen.

—MARY MCLEOD BETHUNE

would print them, distributed leaflets, rode interminable miles of dusty roads on my old bicycle, invaded churches, clubs, lodges, chambers of commerce."

She later wrote, "I considered cash money as the smallest part of my resources. I had faith in a loving God, faith in myself, and a desire to serve."

In 1907, Bethune actually bought the local dump for $250 and on it erected the school's first building—Faith Hall. The motto of "Enter to Learn" and "Depart to Serve" were engraved over the main entrance to Faith Hall—another diamond that emerged from the rough. Bethune's personal motto was: "Be calm, be steadfast, be courageous."

Her choice of Daytona Beach proved a cannier decision than it might have appeared on the surface. Daytona Beach was a popular tourist and vacation attraction for not only locals but well-to-do white's from the north who kept vacation homes in the town. She boldly solicited these people for donations, hitting up tony white society organizations such as the ladies' Palmetto Club, philanthropists, and industrialists like James Gamble of Procter & Gamble and Thomas White of White's Sewing Machines, who presented the school with a brand-new machine to replace one that was broken.

Society ladies became actively involved in fund-raising. In turn, Bethune sent her students to do housework and serve cookies and tea at society luncheons or to perform cultural black music at fashionable hotels. These interactions between Bethune's students and the white Daytona resort community were bolstered by Bethune's appearances. A charismatic and persuasive speaker, she gave compelling public talks that extolled her vision of her school as "a crossroads of culture and human relations" and won over the locals.

Bethune's sincerity and emphasis on Christian love served her well as she broke down barriers between the races in Daytona Beach. As Dr. Texas A. Adams, the school's physician, recounted in a paper titled "As I Recollect," a white man wielded a Winchester rifle at Bethune's students as they walked by his house. Bethune sought out the man, listened to him with courtesy and respect, and ultimately won him over. In the end, the man made it a point to protect Bethune's students and was heard to declare, "If anybody bothers old Mary, I will protect her with my life."

Bethune ran her school in the head-hand-heart tradition. As Halasa writes, she explained, "Their heads to think, their hands to work, and their hearts to have faith." Initially, the school offered courses in home economics and such industrial skills as sewing, millinery (hat making), cooking, chair caning, rug weaving, broom making, gardening, and other practical abilities that emphasized the core value of self-sufficiency that Bethune shared with her hero, Booker T. Washington. Like Washington, McLeod believed that industrial training would help blacks gain economic independence and self-respect that would ultimately win them social and political equality. Hearkening back to her own early childhood task of picking cotton to help feed her family, she argued that there was no menial work, only menial spirit.

Eventually, her efforts expanded the school's enrollment, staff, and curriculum, which now included high school math, foreign languages, English, and Bible study. This curriculum was practically unthinkable for black children when Bethune founded the school. She performed missionary outreach to the children of local turpentine workers to provide them with an education they otherwise never could have imagined.

When one of Bethune's students fell ill with appendicitis, she took the girl to a local, whites-only hospital, where only her stubborn insistence got the child admitted for treatment. On a later visit, Bethune was shocked and incensed to find the child recuperating on a cot on a back porch, where she was largely ignored by the white staff. Bethune vowed to rectify this situation and made good on her promise in 1911 by establishing a small hospital at the school and providing training for black nurses.

By 1912, Bethune's successes attracted the attention of Booker T. Washington himself, who visited her and encouraged her to cultivate more white benefactors. By then, Bethune was landing impressive donations such as $62,000 from John D. Rockefeller.

As part of her ongoing outreach in Daytona Beach, Bethune opened her school to tourists on Sundays to showcase student accomplishments and present national speakers on issues important to black Americans. Bethune deliberately arranged these community open houses to be integrated. There were no special seating sections for white visitors at these popular events. In 2004, as the college celebrated its centennial, the school's vice president commented, "During Mrs. Bethune's time, this was the only place in the city of Daytona Beach where whites and blacks could sit in the same room and enjoy what she called 'gems from students'—their recitations and songs. This is a person who was able to bring black people and white together."

The Freedom Gates are half-a-jar. We must pry them fully open.

—Mary McLeod Bethune

With her successes and increasing community activism, Bethune shook up the status quo in Daytona Beach, which drew some powerful enemies, including the Ku Klux Klan. One chilling attempt to halt Bethune's black voter registration drive underscores just how courageous she could be.

As Bethune caught up on paperwork in her office early one November night in 1920, she noticed that all the street lights had gone out outside the campus. She then heard car horns and, more ominously, horses' hooves. Members of the Ku Klux Klan approached the school, carrying the emblem of their hatred—a burning cross. The Klan's message to Bethune and her staff was clear: you will not vote!

The only other people with Bethune at the time were several female students who lived on campus. The students looked to the woman they called "Mama Bethune" to protect them. Halasa records that Bethune told them, "When you see a burning cross remember the son of God who bore the heaviest cross of all."

Instead of giving in to terror, Bethune ordered all the school's indoor lights turned off and all the outdoor floodlights turned on. The Klan found itself in the glare of an unwanted spotlight for all to see. Bethune directed her girls to sing spirituals, which sent the Klansmen skulking away, thwarted. Armed only with light, resolve, and a choir of frightened girls, Bethune successfully stared down the KKK and made them blink. She and her staff went on to vote in the local election. It was the kind of nonviolent resistance that was practiced in India by Mahatma Gandhi and would eventually become the hallmark of the Civil Rights movement, as led by Dr. Martin Luther King Jr.

In 1923, the Methodist Episcopal Church helped to merge Daytona Normal and Industrial Institute with the Cookman Institute for Men from Jacksonville, Florida. The church hoped that, under Bethune's direction, the new, coeducational Bethune-Cookman College would develop into a two-year, and then a four-year college. By this time, the campus boasted eight buildings, which were eventually reassessed at $250,000—a splendid return on the $1.50 Bethune had invested nineteen years earlier. In 1943, the school would award its first bachelor's degree.

"Not only the Negro child but children of all races should read and know of the achievements, accomplishments and deeds of the Negro. World peace and brotherhood are based on a common understanding of the contributions and cultures of all races and creeds."

Education had been Bethune's true calling, but it also became a bridge to something greater. She saw her school as the center of Daytona's black community. As community outreach became an intrinsic part of the college's mission, Bethune became more involved with the welfare of Daytona's people. As she forged community and business ties, her sphere of influence grew. Her travels across the United States not only gained funds for her school but also national prominence.

Bethune became heavily involved in black women's clubs, both as an organizer and a leader. She made her school a key venue for local and state club events. From 1917 to 1924 she presided over the Florida Federation of Colored Women. In 1920 she founded and led what would become the Southeastern Federation of Colored Women. By 1924, she was president of the ten thousand-member National Association of Colored Women (NACW). Throughout her tenure with these organizations, she traveled nationwide to give speeches and present to the world a new and more positive image of black women.

Understanding the power of numbers, Bethune united the major national black women's associations in 1935 to form the National Council of Negro Women (NCNW) and became its long-term president. In the NCNW Annual Report of October 1941, she explained, "The scattered work and independent programs of national organizations of Negro women needed the strength that unity could bring."

Through these women's clubs, Bethune set her sights higher than ever.

During World War II, she helped to integrate the American Red Cross. She led marches on Washington, D.C., businesses that would not hire blacks. She rallied to free the Scottsboro Boys—nine young black men who were accused of raping two white women on a freight train and were tried and convicted on shaky evidence in Scottsboro, Alabama, in 1931. She campaigned against lynching and demonstrated for black sharecroppers' rights. She also worked with the Southern Conference for Human Welfare, the National Urban League, and the NAACP, which awarded her its Spingarn Medal for distinguished achievement in 1935.

Bethune developed a public persona similar to that of Booker T. Washington. She preferred to adopt a tone of conciliation over confrontation in her efforts to achieve black equality. She came across to white audiences as friendly, down-to-earth, warm, and positive. She emphasized cooperation in her outreach to white leaders, but she maintained and communicated a clear, strong vision of racial equality for all Americans. Her public appearances and speeches generated great demand, providing her a platform to reach wider audiences about such crucial issues as black voting rights and education. To those who felt she was not aggressive enough, she gently counseled, "Faith and courage, patience and fortitude."

What came next was exceptional: the opportunity to advise American presidents. In 1928, President Calvin Coolidge invited Bethune to attend the Child Welfare Conference. Coolidge's successor, President Herbert Hoover, appointed her to the White House Conference on Child Health, the National Commission for Child Welfare, the Hoover Commission on Home Building and Home Ownership, and the Planning Committee of the Federal Office of Education of Negroes. As a women's rights activist, Bethune eventually met and become friends with Eleanor Roosevelt. Bethune became instrumental in advancing Mrs. Roosevelt's position on civil rights. Mrs. Roosevelt, in turn, often described Bethune as "her closest friend in her age group."

With Franklin D. Roosevelt's election to the White House, Bethune achieved the greatest platform yet from which she could further the cause of civil rights. On Eleanor Roosevelt's recommendation, President Roosevelt appointed Bethune to the National Advisory Committee to the National Youth Administration (NYA), a federal agency created under Roosevelt's

New Deal to help Americans ages sixteen to twenty-four with unemployment during the Great Depression. Its purpose would shift during the war to provide this demographic with vocational training and placement in crucial defense industries.

Now a Washington insider, Bethune held the highest position ever attained by a black woman in the federal government. She intended to make the most of her newfound power to guarantee better opportunities for her people. She had the

There can be no divided democracy, no class government, no half-free country, under the Constitution. Therefore, there can be no discrimination, no segregation, no separation of some citizens from the rights which belong to all. . . .
We are on our way. But these are frontiers which we must conquer. . . .
We must gain full equality in education . . . in the franchise . . . in economic opportunity, and full equality in the abundance of life.

—MARY McLEOD BETHUNE

president's ear, discussing the needs of black Americans with him six to seven times a year and sometimes criticizing the administration for being slow to assist. She ensured that a fair share of the agency budget went to programs for blacks and convinced the NYA to hire blacks for federal and state government jobs. She helped to create school-aid programs and funding for black colleges and graduate students. Under her leadership, over 150,000 black teenagers went to high school, and 60,000 went on to college. By 1939, she established herself as the director of the Division of Negro Affairs.

During World War II, Bethune successfully lobbied for jobs for black youths in the defense industries, resulting in President Roosevelt's 1941 executive order to require equal hiring practices for blacks seeking work in defense factories. In 1942, she lobbied the War Department to commission black women officers in the Women's Army Auxiliary Corps (WAAC). She made sure that black Americans got to take part in the Civilian Pilot Training Program, which paved the way for black pilots in the military (most notably, the heroic Tuskegee Airmen). A telling measure of her clout was the fact that she was the only black American in the Roosevelt Administration who controlled the use of money. As Aubrey Willis Williams, the director of the NYA, put it, "No one can do what Mrs. Bethune can do."

The tireless Bethune also founded the Federal Council on Negro Affairs, an informal group of prominent, talented D.C.-based black administrators who came to be known as President Roosevelt's "Black Cabinet." Meeting at Bethune's Washington, D.C., home, the group did not dictate policy, but it influenced political appointments and federal funding to benefit black people. They successfully eliminated segregation in Virginia's Shenandoah National Park and in government cafeterias.

As Broadwater documents, at the outset of establishing the cabinet, Bethune advised them, "Let us forget the particular office each one of us holds. We must think in terms as a 'whole' for the greatest service of our people."

For his part, President Roosevelt got America's most influential black woman to serve as one of the most vigorous and effective advocates for his New Deal policies. Her message to black America proclaimed that the New Deal signaled the dawn of a new day. She advised Democratic strategists on effective ways to appeal to black voters and encouraged blacks to join the Democratic Party. During World War II, she rallied blacks to join the military to defeat the Axis powers.

President Roosevelt said of her, "Mrs. Bethune is a great woman. I believe in her because she has her feet on the ground: not only on the ground, but in the deep down ploughed soil."

Yet, throughout her service to Roosevelt, Bethune stayed on message, always pressing for concrete civil rights initiatives. As she encouraged black Americans to join the war effort, she declared, "We must not fail America, and, as Americans, we must insist that America not fail us!"

While poor health led her to resign the presidency of Bethune-Cookman College in 1942, and she left government service in 1944, Bethune did not stay retired for long. The Truman Administration called upon her to join Eleanor Roosevelt at the San Francisco organizing conference that framed the charter for the United Nations in 1945.

She resigned as NCNW president in 1949 and made a show of retiring to her home in Daytona Beach, but she remained active, despite her doctor's warnings, until the day she died.

Her activities ranged from travel to Haiti and Liberia as a guest of honor, to ownership of the *Pittsburgh Courier*, a black newspaper. She even found time to join other business owners in purchasing Paradise Beach, which they turned around to sell to black families so that they could enjoy a Florida seaside resort that had earlier been closed to them.

The lesson of Mrs. Bethune's life is that genius knows no racial barriers.

—DAYTONA BEACH
EVENING NEWS

Shortly before her death in 1955, Mary McLeod Bethune penned an article for *Ebony* magazine titled "My Last Will and Testament." In it, she outlined her legacy to black Americans.

"I leave you love. I leave you hope. I leave you the challenge of developing confidence in one another. I leave you a thirst for education. I leave you a respect for the use of power. I leave you faith. I leave you racial dignity. I leave you a desire to live harmoniously with your fellow men. I leave you, finally, a responsibility to our young people."

But most of all, she noted, "If I have a legacy to leave my people, it is my philosophy of living and serving. As I face tomorrow, I am content, for I think I have spent my life well."

How to Be Like Mary McLeod Bethune

1) **Understand the value of an education.** As a small child, Bethune recognized that even a grasp of the basics—elementary reading and math—could pay dividends for her family. The owner of the cotton mill could no longer get away with cheating her father on the price of cotton when young Mary learned to read the scale. As an adult, Bethune recognized the only way most black Americans could improve their position in life was through education. Her vision was a grand one: education would be the primary means for her people to advance and prosper.

2) **Do what it takes to pursue your passion.** Education was Bethune's passion. As a nine-year-old girl, she was more than willing to walk the five miles each way to school to learn to read and write. Her hard work in school paved the way for her to receive the education she wanted and needed to then make a difference for black Americans. And she was willing to leave behind her closely knit family in South Carolina to go the distance for her dream.

3) **Find mentors who will cultivate your potential.** Bethune benefited from the assistance of her first teacher, Emma Jane Wilson, who found a benefactor to pay for the next step in Bethune's education. She was profoundly inspired and influenced by her second mentor, Lucy Craft Laney, who embodied the type of educator Bethune wanted to be.

4) **Don't be sidelined by disappointment.** When Bethune learned that she would not be able to become a missionary in Africa, she called it the greatest disappointment of her life . . . until she realized that she could—and should—perform that very role in her own country. "My life's work lay not in Africa but in my own country," Bethune said.

Cont'd

5) **Stay on your course.** Bethune gave up teaching for a time when she gave birth to her only child in 1899, but she never gave up her ambition to establish her own school. While she was a loving and devoted mother to her son, she insisted, "This married life was not intended to impede things I had in mind to do. The birth of my baby boy had no tendency whatever to dim my ardor and determination."

6) **Be resourceful.** A dream in which Booker T. Washington gave Bethune a diamond in a dirty handkerchief and told her to build her school provided just the metaphor she needed to turn junkyard items, broken furniture, hotel discards, and simple boxes into the rudimentary means to start her school. A swampy landfill eventually became the grounds of Bethune's college. When nothing with potential was wasted, nothing but potential resulted.

To purchase land to expand her college, Bethune rallied parents of students and local black churches to help her make foods and desserts to sell. To garner publicity about the school, "I wrote articles for whoever would print them, distributed leaflets, rode interminable miles of dusty roads on my old bicycle, invaded churches, clubs, lodges, chambers of commerce," she said.

7) **Ask and you shall receive.** Bethune solicited local businesses for furniture, and then for money. "I rang doorbells and tackled cold prospects without a lead," she said. She boldly solicited well-to-do white people and others for donations. It paid off. For example, industrialists like John D. Rockefeller, James Gamble of Proctor & Gamble, and Thomas White of White's Sewing Machines contributed significant amounts of money and other necessities.

8) **Know your strengths.** Bethune's personal motto was: "Be

Cont'd

calm, be steadfast, be courageous." She said, "I considered cash money as the smallest part of my resources. I had faith in a loving God, faith in myself, and a desire to serve."

9) **Stand up to bullies.** Bethune's thoughtful treatment of an angry man with a rifle not only persuaded him to stop terrorizing her students but won him over as a protector. Her courageous stand against the Ku Klux Klan, armed only with lights, resolve, and a choir of frightened girls not only saved her school and her students, it literally and figuratively shed light on their cowardice and sent them skulking back into the darkness.

10) **Realize that you may have more than one mission in life.** Bethune's life encompassed three different careers, any one of which was a lifetime's work unto itself. She was an important educator who created an institution for quality education for black students; she was a leading activist whose leadership helped establish a black women's organization movement and strengthen its power; and she was a powerful and distinguished political adviser to several American presidents.

Once she had met her life's goal in founding her school, her accomplishments and the talents for speaking and fund-raising set her onto the path of social activism, which in turn caught the attention of the most powerful figures in Washington, who were impressed enough with her to seek her advice and input.

Once she became a Washington insider, Bethune optimized and leveraged her power to create lasting, positive change for black Americans in the military, in education, in job opportunities, and in government. Her refusal to waste her opportunities resulted in unprecedented numbers of black men receiving high school diplomas and college educations, the end of segregation in many government agencies, and the creation of programs that allowed black pilots, such as the Tuskegee

Cont'd

Airmen, to play heroic roles during World War II.

11) **Forge alliances.** One of Bethune's greatest skills was her ability to build alliances on both sides of the color line, winning the backing and funding of influential whites while securing cooperation from influential blacks.

She preferred to adopt a tone of conciliation over confrontation in her efforts to achieve black equality. She came across to white audiences as friendly, down-to-earth, warm, and positive. She emphasized cooperation in her outreach to white leaders, but she maintained and communicated a clear, strong vision of racial equality for all Americans.

12) **Look to your legacy.** Decide and know what you stand for, and determine what legacy you want to leave for your family, friends, and the world. The article Bethune wrote shortly before her death in 1955 outlined her legacy to black Americans: "I leave you a thirst for education. I leave you racial dignity. I leave you a desire to live harmoniously with your fellow men. I leave you, finally, a responsibility to our young people. . . . If I have a legacy to leave my people, it is my philosophy of living and serving."

14

Lorena Ochoa
1981–

Service

You will never regret making a sacrifice.
It will always pay you back.

—LORENA OCHOA

*L*orena Ochoa recognized early in her life that she had a love and ability for golf, but she came to realize that her gift would mean even more for others. A product of privilege but with a work ethic and focus that matches a rags-to-riches story, Ochoa took advantage of the opportunities afforded her in life by achieving her dream of golfing excellence.

Ochoa, born in Mexico, is the number one ranked female golfer in the world, and with every swing of her club, she comes closer to helping the less fortunate in her country through the Lorena Ochoa Foundation. She reached $12 million in career earnings faster than any other player in Ladies Professional Golf Association (LPGA) history.

"I play golf for a reason," she said to Paul Forsyth of the *Sunday Times* in a 2008 article, "to be able to reach other people. I'm very fortunate to have an image that allows me to do that. The more tournaments I win, the more I can help. If you can change one person's life, it is worth it. If you change more and more . . . well, that's what I'm trying to do. I want to give to the people who don't have."

Her drive to excel was evident early on. "When she was twelve, Lorena told me she wanted to be the best player in the world," said her mentor and coach, former PGA pro Rafael Alarcon, to the *Virginian-Pilot*.

"I didn't struggle doubting or spending time debating on what I should do," Ochoa said. "It was clear to me that I wanted to be a golfer and I wanted to be the best."

Named the LPGA Player of the Year in 2006 and 2007, Ochoa was also the leading money winner on the tour in those same years. She was the LPGA Rookie of the Year in 2003 after being the National Collegiate Athletic Association (NCAA) Player of the Year in 2001 and 2002.

In addition to diligent practice, Ochoa improves her game by running and doing leg workouts. On the small side for a professional golfer at 5 feet, 6 inches and around 120 pounds, she still has one of the longest drives, 290 yards, on the LPGA tour by emphasizing technique.

"You don't have to be big or swing crazy fast to hit it long. You just need to make a good turn going back, and let your lower body lead coming down, your legs and hips pulling everything through," she told *Golf Digest*. "All the power in my golf swing comes from my hips and legs."

When she wins on the course, her foundation, created in 2004, does also. It places an emphasis on health and education issues for children in Mexico. Over the last several years the foundation has been paying 325 annual scholarships to La Barranca, a school for children ages six to fifteen in Guadalajara.

Education is the only way to teach [students] values. It's the only way to make them a better son, a better daughter, a better father, or mother. You want them to feel worth it, even if they grew up in a hard place.

—LORENA OCHOA

More than an absentee benefactor, often when she is town Ochoa will stop by the school unannounced. She'll talk to the kids and even play the national pastime, fútbol, with them.

"The teachers say it is good for the students, but I think I am the one who gets inspired," Ochoa said to Alan Shipnuck of *Sports Illustrated* in 2008.

The foundation has other projects, including subsidizing a school in Tapalpa for at-risk youths and providing funds for a Guadalajara program that gives treatment and support to children with cancer. It also promotes athletics by bringing sports like golf to children, especially girls, that otherwise would never have an opportunity to participate.

The totality of her achievements led to Ochoa being chosen by *Time* magazine in May 2008 as one of the world's one hundred most influential people. In November 2001, Mexico's president Vicente Fox bestowed upon Ochoa her nation's National Sports Award. She was the youngest recipient and first golfer to ever receive the country's prestigious athletic award. The people of Mexico City, who have an undying love for her, held a parade in her honor.

"I feel lucky to have the opportunity to represent my country and to be an example for the children of Mexico; it is a responsibility that I accept with honor," Ochoa said on her website.

"As good as Annika [Sorenstam] has been for the game, Lorena is changing a country," Dave Brooker, Ochoa's caddie, said to Forsyth. "Building schools, giving kids an education: it's not just about getting the ball in the hole. You wouldn't believe how popular she is in Mexico. From the moment you arrive at the airport, it seems like she is on every billboard. Many people there don't have access to television, but they know this girl is special."

> She is by far the sweetest, kindest, most giving person walking the earth. . . . She has that inner light. I think she's been touched by God. Honestly, I'm surprised she hasn't been canonized yet. I'm not exaggerating—she is the greatest thing ever: a cross between Tiger Woods and Mother Teresa.
>
> —CHRISTINA KIM, LPGA PLAYER.

"She is the girl that does this," Brooker said, referring to swinging a golf club. "Even if they don't know what 'this' is. [Her countrymen] understand that she is not doing it for herself; she is doing it for them. When she wins, they win."

Born in 1981 in Guadalajara, Mexico, Ochoa did not overcome great adversity, nor did she have to rise from poverty. Her father, Javier Ochoa, was a real estate executive, and her mother, Marcela, worked as an abstract artist. Lorena grew up in a five-bedroom house right next to the Guadalajara

Country Club with her parents, two older brothers, and younger sister. The family belonged to the adjacent country club. Her older brothers, Javier and Alejandro, were already playing golf, and little Lorena insisted on following suit.

Her family is a close one, and she keeps a photograph of them in her golf bag while on tour. Big brother Alejandro works as her manager.

She says the best advice she ever got from her family and close friends is to "never lose the real Lorena. Be humble as you have been. Always fight to keep some time for things you love to do."

Ochoa sticks firmly to her beliefs and stays true to herself. She was educated in Catholic schools and spent weekends distributing food to Guadalajara's poor communities and teaching people the power of prayer. Rather than just speaking about doing great things, she has, in fact, done them herself. Ochoa is a doer and not a talker.

"I don't think talking about it is the best way. It's about letting people see for themselves what kind of person you are," she said. Inspiring by example makes the most sense to her.

Both of Ochoa's parents shared their love of the outdoors with their children. Ochoa learned to take on an active lifestyle from a very young age and had a memorable childhood. At the family cabin in the Sierra Madre mountains, she enjoyed spending time hiking, climbing, horseback riding, and mountain biking.

But from the moment she first decided to pick up a golf club and persuaded her dad to let her play, she was at home. At the time, she was the only girl playing at the Guadalajara Country Club. The club's manager, Carlos Gutierrez, was a witness to her dedication. "I'd leave at night, and she'd still be there. [Lorena] just loved it, and her enthusiasm made you love her," he said.

There is no "quit" in Ochoa the competitor. One time, her brother Alejandro convinced her to join him for a four-day ecothon, featuring running, mountain biking, kayaking, swimming, and abseiling (climbing). She committed herself to finishing the competition.

The swim was 5 kilometers through an icy lake. She was only seventeen at the time, the youngest of the 144 entrants who made the attempt. Many of those pulled out of the competition, but Ochoa completed the race.

She said of the overall ecothon, "I love that feeling of keeping going, of not giving up." She feels the mental conditioning is the key with ecothons and marathons: "It's about pushing yourself as far as you can. You learn to be tough, even though you are having a hard time, and you try and do your best. Sometimes I ask myself why I play golf when I like to do so many outdoor things, but golf is more complete. It's hard to do well, and I like the challenge of managing my mind."

An avid outdoorswoman, Ochoa and her family continue to regularly visit Tapalpa, a town in the Sierra Madre mountain range that provides the perfect surroundings to feed her outdoor activities, such as climbing. Already, she has conquered such peaks as Mexico's Mount Iztaccihuatl (17,343 feet) and Japan's Mount Fuji (12,388 feet).

"If you don't challenge yourself, you don't know how far you can go. If you are going to run 35 minutes, why not run 45 minutes? Don't just say you can do it, do it. I always like to prove it, so that when you are in a bad situation, you have that extra something. Without the mind, the body only goes so far," she told the *Sunday Times* in an interview.

While attending the University of Arizona, she was known for often waking up in the wee hours of the morning to take a 10-kilometer run before the women's golf team convened practice at 6:30 AM.

With all of her talent, there is an equal part humility. "I've never been around someone who is more humble," Brooker said. "When she meets people, she is the one asking the questions. She doesn't want the conversation to be about herself."

Nancy Lopez, a member of the LPGA Hall of Fame, said to *Time* magazine: "There's no way around the fact that Lorena . . . dominates her sport. And yet when you meet her for the first time, you experience a remarkable warmth and modesty. When you meet her for the second time, and she remembers not only your name but also the slightest detail from the last time you spoke, you understand just how exceptional this young woman is."

Even while besting opponents on the green, Ochoa is down to earth and likes to have a good time, which might mask her competitiveness.

"We were having so much fun [during a match] . . . . I barely noticed she was kicking my butt," said Swedish professional golfer Helen Alfredsson about Ochoa.

She enjoys competition, enjoys the pressure, as much as anybody I've ever seen.

—Dave Brooker, Ochoa's caddie

Ochoa will frequently interact with the crowd at golf tournaments. When Tom Henry and his wife, Christ, were watching Ochoa play in Illinois in 2004, the golfer made eye contact and greeted them. The Henry's started going to see Ochoa play at different tournaments and developed a relationship with her. When Christ Henry fell ill, Ochoa stayed in contact with positive e-mails to her. In June 2008 she sent Christ the cap she had worn at the LPGA Championship earlier in the month on a day she shot a 65. "She makes you feel special," Henry said to Karen Course of the *New York Times*.

"She is a breath of fresh air. . . . Thinking about others right in the middle of a golf tournament is so unusual. I'm a real fan of hers. I hope for her to break every record that there is," said Mickey Wright, winner of eighty-two LPGA titles, to *Course*.

At tournaments, she's known for seeking out the grounds crew who prepare the golf course and the food service workers to personally offer her gratitude. She has even joined in to serve the grounds crew breakfast. Of all the support staff that makes tournament golf possible, she says: "They are good people, and they work hard to help their families. . . . I want them to know I support them and that I play for them."

Rather than behaving foolishly only to have some publicist clean up her reputation, Ochoa takes it upon herself to always be respectful. While playing in the public eye, she chooses not to wear lavish jewelry and expensive clothing. "There are kids starving in Mexico, so of course Lorena wouldn't be caught dead wearing any jewels," LPGA veteran and longtime friend Christina Kim told *Sports Illustrated* in an interview.

The best part about working for Lorena is not the money, the memories, winning the amazing events. . . . It's that being around her makes me want to be a better person.

—Dave Brooker, Ochoa's caddie

"As good as Lorena Ochoa is at golf, she is ten times as good a person off the golf course. Everyone who has ever encountered Lorena loves her," said Greg Allen, University of Arizona women's golf coach.

Ochoa realizes that her career in golf won't last forever. And that's how she wants it. Five years down the line, she plans on leaving the sport so that she can focus on having kids of her own.

"Life is too short," she said in an interview with the *Sunday Times*. "It's not just about golf. I don't want to be too old when I get married, start a family and do my work in Mexico."

"Lorena is one of the rare athletes who just gets it," Alfredsson said about Ochoa. "She's like an Arnold Palmer or Nancy Lopez or Muhammad Ali— she understands the power she has to change the world."

How to Be Like Lorena Ochoa

1) **Give back.** Ochoa created the Lorena Ochoa Foundation in 2004, which focuses on health and education issues for children in Mexico. "The more tournaments I win, the more I can help. If you can change one person's life, it is worth it. If you change more and more . . . well, that's what I'm trying to do. I want to give to the people who don't have."

2) **Shoot for the top.** From the time Ochoa was twelve-years-old, she told her golf coach, former PGA pro Rafael Alarcon, that she wanted to be the best player in the world. "I didn't struggle doubting or spending time debating on what I should do. It was clear to me that I wanted to be a golfer and I wanted to be the best."

3) **Practice proper techniques.** Ochoa is not big physically at 5 feet 6 inches and 120 pounds, but she's got one of the longest drives on the LPGA tour. She explains how she achieved her golden swing by learning to properly use her lower body. "All the power in my golf swing comes from my hips and legs."

4) **Be a role model.** In November 2001, Ochoa was the youngest person and first golfer to receive Mexico's National Sports Award, and in May 2008, *Time* magazine named her one of the world's one hundred most influential people. "I feel lucky to have the opportunity to represent my country and to be an example for the children of Mexico; it is a responsibility that I accept with honor."

5) **Don't squander opportunities.** Rather than having to overcome disadvantages, Ochoa grew up in privileged circumstances. While there are those who waste such golden opportunities, Ochoa didn't. She stayed on her educational and athletic career path to become the number one ranked female golfer in the world.

Cont'd

6) **Don't be self-conscious.** When she first started playing golf at age nine at the Guadalajara Country Club, she was the only girl playing. Some might have been intimidated, but it did not stop Ochoa—and it should not stop anybody.

7) **Be mentally tough.** "Sometimes I ask myself why I play golf when I like to do so many outdoor things, but golf is more complete. It's hard to do well, and I like the challenge of managing my mind. . . . Without the mind, the body only goes so far."

8) **Pay the price.** Ochoa's discipline has always been firm. She is not afraid to put in the extra time to get things right. The manager of the country club where Ochoa played as a child remembers her dedication even then—she'd still be there practicing when he left for the night. At college, Ochoa was known for getting up in the wee hours of the morning to run before the golf team's early morning practices.

9) **Have humility.** Ochoa is recognized the world over for displaying humility, even after crushing opponents on the green. Her caddie David Brooker says that when Ochoa meets people, she's the one asking the questions because she doesn't want the conversation to be about her. LPGA Hall of Fame's Nancy Lopez describes Ochoa as having remarkable warmth and modesty: "When . . . she remembers not only your name but also the slightest detail from the last time you spoke, you understand just how exceptional this young woman is."

10) **Recognize other people.** Recognizing people and saying "thank you" is something Ochoa always does. She's known for seeking out the grounds crew and food service workers at tournaments to personally thank them for their efforts. Ochoa also acknowledges her fans in the crowd, making personal connections with many of them, and as in the case of the Henrys, offering encouragement and comfort in difficult times.

Cont'd

15

Condoleezza Rice
1954–

Optimism

Thomas Jefferson—who said my favorite line,
"The God who gave us life, gave us liberty at the same time"—
was a slave owner. And so, these were not perfect people
who created America's institutions, but they did
create institutions that allowed people like Frederick Douglass
or Rosa Parks or Martin Luther King to appeal
from within those institutions.

—CONDOLEEZZA RICE

C ondoleeza Rice was no stranger to the horrors of wanton terrorism, or the lessons that emerge in its aftermath. On Sunday, September 15, 1963, at 10:22 a.m., nineteen sticks of dynamite on a time-delayed detonator exploded outside the basement of the 16th Street Baptist Church in Birmingham, Alabama. The church had been a rallying point for civil rights activity and, therefore, it had been targeted by the Ku Klux Klan.

The bomb exploded as twenty-six children walked into the basement for Sunday school. Twenty-two people were injured. Four girls were killed: Addie Mae Collins, Carole Robertson, Cynthia Wesley, and Denise McNair. The explosion blew a hole in the church's back wall, destroying all of the stained-glass windows except one, which depicted Jesus Christ leading young children, though Christ's face was blown away.

Several blocks away, young Condoleezza Rice was also in church, listening to her father, a Presbyterian minister, deliver a sermon when the sound of the explosion spread fear in the congregation. She can still hear that sound today and remembers how her father and other men of the community began patrolling the neighborhood carrying shotguns during the summer and fall of the bombings, a reason she is a staunch believer in the Second Amendment to the Constitution, the right to bear arms.

"Denise McNair was my little friend from kindergarten," Secretary of State Rice told CBS's Katie Couric on *60 Minutes*. "She was a playmate, and I just couldn't believe that she was dead. . . . Addie Mae Collins was in my uncle's homeroom in school. These were innocent children. . . . These little girls weren't going to hurt anybody. They didn't have any political power. This was just meant to terrorize the community."

The terror for black people, and especially for children, she felt in Birmingham in 1963 has never left Rice. "Those terrible events [are] burned into my consciousness," said Rice. "I missed many days at my segregated school because of the frequent bomb threats."

In spite of the volatile environment of her childhood, Rice's parents infused her with their optimism and instilled in her the belief that she could become whatever she wanted to be through education. She might not be able to buy a hamburger in a "white's only" restaurant or go to the petting zoo at the state fair, but in the future she could become president of the United States if she purposed to do so. She would just have to work for it and be twice as good as a white person, due to the racist societal expectations for black people.

My parents were very strategic. I was going to be so well prepared . . . and I was going to do all of these things that were revered in white society so well, that I would be armored somehow from racism. I would be able to confront white society on its own terms.

—CONDOLEEZZA RICE

The lesson took form at an early age. When Rice was ten years old, her family took a trip to Washington, D.C. Taking pictures in front of the White House, she told her father that while she might be barred from it now because of her skin color, one day she would be inside of it, working.

As an adult, Rice would again experience the horrors of terrorism, confronting it from inside the White House on September 11, 2001, as President George W. Bush's national security advisor. She was the first woman to be appointed to that position. When she was appointed by President Bush to become secretary of state in 2004, she became only the second woman to hold that position.

"We've been a country that's been fortunate to be protected by two oceans, to not have serious attacks on our territory for most of our history. And we were unfortunately reminded in a very devastating way of our vulnerability," Rice said following the attacks on the World Trade Center and the Pentagon. "I think, if September 11 taught us anything, it taught us that we're vulnerable, and vulnerable in ways that we didn't fully understand."

Rice went on to say: "We have been reminded in a dramatic and terrifying way of what happens when difference becomes a license to kill. Terrorism is meant to dehumanize and divide."

Thirty-eight years almost to the day after the 16th Street Baptist Church bombing, another lesson of terrorism was repeated: innocent people die. "If you were in the Twin Towers [on September 11], it didn't happen to matter what your skin color was," she said to *Ebony* magazine. And while Rice is a diplomat always searching for ways to end conflicts peacefully, the lessons of history are not lost on her.

"We all live with the specter of World War II, and we all live with the fact that the great democracies were not able to muster the will to act even when the handwriting was pretty clear on the wall that Adolf Hitler was unstoppable except by force," Rice said, as quoted by Gloria Blakely in *Condoleezza Rice*.

Birmingham, Alabama, the city in which she was born in 1954, was one of the most segregated cities in the Deep South. Rice grew up in the racially cloistered community of Titusville, once commenting that she didn't have a white classmate until 1965 when she became the first African-American to attend music classes at Birmingham Southern Conservatory of Music.

Despite carrying the seemingly overwhelming burden of prejudice reinforced by constant reminders of racial hatred in the community of
Birmingham at large, Rice's parents refused to let their daughter grow up
feeling pessimistic or as a victim. They shielded and protected her from as
much of the hatred as they could. Rice's cousin Connie explained to the
Sunday Times that Rice's parents "simply ignored the larger culture that said
you're second-class, you're black, you don't count, you have no power."

It left a lifetime impression on their daughter: "One thing I really hate
is pessimism," Rice told *Vogue* magazine. "I mean, I just detest it. Let's take
my grandfathers. One managed to get himself a college education by agree-
ing to become a Presbyterian minister, although I'm sure that was the last
thing on his mind. The other got himself several skills so that he could raise
his family impressively and did very well even in the Depression. Now,
those are men who had reasons to be pessimistic—black men in the Deep
South in the twenties and thirties."

"Condi is one of those happy-go-lucky kinds of people," said her former
University of Denver professor, Karen Feste, to the *Sunday Times*. "She
doesn't have an unhappy side to her; at least I've never seen it." Rice
explained: "I'm a really religious person, and I don't believe that I was put
on this Earth to be sour, so I'm eternally optimistic about things."

Her parents, Angelena, a science and math teacher, and John, who in
addition to being a minister was an athletic coach and guidance counselor,
instilled within her the belief that the vigorous pursuit of education was the
key to successfully overcoming prejudice and gaining equality. They backed
up their words with action. For example, when the local school felt her
daughter was too young to begin, Angelena took time off to home school
her daughter.

Education played a large role in the Rice family lineage. Condoleezza's
grandfather, John Wesley Rice Jr., had been determined to better himself,
and in 1918 he saved enough money to attend Stillman College. When he
ran out of money during his first year, he discovered that if he wanted to
become a Presbyterian minister he could receive a scholarship. Since then,
Rice's family has been college educated and Presbyterian.

To that end, her family gave her all the encouragement they could,
which resulted in her near Spartan-like self-discipline and drive. While they

could not shelter her from the effects of a society's double standards, they could get her to focus on the greater opportunities that lay ahead through education, ones foreign to her Birmingham social climate.

My personal heroine is Dr. Dorothy Height [African-American administrator, educator, social activist]. People who had that foresight to see, as the struggle unfolded, that education was the key to having a whole generation of people who were ready to take advantage once the United States came to terms with segregation were my heroes."

—CONDOLEEZZA RICE

"They explained to me carefully what was going on," she told the *Sunday Times*. "And they did so without any bitterness. It was in the very air we breathed that education was the way out." Her father impressed upon her that being highly educated was one thing no one could ever take away from her, because knowledge resides inside a person.

Rice began reading at a very early age, though she says that she learned to read music through her grandmother's instruction long before she learned to read words. Her parents ensured that she could pursue whatever she wanted, such as studying ballet, piano, violin, and French. Today, Rice speaks fluent French, Russian, German, and Spanish, a huge asset in her role as secretary of state. She became the second African-American to hold the post, following Colin Powell, both of whom were appointed by President Bush.

After Rice's father accepted the position of vice chancellor at the University of Denver in Colorado, the family left Alabama. Rice then attended her first integrated school, St. Mary's Academy, a private Catholic school.

She was a different kind of kid . . . she was more mature and very, very, very—how can I explain it for a kid? Very focused.

—JOHN CANTELOW, FORMER ELEMENTARY SCHOOL TEACHER

She produced an academic record of straight As and skipped two grades. Rice was also on the tennis team in addition to being a competitive figure skater. A lifelong football fan, she sees great value in participating in sports.

"Athletics gives you a kind of toughness and discipline that nothing else really does," Rice said in the *Sunday Times*.

However, after not scoring as high as she could have on the scholastic aptitude test (SAT), a guidance counselor took it upon himself to tell her that she was not "college material." He suggested getting a job after high school rather than pursing higher education.

Rice has since said that the guidance counselor only saw before him a black girl with a low test score, rather than who she was as a person and what she had accomplished overall.

At first heartsick and stunned by the counselor's opinion, her parents reassured her, telling her to disregard what he had said and to press on. The result: Rice became a freshman at the University of Denver at the age of fifteen. She graduated cum laude and Phi Beta Kappa at nineteen with a degree in political science. A year later she completed her master's degree in government and international affairs at Notre Dame.

Rice had at first planned to become a concert pianist and initially studied piano performance. It seemed to be a natural pursuit since she had been playing piano since age three. However, Rice soon felt she would never be a great pianist, and because she grew up in a family that discussed politics, she drifted toward political science. She became fascinated by the complexities of the Soviet Union and international affairs through a lecture by Dr. Josef Korbel. A former member of the Czech diplomatic service, Korbel had fled Prague with his family in 1948 when the Communists took over. Among his family was his daughter, another future secretary of state, Madeleine Albright.

In America, with education and hard work, it really does not matter where you came from; it matters only where you are going.

—Condoleezza Rice

When Rice heard Korbel's lecture on Soviet dictator Joseph Stalin, she recognized she had found her calling and passion. Rice has referred to Korbel as "one of the most influential figures in my life, next to my parents."

The respect was mutual. In her autobiography, *Madam Secretary,* Albright said that her mother had told her that Rice was her father's favorite student. When he died, Rice gave the family a planter shaped like a piano, symbolic of how her life's path had been changed by Dr. Korbel.

Rice would return to the University of Denver to earn her Ph.D. from the Graduate School of International Studies in 1981. She then accepted a job teaching political science at Stanford University, where she was a member of the Center for International Security and Arms Control from 1981 to 1986 (currently the Center for International Security and Cooperation). She quickly distinguished herself and received one of the school's highest teaching awards, the Water J. Gores Award for Excellence in Teaching in 1984 and the 1993 School of Humanities and Sciences Dean's Award for Distinguished Teaching. She was also a Hoover Institution national fellow in 1985 and 1986.

Her salient area of expertise was the Soviet Union, and she published several books, including *The Soviet Union and the Czechoslovak Army, 1948–1983: Uncertain Allegiance*, which she dedicated to her parents and Dr. Korbel, and *The Gorbachev Era*, which she coedited with Alexander Dallin.

Rice also switched her party affiliation, from Democrat to Republican. Her father was a Republican because he had been denied voter registration in 1952 by a Democrat who had told him he could only register if he could guess the correct number of beans in a jar. After some discussion among the black community, her father learned of a Republican in the registrar's office who registered African-Americans in secret. John Rice became a Republican. Condoleezza changed because of foreign policy issues and because, as she said, "I found a party that sees me as an individual, not as part of a group."

At a 1985 meeting of arms control experts at Stanford, Rice's educational expertise impressed former Ford administration national security advisor, General Brent Scowcroft, so much that when he was asked to fill the same role for President George H. W. Bush, he asked Rice to become his Soviet expert on the United States National Security Council. President Bush named her director of Soviet and East European Affairs. Rice had her first experience with government service.

Of their first meetings with Rice, Scowcroft was impressed and recalled in the *New Yorker*: "I thought, this is somebody I need to get to know. It's an intimidating subject. Here's this young girl, and she's not at all intimidated."

A famous Rice story on not being intimidated happened at the White House in 1989, when Russian president Boris Yeltsin arrived, insistent that he must see President Bush. Even though he had the title of president,

Yeltsin was not the head of the Soviet government. Mikhail Gorbachev, general secretary of the Communist Party of the Soviet Union, was.

Rice stood in the doorway blocking the physically imposing Yelstin, who was almost twice her size. More imposing than his size was his stature; he not only had the title of President of the Soviet Union, he was a respected world figure. Rice told him in perfect Russian that his interview was with General Scowcroft. After a few minutes, Yeltsin relented and met with Scowcroft.

I don't do life crises. I really don't. Life is too short. Get over it. Move on to the next thing!

—CONDOLEEZZA RICE

Rice would return to Stanford in 1991 to continue teaching while serving as a consultant on the former Soviet Bloc for numerous public and private sector clients. Then in 1993, Stanford University President Gerhard Casper asked her to accept the position of provost at Stanford. Casper recalled that when he offered the position to her over the telephone, there was stunned silence. In the end, she accepted, and became the youngest provost in the history of Stanford. In addition, she achieved two other milestones. She was Stanford's first woman and first African-American to hold the position, second in command to the university president.

The new position was fueled with huge challenges, among them the daunting task of handling a budget the size of Stanford's. Stanford's Institute of International Studies deputy director, Coit Blacker, recalled in a 1999 article that "there was a sort of conventional wisdom that said it couldn't be done . . . that [the deficit] was structural, that we just had to live with it. She said, 'No, we're going to balance the budget in two years.' It involved painful decisions but it worked, and communicated to funders that Stanford could balance its own books and had the effect of generating additional sources of income for the university. . . . It was courageous."

Forbes later reported that "in her first year, Rice, 39, balanced the university's $410 million unrestricted budget without dipping into reserves for the first time in six years." When she left as Stanford's provost in 1999 to become a senior fellow at the Hoover Institute, she left behind a budget with a $40 million surplus. Her balancing of the budget did result in making a few enemies, but it also demonstrated the talents she would later fully utilize in her most demanding roles for President George W. Bush.

As Blacker would aptly summarize, "[She has] a kind of intellectual agility mixed with velvet-glove forcefulness."

To get the job done at Stanford, Rice sometimes had to take others' jobs away from them. Always compassionate about it, she found no joy in firing people. "It's never pleasant. You feel bad for the dislocation of lives. . . . When I had to lay people off, I eased the transition for them in any way I could. But sometimes you have to make difficult decisions and you have to make them stick. I think those were probably the toughest couple of years I went through. There were so many doubters," Rice said, quoted by Christin Ditchfield in *Condoleezza Rice: National Security Advisor*.

At the Hoover Institute, she soon found herself advising Texas governor George W. Bush who was launching his presidential bid and whom she had met during a visit to the Bush's father's home in Kennebunkport, Maine, in 1998. Rice said that they got along well right away, quickly discovering each other's love for sports. During the 2000 presidential race, she served as a member of Bush's foreign policy and campaign response teams.

When Bush was elected president, he appointed Rice his national security advisor. It was also a role that caused her to become a member of a team facing the direst threat to America since World War II or the Cuban Missile Crisis.

As national security advisor, she worked diligently with the president and the Departments of Defense and State on America's responses to Al Qaeda in Afghanistan and elsewhere. Following the beginning of the war in Iraq, Rice became as visible a spokesperson for Bush's foreign policy as Secretary of State Colin Powell, always retaining her calm and reasoned demeanor through numerous confrontational situations with the press and members of Congress.

When Powell resigned in 2004, President Bush nominated Rice to replace him. In his nomination of Rice, President Bush said, "The secretary of state is America's face to the world, and in Dr. Rice, the world will see the strength, the grace and the decency of our country."

The confirmation hearings afforded critics of President Bush's policies an opportunity to vent their frustration with Bush via Rice. She approached the grilling from some Senate Democrats with the same calm she had demonstrated on numerous occasions throughout her various careers. She was confirmed by a vote of 85 to 13.

In 2003 Rice spoke of her strong optimism for peace in the Middle East and how it would be achieved, saying, "The people of the Middle East share the desire for freedom. We have an opportunity—and an obligation—to help them turn this desire into reality. And we must work with others to create a world where terror is shunned and hope is the provenance of every living human. That is the security challenge, and moral mission, of our time." In these comments, it is very easy to see the manifestation of her, as well as her parents', beliefs, instilled within her so long ago.

As secretary of state she has clocked a record amount of flight time visiting foreign countries, mending fences, building bridges, and tearing down walls as America's special envoy. Her parents were indeed correct in their optimism for her in the world of tomorrow. She became one of the most powerful women in the world. Using all her education, training, "intellectual agility and velvet-gloved forcefulness" she has secured cooperation in some of the most complex alliances. She has also advised on and confronted some of the most terrifying and tragic events of the modern era, including being dispatched to Georgia to help negotiate an end to the Russian invasion in August 2008. Not bad for a young girl who had once been told she was not college material.

In accepting the 2002 President's Award from the NAACP, Rice said, "As I travel with President Bush and as we meet with leaders from around the world, I see America through other people's eyes. I see a country that still struggles with the true meaning of multiethnic democracy, that still struggles with how to accommodate, and indeed, how to celebrate diversity. But it's a country that is admired because it *does* struggle to become better. It's not perfect, but it is a long, long way from where we were."

How to Be Like Condoleezza Rice

1) **Pursue excellence.** Raised in a community teeming with prejudice and hate, Rice's parents instilled in her that she could become anything she wanted, even president of the United States, if she worked determinedly. But they also counseled her that she would probably have to work twice as hard as a white person to receive the same opportunities. Rice's parents "simply ignored the larger culture that said you're second-class, you're black, you don't count, you have no power."

2) **Find optimism.** Rice witnessed positive examples in her own family as both of her grandfathers optimistically persevered through difficult circumstances. Another source of Rice's optimism might be her incredible work ethic. She simply has outworked problems in her life. "I'm a really religious person, and I don't believe that I was put on this Earth to be sour, so I'm eternally optimistic about things."

3) **Pursue education.** Rice's parents were educated professionals. They instilled within her the belief that the vigorous pursuit of education was the key to overcoming prejudice and to gaining equality. Rice put it this way: "In America, with education and hard work, it really does not matter where you came from; it matters only where you are going."

4) **Compete athletically.** In high school, Rice was on the tennis team in addition to being a competitive figure skater. A lifelong football fan, she sees great value in participating in sports. "Athletics gives you a kind of toughness and discipline that nothing else really does," she said.

5) **Don't be discouraged by others.** After a disappointing SAT score Rice was told by a guidance counselor that she was not "college material." With her parents' encouragement, however,

Cont'd

she disregarded what he had said and pressed on to college. Rice earned a degree in political science from the University of Denver at age nineteen, and a year later completed her master's degree in government and international affairs at Notre Dame. In 1981, Rice returned to the University of Denver and earned a Ph.D. in International Studies in 1981. (There is no word on where her "guidance counselor" is today.)

6) **Recognize your passion.** When Rice became fascinated by the complexities of the Soviet Union and international affairs through a lecture by Dr. Josef Korbel, she knew she'd found what her life's work would be. Korbel, father of the first female secretary of state, Madeleine Albright, became Rice's mentor, and she his favorite student.

7) **Don't be intimidated.** President George H. W. Bush's national security advisor, Brent Scowcroft, asked Rice to become his Soviet expert on the United States National Security Council, in part because he was impressed by the expertise and confidence she demonstrated at a 1985 meeting of arms control experts at Stanford. Of their early meeting, Scowcroft recalled:

"I thought, this is somebody I need to get to know. It's an intimidating subject. Here's this young girl, and she's not at all intimidated." Rice later demonstrated that same refusal to be intimidated in her White House encounter with Boris Yelstin.

8) **Show compassion.** In her position as provost at Stanford, Rice had to implement layoffs to balance the budget. Always compassionate, she found no joy in firing people. "It's never pleasant. You feel bad for the dislocation of lives," she said, "but I eased the transition for them in any way I could."

9) **Do not dwell on the past; look to the future.** This is a frequent comment from Rice, whose parents instilled in her an optimistic regard for the future. When thinking of present-day race

Cont'd

relations, Rice said on NBC's *Meet the Press*, "I would hope that we would spend our time thinking how to educate black children, particularly black children who are caught in poverty. I would hope that we would spend our time, as the president has said, 'turning back the soft bigotry of low expectations against our children.'"

"Look at where people in my generation are," she told *Ebony* magazine. "We've broken ceilings as CEOs and as presidents of universities and secretaries of state. It shows how change can happen, and how fast it can happen."

❧ 16 ❧

Suze Orman
1951–

Financial Responsibility

People first, then money, then things.

—Suze Orman

Ⓘt is difficult to imagine that financial advisor Suze Orman, the warm, confident, articulate, supersavvy expert on everything from Roth IRAs to margin calls, was once a shy little girl with speech and reading disabilities whose family struggled constantly against calamities and disaster to make ends meet. Today she's a six-time *New York Times* bestselling author; newspaper, magazine, and Internet columnist; and Emmy-winning television personality who has guided untold millions of people to become smarter with their money, wiser with their investments, and more secure in taking charge of their financial destinies.

Growing up on the South Side of Chicago, Susie Lynne Orman was the youngest child and only daughter of Morris and Ann Orman, a Jewish couple who also had two sons. Morris, who immigrated to the United States with his family from Russia, plucked chickens and owned a take-out chicken shack. Orman's mother, Ann, whose family immigrated to the

221

United States from Romania, worked as a secretary for a rabbi. The chickens Morris plucked were not kosher, so the Ormans would hide their chicken dinners whenever the rabbi stopped by for a visit.

In her book *The 9 Steps to Financial Freedom*, Orman recounts a defining moment of her life. When she was thirteen, her father's little chicken stand caught fire and burned to the ground. Her father had escaped the building unscathed, but then he took an incredible risk. "All of a sudden my dad realized that he had left his money in the metal cash register inside the building, and I watched in disbelief as he ran back into the inferno, in the split second before anyone could stop him. He tried and tried to open the metal register, but the intense heat had already sealed the drawer shut. Knowing that every penny he had was locked in front of him, about to go up into flames, he literally picked up the scalding metal box and carried it outside. When he threw the register on the ground, the skin on his arms and chest came with it."

Morris Orman acted because he believed his responsibility was to protect his business and his family's security. Orman notes that not only did her father suffer severe burns from the ordeal, but he developed emphysema, which would plague him for the rest of his life. From this episode, young Suze drew a telling conclusion that for some, "money is obviously more important than life itself." And she notes, "from that point on, earning money, lots of money, not only became what drove me professionally, but also became my emotional priority. Money became, for me, not the means to a life rich in all kinds of ways; money became my singular goal." This is not surprising given what she experienced in her childhood. Later in her life, she realized what is truly important and today her philosophy is: "People first, then money, then things."

> *My experience is that most people who don't respect money don't respect themselves. How we treat money is symptomatic of how we feel about ourselves.*
>
> —SUZE ORMAN

Morris and his father also owned a boardinghouse, but they lost the rental property when a tenant fell from a staircase, became paralyzed, and sued the Ormans for everything. "From then on," Orman told Fortune.com, "everything my father did turned to dust."

With three children to feed, the Ormans pressed on. Morris focused his efforts on running a chicken stand and contended not only with pressure from big-chain competitors but also landlords who would force him to relocate. Ann worked as a legal secretary, an *Avon* lady, and a school nurse. In an interview with *Jewish Woman Magazine*, Orman recalled how very keenly palpable her parents' anxiety was. "Money wasn't really discussed, but I knew the reason my parents were so unhappy was not because they didn't love each other. It was because they didn't have any money."

She also noticed the costs of her mother's hard work. As she told *Yahoo Shine*, "My mother is the one who is taking care of my father, her mother, taking care of us, taking care of everybody, and still volunteering at the PTA. Never once do I remember her taking time to read a book, taking time to do something she wanted. Her entire life was dedicated to taking care of everyone else but her. She lost herself."

Observing her mother's efforts and willingness to work even harder, Orman would develop an appreciation for the different attitudes men and women bring to matters of money and the widely disparate ways society and culture value their work. And while Ann Orman placed the well-being of others before her own, she also taught her daughter to take pride in her work. Orman notes, "I came of age with a mom who enjoyed her work, was an equal partner with my dad on family finances and everything else, and who nudged me to always think about what I wanted to do for a living when I grew up."

Growing up poor left a lasting impression on Orman. She would miss out on small, but significant childhood experiences, such as being able to go out with her friends or have her picture taken on a pony, because her parents simply didn't have a dollar to spare for the types of treats that many baby boomer era children could take for granted during the prosperous Eisenhower years. She felt left out, set apart from her peers, and she inherited her parents' anxiety over money issues, fearing that her friends wouldn't like her if they knew how poor she was.

Tellingly, Orman once stole a dollar from her mother to go swimming with her friends—anything to maintain her worthiness in the eyes of her peers. It was a choice she would revisit later in her life.

Decades later, after her father's death, Orman would learn a stunning surprise about her father, the chicken plucker. A casual conversation with a cousin revealed to Orman that, for a time, her father had actually attended law school during the Depression. In *The Courage to Be Rich*, she writes, "As the story came out I learned that my father had, indeed, gone to law school, working at a flower shop between classes and selling produce from a cart on weekends to pay his tuition. He lived at home, in a one-bedroom apartment with his parents and brother, and contributed his share toward the family's household expenses. Just as he was about to start his last year of school, however, my grandfather asked him for money to help open a new chicken store. My dad gave up his dreams, gave his tuition money to my grandpa, joined him in the chicken business, and never became a lawyer. . . . Regardless of why, ultimately he convinced himself that this was his destiny, not the one he dared, for a time, to imagine."

The revelation changed the way Suze Orman saw her hardworking father and her own life expectations. "My dad had played such a vital role in my life, and I had learned the lesson of my childhood well. This was the plan for us. Who was I to think I could have more, be more? In retrospect, I can see that for a long time I thought his destiny was mine as well, because the message he'd passed on to me was the lesson of less and the thoughts of *I can't*."

Suze Orman equips readers with financial knowledge, especially as it relates to the emotional attachments we all have with money.

—JOE MOGLIA, CEO AMERITRADE, INC.

While further calamities (including a second fire) befell Orman's father, she eventually understood that he was not just the victim of incredibly bad luck. "I now realize that my dad's thoughts were always thoughts of poverty, that his internal voice told him *you can't*. It wasn't as if he didn't try, because he did try. He worked harder than anyone I've ever known, every day of his life . . . he had amazing courage. Despite this, my brothers and I also heard him say, more than once, 'This is just the way it was meant to be, and there's nothing I can do about it.'"

Orman came to understand that her father had dared to defy a lifetime of low expectations for himself by attending law school, but he lost his resolve once his father turned to him for help, effectively pulling him back into the cycle of struggle. She pinpointed this disappointment as the pivotal moment of her father's life, setting him on the road to a series of business failures and a lifetime of financial struggles. The episode was pivotal not only for her father, but for Orman and the rest of her family as well, as his attitude eventually became their attitudes. She concludes, "With his thoughts he created his destiny, as do we all."

Susie also faced challenges of her own, starting with a speech impediment that hampered her ability to pronounce the letters *r, s,* and *t.* Her speech problems carried over into trouble with reading, and the future bestselling author found herself scoring poorly in public school reading exams. In her official website biography, *Suze's Story,* Orman recalls, "One year a teacher decided that he would seat us according to our reading scores. There were my three best friends in the first three seats of the first row, while I was banished to the last seat in the sixth row. If I always secretly felt dumb, it was now officially confirmed for everyone to see. Talk about feeling ashamed."

Despite economic hardships, Orman's parents did not entertain low expectations for their children, and they insisted that their daughter would attend college. All Suze Orman could afford was a state college, so she applied to the University of Illinois at Urbana-Champaign and was accepted (despite her low SAT scores). She chose what she perceived would be the easiest major: social work.

While she was in college, Orman changed the spelling of her name from Susie, which she found too plain to wear into the exciting future she envisioned for herself, to Suze (pronounced the same as Susie). She reckoned that if she kept the original pronunciation of her name, she could change the spelling without her mother ever finding out about it. She never imagined that her mother would ever see her new name in print.

During her second year of college, Orman shared a one-bedroom apartment with her dorm pals, Carole Morgan and Judy Jacklin. With Judy came her boisterous, fun-loving boyfriend (and future husband), John Belushi. The rest of Orman's college days were marked by amusing adventures with the future *Saturday Night Live* comedy legend (Judy Jacklin would later become a staff writer on the same show), but then Orman hit a roadblock.

Convinced that she just wasn't capable enough, she was unable to fulfill the college's foreign language requirement. She left school in 1973 without taking her degree, and spent time traveling, searching for the next direction her life would take. She would travel great distances to find her true purpose.

The search for spiritual fulfillment would remain an important issue in Orman's life and would later inform her quest to help others. As she later told the *Jewish Daily Forward*, "Faith plays a prominent role in my life. Without faith, nothing matters."

Seeking to explore her Jewish background for answers, Orman journeyed to Israel. At the time, she thought that she would find God. As she recalled in her interview with Robert Frick of *Kiplinger's*, a man she met on a bus advised her that the best way to find God was to "just spit." He told her, "What are you looking for? God is in the earth. God is in you."

That answer, while underwhelming for a young woman looking for epic revelations, would suffice for Orman to carry with her back to the States. She then hit the road to continue her journey and take in the cross-country splendors of America. She had a Ford Econoline van, $300 in her pocket, and a trio of girlfriends for company.

Eventually, Orman put down her roots in the Bay Area, quite literally, finding her first paying job (at $3.50 an hour) with a tree service company. During that time, she lived inside her van. She finally settled into a job she enjoyed as a waitress at a popular Berkeley restaurant called the Buttercup Bakery. In 1976, she was making about $400 a week, which enabled her to buy a small house in Oakland (which she still owns). Yet, her father's low expectations lingered with her. As she told *Kiplinger's* "I never felt I would ever be anything more than a waitress. I was getting by. I loved serving people." Still, Orman loved Berkeley, enjoyed delving into crystals and astrology, and her irrepressible high spirits and warm personality one day earned her an unexpected display of appreciation from her many regular customers.

One of Orman's favorite tales to share with her audiences is how she got started as a professional in the financial sector. She had dreamed of opening her own restaurant one day, but when her parents could not stake her the $20,000 seed money she would need, she faced the prospect of another Orman family dream deferred. When she shared her disappointment with one of her favorite customers, a man named Fred Hasbrook, he took it upon himself to share Orman's dream with several other Buttercup Bakery customers who were in for their regular morning breakfast. Before the breakfast shift was over, Hasbrook returned to Orman with a stack of checks (including his own check for $2,000) and personal commitments totaling some $50,000. According to Orman's website, the windfall came with a note that read: "This is for people like you, so that your dreams can come true. To be paid back in ten years, if you can, with no interest."

Orman was bowled over by the generosity of her customers and friends, and she set out to do the smart thing with her seed money and the right thing by her trusting investors. On Fred Hasbrook's advice, she went straight to a local Merrill Lynch office and invested it so that it would be safe while she shopped around for potential locations and looked at floor plans for her new restaurant. And yet, like the road to her house high in the Oakland hills, Orman's path would become a twisty one leading her in unexpected directions.

The broker to whom Orman entrusted her $50,000 (she has called him "Randy" in her books) placed the money in risky investments. Because Orman knew nothing about investing and trusted that Randy would know everything she didn't, she signed blank authorization forms allowing him to use his discretion with her funds. At first, the investments yielded some solid earnings, but Randy recklessly mismanaged her account, and within four months the entire $50,000 was gone—and along with it went her dreams of her own restaurant. Financial calamity had struck again, but this time, it had chosen Suze Orman, not her father, Morris.

It's better to do nothing with your money than something you don't understand.

—Suze Orman

One of Morris's many positive qualities was his willingness to keep going, no matter what. Orman proved herself very much his daughter by immediately seeking work so that she could pay back her investors. She wouldn't be able to do this on her wages at the Buttercup Bakery, so she decided to tackle her financial matters head on and sought employment from the Merrill Lynch office where Randy had swindled her.

After all, Orman reasoned with her characteristic humor, "If Randy can be a broker, I can be a broker, too—after all, it seems like they just make people broker!"

By all reason, Orman should never have gotten the job. She had no idea what it took for women to dress for success in those days, so she showed up for work in her patriotic best: a bright blue blouse and red and white striped Sassoon pants tucked into white cowboy boots. The interview process was simply mortifying. "You should have seen the looks on all the interviewers' faces," she writes in *The 9 Steps to Financial Freedom*. "When they saw me, they actually asked if I had dressed that way to insult them. If there had been a rock in that conference room, I would have crawled under it."

To add insult to injury, one manager who interviewed Orman told her that he believed women didn't belong in the investment game and should stay barefoot and pregnant. Orman deflected the insult by asking how much he'd pay her to get pregnant. And then Orman received another surprise. The manager hired her starting at $1,500 a month, warning her that he expected her to fail within six months.

Whether Merrill Lynch needed to fill a hiring quota for women during those early years of affirmative action programs, or the company simply wanted to avoid a lawsuit because of Randy's shenanigans with her investment, Orman entered the company's training program to become an account executive. Orman was eager to learn everything she could about money, but she was also terrified. "Taking that job was breaking away from everything I had ever known. I was so out of my league."

Still, Orman put her own personal flair into her new career, bringing a large crystal to work to consult on the merits of certain investments. Clif Citrano, a Merrill Lynch broker who mentored Orman, told *Kiplinger's* that "everybody was saying, 'I hope that's a paperweight.'" But, as Citrano came to appreciate, Orman also had a knack for taking investment concepts and terms and putting them into language that was helpful and reassuring to her customers. Citrano remarked of Orman, "I've met much better investors in my time, but no one who could market to investors better."

Orman's crystal may have been more a security blanket than a prognostication tool during the period in which she learned her very complex trade. She became an extremely effective account executive for Merrill Lynch, but she was also plagued by those childhood-rooted feelings of unworthiness. While other brokers dined in nice restaurants at lunch, Orman would hit Taco Bell and eat in her car, feeling that this was where she belonged.

Additionally, she felt the weight of great responsibility toward her customers (many of whom were elderly and vulnerable to risk), and she cared a great deal about them. As she puts it in *The 9 Steps to Financial Freedom*, "It can be a scary business, investing other people's money."

But Orman proved to be not only a superlative student of finance but also eager to learn new ideas to replace the notions that didn't serve her well. At her core, she valued the truth. It is what drove her to seek answers to her spiritual questions, to find out what made good investment strategies tick, and to check out different philosophies to see if they offered anything of value to her. If something didn't produce the answers or results she desired, she would continue to search for what she wanted rather than give up.

Eventually, she relinquished relying on her crystal because she came to the realization that "it was a crystal." Her own experience, common sense, and willingness to expand her knowledge would guide her. She began to follow the tenets of author Norman Vincent Peale and his book *The Power of Positive Thinking*. In a way, the Israeli pilgrim's words to Orman in 1973 proved true: the crystal was in her. She started to embody positive thinking in action. She manifested God within herself whenever she took mindful action and therefore remained forever guided by her spiritual beliefs.

Orman developed a positive mantra of her own: "I am young, powerful and successful, and I produce at least $10,000 a month." (Orman notes that she added "at least" to allow for the possibility of making more than $10,000 a month.) Whatever that thought triggered in her, she began to consistently reach this monthly goal. She also extended her client outreach by conducting retirement seminars with the employees of the local utilities company, Pacific Gas & Electric.

Orman also sued Merrill Lynch to recover the funds Randy had mismanaged. Another situational twist played in her favor. During the lawsuit, Merrill Lynch could not fire her. She had become such a productive account executive that it was in the company's best interests to settle out of court by repaying her the lost money, with interest. Orman was able to repay her Buttercup Bakery investors, including Fred Hasbrook, who—having suffered a stroke—found the money Orman returned to be a godsend before he died.

After another spiritual quest, a more inspiring visit to India and Nepal, Orman began working at Prudential Bache Securities in 1983. But she felt that she wanted to offer her clients more options for their investments. Within four years, she founded her own financial planning firm, the Suze Orman Financial Group. At first, Orman's new firm showed great promise. Retirees from Pacific Gas & Electric, who had attended her retirement seminars, invested in annuities through her new company. But once again, calamity struck!

This time, disaster came in the form of a disgruntled employee who had gone with Orman to become her assistant at the Suze Orman Financial Group. Because Prudential Bache retained Orman's license for a month after her final day with them, her assistant was the one who signed on the large number of Pacific Gas & Electric employees who were taking an early retirement option. When she and Orman had a falling out over compensation, the assistant stole the clients' annuity checks, copied all of Orman's client files and business records, and then systematically set out to destroy Orman's business and set up her own by slandering Orman to her clients. Orman's new company was almost obliterated.

For a time, Orman became despondent and took to spending her own money recklessly. She went into serious credit card debt as she tried to stave off depression by living extravagantly. She feared that her friends would only like her for what she had, not for who she was. Thus, she spent lavishly, depleting her retirement accounts. She was repeating the traumas of her childhood, but instead of stealing a dollar from her mother to keep up appearances, she was stealing the money from her own future.

As Orman explains in her book *The Laws of Money, the Lessons of Life*, "The straw that broke the camel's back: 'I got a speeding ticket. I remember that the ticket was for only $40. But I did not have $40—I didn't have $20, or even $10. . . . As I drove away from the bridge in my high-end leased car, wearing my $8,000 credit-card charged watch and my $2,000 department-store-charged leather jacket, the magnitude of my lies became real to me for the first time. I was speeding down the highway to financial ruin.'"

Self-worth equals net worth.

—SUZE ORMAN

Orman put the brakes on her downward spiral and faced adversity by moving forward. She began by facing up to the truth about her own situation: her own behavior was destroying her well beyond what her employee had done. She took responsibility for her bad decisions and began to put her financial house back in order. Then, she sued her betrayer and won two long, difficult court cases against her.

More important, Orman learned that she could not recover and move on with her life until she forgave herself for her mistakes. After she forgave herself, she faced off with her former employee and did something extraordinary. As she recounted the moment to *Kiplinger's*, she told the woman, "I said, 'Listen to me. I don't know what I did to you to cause what you did to me. But I just want to tell you that I'm sorry.'" Of course, Orman might have done nothing that justified her former employee's actions. But she gave her the benefit of the doubt and the opportunity to examine her own conscience with respect to what she did to Orman.

Orman's ability to break the patterns of calamity and resignation that had bedeviled her and her father helped her to forge a path to greater personal prosperity. She understood, from her spiritual travels, that while she could not control the bad hands that fate might deal her, she could control her response to disaster and learn to make the right decisions in her responses. More important, she could take full responsibility for her responses, which put her in charge of her fate in a way that would make it harder for disaster to knock her down. With smart financial planning and an understanding of what crazy turns the road might take, she could plan for disaster and have the resources available in case she ever needed them. This core understanding not only made for a more mature and confident woman, it made for a terrific financial advisor who could help people face their own calamities.

True to Suze Orman form, she kept going. Her business recovered and began to prosper as her warmth, caring, and clear-eyed, no-nonsense approach to helping people make the most of their money struck a chord with people in need of guidance. Orman asked her clients to pay her what they thought her advice was worth. Apparently, they felt her advice was valuable, and she was back on track.

Pacific Gas & Electric brought more business to Orman's door in 1994 when they approached her to expand her retirement workshops by doing a satellite pitch for an audience of seven thousand employees. The seminar materials she developed for these presentations sent Orman's career in a whole new direction. That same year, she put these financial life lessons into her first book, *You've Earned It, Don't Lose It.* With the help of her publisher, Newmarket Press, she began to promote the book through an unexpected outlet: the QVC shopping channel on cable—a place where impulse buying is the name of the game. During one early morning show in 1995, Orman sold her entire stock of twenty-five hundred books. Newmarket had to print a new run. Orman's powers of persuasion struck gold again on Super Bowl Sunday in 1996, when she sold ten thousand copies of the book in a breathtaking twelve minutes.

Although she was quickly pulled off the air because the inventory had been exhausted, Suze Orman had launched her media career in a big way. She was able to tap into personal qualities that struck a chord with QVC's largely female demographic. She was warm, funny, mediagenic (the camera loved her), and convincing, particularly because—like many in her viewership—she had started from poverty and worked her way up to prosperity.

That she could poke fun at herself with anecdotes about her own life reassured her audience that even the most fiscally clueless among them could take charge of her financial future and achieve security. And she was honest, particularly about the very emotional component of money, which her audience understood. Her ability to inject the deeply personal into what were otherwise dry, economic concepts helped to ignite popular interest in investing.

Orman has a knack for making us feel the depth of the client's confusion and even terror about money, making each step toward financial independence all the more vivid and memorable.

—PATRICIA HOLT,
SAN FRANCISCO CHRONICLE

QVC gave Orman her own show, the *Financial Freedom Hour.* By the time her second book, *The 9 Steps to Financial Freedom,* was published in 1997, she could sell twenty-five thousand copies in one show. In book publishing, bestsellers (unlike movies or records) are reckoned in sales of the hundreds of thousands, not millions, of copies. For a book to sell twenty-five thousand copies in a single hour was nothing short of phenomenal. More books would follow: *The Road to Wealth* (2001), *The Laws of Money, the Lessons of Life* (2003), *The Money Book for the Young, Fabulous and Broke* (2005), and *Women and Money: Owning the Power to Control Your Destiny* (2007).

While her books are packed with detailed guidelines on investment strategy, worksheets, and other features one can find in many books on personal finance, what sets them apart from other bestsellers in the field are the personal stories of Orman's clients and Orman's own tales of her mistakes, her family's financial hardships, and the lessons she has learned from them. Many of the clients' stories are heartbreaking narratives of lost opportunities, lost lives, marital and family intergenerational despair, chilling evil, great kindness, and how attitudes, rather than money itself, have forged and destroyed destinies. What Orman communicates so effectively in these books is her passion for helping others, her deep concern for her clients and for people in general, and her hope that the life lessons will inform, inspire, and guide others to do better for themselves and their loved ones.

Orman's next move was to public television, where offers of her book and a related video as a membership premium raised an unprecedented $2.3 million for PBS stations. She became the largest individual fund-raiser in the history of PBS pledge drives and went on to create and host six PBS specials based on her books. Later, she expanded to the CNBC weekend lineup with *The Suze Orman Show*. Orman wasn't quite finished with her conquest of television, however. She won two daytime Emmy Awards and five Gracie Awards (presented by the American Women in Radio and Television and named for another popular blonde TV star known for her humor and positive image—comedienne Gracie Allen). To date, Orman has won more Gracie Awards than any other winner.

The next media boost for Orman was her appearance on *The Oprah Winfrey Show*, where Oprah's audience—well established as book lovers and book buyers—would help propel *The 9 Steps to Financial Freedom* to the top of the *New York Times* Best Seller List. (It would finish 1998 as the year's top-selling nonfiction title.) Her popularity with Oprah's audience secured for her the position of contributing financial editor to *O, The Oprah Magazine*. She would land the popular, biweekly *Money Matters* column on Yahoo Finance, contribute regularly to *Costco Connection* magazine, and serve as the editor-in-chief of Condé Nast's *Currency* magazine supplement, which achieved a record-breaking, one-time publication run of 9.3 million copies.

To date, Orman's ability to reach unprecedented numbers of people online, in print, and on television has reached a critical mass. But having access to all those eyes, ears, and computer screens has not been the clincher of her success. What has helped her become one of *Time* magazine's most influential people for 2008 is her ability to engage her audience and speak to them truthfully, without condescension, about one of the most emotionally volatile areas of their lives—money.

Money is often at the root of the conflicts, tragedies, triumphs, and phenomenal journeys in people's lives. It can secure a person's future or wreak untold havoc and suffering. It can be the preserver of communities or the destroyer of families, and yet, like sex, religion, and politics, it remains one of the more difficult topics for people to discuss openly or face up to as a measure of personal worth. Author Ayn Rand observed that "money is only a tool. It will take you wherever you wish, but it will not replace you as the driver." Orman has spent her lifetime learning how to drive and how to teach others to do so safely and confidently. Two important lessons remain constant refrains in Orman's books: responsibility and giving back.

Orman asks her clients and readers to be responsible to themselves first and to do whatever it takes to stop harming themselves and others with destructive financial behaviors. She is particularly forceful about the dangers of credit card debt and the lack of planning for the future. She also emphasizes that people must be responsible to their loved ones: teach their children healthy spending habits, provide for potential disasters by saving for rainy days and buying the right kind of insurance, and leave behind intelligently planned estates so that they don't hand down headaches and heartaches.

My work empowers both men and women equally. I do not believe in segregating money. Women should become powerful with it, but not to the exclusion of men. When you empower partners equally, that's how the problems of money go away in a family.

—SUZE ORMAN

The second lesson is to give back, which harkens to Orman's core belief that faith permeates and guides every aspect of her life. From her travels to India, she learned the Hindu religious tenet that acts of charity generate "righteous action," which opens up the opportunity for more money to come to the giver. She says that giving inspires us to feel "rich, lucky, grateful, expansive, vital." To wit, the more we give, the more we receive.

One bit of advice that dovetails with Orman's recommendation to give back is that there is one group of people we should always feel free to give money to without reservation: our parents. Orman's strong ties with her own parents—whose poverty provided some of the best education of Orman's life—has inspired her to encourage people to give back freely to those who have given them the most—mom and dad. If, indeed, the American dream is for us to do better than our parents have done, what better way to enjoy the successful achievement of that dream than to share those fruits with our parents?

It is true that Orman owes a significant part of her success to the technology that has allowed her to spread her ideas to a great number of people never before reachable. Yet, it is also true that all of the technology in the world would bring her few results if her message did not resonate for so many in their hearts as well as their heads.

It is fitting that Orman's profile quote on her MySpace page sums up so much of what she strives to teach others. She writes: "A big part of financial freedom is having your heart and mind free from worry about the what-ifs of life."

How to Be Like Suze Orman

1) **Take time for yourself.** Orman said her mother took care of her husband and children as well as her own mother, and still volunteered at the PTA. "Never once do I remember her taking time to read a book, taking time to do something she wanted. Her entire life was dedicated to taking care of everyone else but her. She lost herself."

Orman came to understand her father had also lost himself when he gave up his dream of becoming a lawyer. "He lost his resolve . . . effectively pulling him back into the cycle of struggle." She pinpointed this disappointment as the pivotal moment of her father's life, setting him on the road to a series of business failures and a lifetime of financial struggles. The episode was pivotal, not only for her father, but for Orman and the rest of her family, as well, as they inherited his attitudes. She concludes, "With his thoughts he created his destiny, as do we all."

Take care of your responsibilities, but don't forget your responsibility to yourself.

2) **Never let others define you.** Not even those closest to you. Orman came to realize that the message her father passed on to her wasn't a positive one. "Who was I to think I could have more, be more? In retrospect, I can see that for a long time I thought his destiny was mine as well, because the message he'd passed on to me was the lesson of less and the thoughts of *I can't*."

3) **Don't buy into negativity.** Orman further wrote of her father's positive and negative influence: "I now realize that my dad's thoughts were always thoughts of poverty, that his internal voice told him *you can't*. It wasn't as if he didn't try, because he

Cont'd

did try. He worked harder than anyone I've ever known, every day of his life . . . he had amazing courage. Despite this, my brothers and I also heard him say, more than once, 'This is just the way it was meant to be, and there's nothing I can do about it.'"

When she became a stockbroker, Orman began to follow the tenets of author Norman Vincent Peale and his book *The Power of Positive Thinking*. She started to embody positive thinking through her actions. Orman developed a positive mantra of her own: "I am young, powerful and successful, and I produce at least $10,000 a month."

4) **Seek education.** Despite economic hardships and some learning difficulties, Orman's parents did not entertain low expectations for their children, insisting that their daughter would go to college. Orman attended the University of Illinois at Urbana-Champaign, and while she left school before graduating, her college years provided a foundation for her later study to become a broker and financial planner.

5) **Examine your faith.** Orman spent time after college seeking spiritual meaning and her life's purpose. Her faith is central to who she is. "Faith plays a prominent role in my life. Without faith, nothing matters."

6) **Cultivate an engaging personality.** As a waitress, Orman loved serving people, and her irrepressible high spirits and warm personality earned her an unexpected display of appreciation from her many regular customers. Those customers gave Orman $50,000 in seed money to start her own restaurant.

Orman's warm personality helped her succeed in the investment business and in connecting with her television audience. What helped her become one of *Time* magazine's most influential people for 2008 is her ability to engage her audience and

Cont'd

speak to them truthfully, without condescension, about one of the most emotionally volatile areas of their lives—money.

7) **Fight through adversity.** After Orman lost the $50,000 her customers gave her to start her restaurant, she "regrouped." One of her father's many positive qualities was his willingness to keep going, no matter what. Orman proved herself very much his daughter by immediately seeking a way to repay her investors. She wouldn't be able to do that on waitress wages, so she ambitiously sought employment from the very Merrill Lynch office where the broker had swindled her.

Orman also sued Merrill Lynch to recover the funds she had lost. Winning an out-of-court settlement that returned her investment plus interest, she was able to repay her Buttercup Bakery investors.

8) **Impose reality checks on yourself.** After an employee betrayed her, seriously damaging her new company, Orman became despondent and began spending money recklessly. She went into serious credit card debt and depleted her retirement accounts. It was when she got a speeding ticket that she couldn't afford to pay that she finally faced the truth: "As I drove away from the bridge in my high-end leased car, wearing my $8,000 credit-card-charged watch and my $2,000 depart-ment-store-charged leather jacket, the magnitude of my lies became real to me for the first time. I was speeding down the highway to financial ruin."

Orman was living a lie, recognized it, and changed. She took responsibility for her bad decisions and took steps to put her financial house back in order.

9) **Forgive yourself and others.** Orman believes that you cannot move on with your life until you forgive yourself for your mis-takes. She forgave herself for her irresponsible spending—and

Cont'd

then changed her behavior. Orman also believes in forgiving others. Although she sued her former employee (and won), she did something extraordinary. She told the woman that she didn't know what she had done to cause the woman's actions, but that she was sorry. She gave her former employee the opportunity to examine her own conscience.

10) **Be responsible, first to yourself, then to others.** Orman encourages people to be responsible to themselves first by eliminating any self-destructive financial behaviors. She cautions especially against credit card debt and failing to plan for the future. She also promotes taking responsibility for loved ones: teaching children healthy spending habits, providing for potential disasters with savings and insurance, and leaving behind an intelligently planned estate..

11) **Be prepared for calamity.** Orman found the path to prosperity when she was able to break the pattern of disaster, and resignation to disaster, that her father had been caught in. Her spiritual searching led her to understand that she could not always control what happened to her, but she could control her response and make the right decisions when disaster struck.

12) **Give back.** Orman's faith permeates and guides every aspect of her life. She believes that acts of charity generate "righteous action," which opens up the opportunity for more money to come to the giver. She says that giving inspires us to feel "rich, lucky, grateful, expansive, vital," and that the more we give, the more we receive.

Ruth Bader Ginsburg
1933–

Equality for Women

When I attended the Harvard Law School,
there was no space in the dormitories for women.
Women were not admitted to the Harvard Faculty Club
dining tables. One could invite one's father, but not one's
wife or mother to the [Harvard] Law Review banquet.

—RUTH BADER GINSBURG

In early August 1993, the United States Court of Appeals for the District of Columbia jurist Ruth Bader Ginsburg was confirmed by the Senate and became only the second female justice of the United States Supreme Court. As the first justice to be named by a Democratic president since Lyndon B. Johnson, only those who were avid Court observers or legal scholars knew the impact this shy, yet fiercely intellectual woman had already had on contemporary American society. In fact, she'd helped change it significantly.

Before President Jimmy Carter had appointed Ginsburg to the federal appellate bench in 1980, Ginsburg enjoyed the reputation of a well-respected law professor at Columbia University Law School. However, it was as the organizer and leader of the American Civil Liberties Union's Women's Rights Project, during the 1970s, that she had made a lasting impression at the federal level. She authored the legal strategy that would in effect force the U.S. Supreme Court to examine gender bias and gender-based classifications that had permitted discrimination on the basis of sex. She did all of this while sustaining a successful marriage and raising a family.

As she prepared her efforts to dismantle the complex, entrenched, and permissible practices of unequal treatment based on gender, Ginsburg also brought her own personal history to this endeavor.

Joan Ruth Bader was born on March 15, 1933, in Brooklyn, New York, the younger of two daughters of Nathan and Celia Amster Bader. The Baders were a classic American immigrant's success story. Nathan was a furrier and haberdasher who had immigrated to the United States from Russia when he was thirteen; Celia was a housewife and avid bookworm whose family came to the United States from Central Europe four months before she was born. Theirs was a comfortably middle-class family situated in the dynamic and ethnically mixed Brooklyn neighborhood of Flatbush. Sadly, their first daughter, Marilyn, died of meningitis, so Ruth was raised as an only child.

Neither of Ruth's parents had attended college, but they impressed upon young Ruth (whom the family called "Kiki") the value of an education and the importance of success. More important, Ginsburg's mother instilled in her a love of learning coupled with the belief that she should have the same opportunities as any young boy. Celia stoked Ruth's intellectual curiosity with regular trips to the public library.

Young Ruth followed her mother's guidance and became a diligent and competitive scholar at Brooklyn's James Madison High School, participating as a cellist in the high school orchestra, writing for the student newspaper, and performing as a baton twirler. Even as she distinguished herself, however, Ruth kept a heartbreaking secret from her classmates: her mother had terminal cancer. Celia Bader succumbed on the eve of her daughter's high school graduation, so Ruth did not attend her graduation ceremony. Years later in 1999, and with very little publicity, she faced her own battle with colon cancer and beat it after surgery, chemotherapy, and radiation treatments.

Celia left her daughter a then-sizeable inheritance of $8,000 for her college tuition, but Ruth had earned sufficient scholarships to support herself throughout school, so she gave the bulk of this financial bequest to her father and embarked for Cornell University.

Of her parents, Ginsburg would later say, "Both taught me to love learning, to care about people, and to work hard for whatever I wanted or believed in."

At Cornell University, Bader earned high honors with her bachelor's degree in government. One classmate described her as "scary smart." She was elected to Phi Beta Kappa (the oldest undergraduate honors society in the United States), and she graduated first among the women in her class. She also met the great love of her life, Martin Ginsburg, who was a year ahead of her in school and who, as Ginsburg put it, was "the only boy I knew who cared that I had a brain." Shortly after she graduated from Cornell in 1954, they married.

Young Ruth's role models were women of accomplishment. For example, she admired the exploits of Amelia Earhart.

—LINDA BAYER, AUTHOR OF
RUTH BADER GINSBURG

For the first couple years of their marriage, the Ginsburgs lived at Fort Sill in Oklahoma while Martin served in the military. His young bride got a job with the local Social Security office while she was expecting their first child. When she told her employers that she was expecting, they demoted her three levels in pay. A fellow coworker, also pregnant, did not tell the Social Security office about her condition, and she was not demoted. Ginsburg was also denied the opportunity to travel to Baltimore for a training seminar because of her pregnancy. When Martin's military service ended, the Ginsburgs both decided to pursue their law degrees and returned to the East Coast with their young daughter, Jane.

While it came as no surprise that Ginsburg, with her record of high academic achievement, would be admitted to Harvard Law School, she found her accomplishments and talents were readily dismissed by the largely male establishment there.

In the mid-1950s, she was one of only eight female students (out of a law school student body of five hundred) at a time when the expectation for most female students was that they would earn not M.A.s, J.D.s, or

Ph.D.s, but the traditional "Mrs." degree (as in matrimony). Ginsburg discovered that both fellow students and what was then a conservative faculty, while tolerant of women, were less than enthusiastic with their presence—there weren't even dormitory rooms for the female law students.

It must have been equally discouraging when the school's dean, Erwin Griswold, complained to Ginsburg and her fellow female law students (again, a mere eight out of five hundred) that they were taking up space "reserved for" more qualified men.

While today it is considered to be the mecca of the liberal eastern academic establishment, Harvard in the "I Like Ike" era presented itself as a bastion of male entitlement to the legal profession; it did not truly welcome women. As a student, Ginsburg recalled that women were likely to be called on in class for fun and games, as though they would serve as comic relief, since the belief was they were not as smart as their male counterparts.

Ginsburg did not provide comic relief. Undaunted, she did what she did best: *she excelled*. When called upon, she provided the correct answers. As a student, she did her due diligence. She earned a place on the prestigious *Harvard Law Review*. As Eleanor H. Ayer wrote in *Ruth Bader Ginsburg: Fire and Steel on the Supreme Court*, classmate Robert Loeb recalled to Ginsburg, "You never missed classes; you were always prepared; your *Law Review* work was always done; you were always beautifully dressed and impeccably groomed; and you had a happy husband and a lovely young daughter."

In the course of performing her duties for the *Harvard Law Review*, Ginsburg once again encountered some of the day's archaic rules distinguishing the sexes. Biographer Carmen Bredeson reports in *Ruth Bader Ginsburg: Supreme Court Justice* that, while source-checking in the school's law library, Ginsburg was denied access to research materials because certain portions of the library were closed to women. That didn't stop her—she got a male colleague to retrieve the material she needed. If a task was assigned to her or preparation for class was needed, "Ruthless Ruthie"—as she was dubbed by her Harvard classmates—could always be counted on to be well prepared.

Even when a serious family crisis struck—Martin Ginsburg was diagnosed with testicular cancer that eventually spread to his lymph nodes at a time when treatments for cancer were nowhere near as successful as they are today—Ginsburg was able to help nurse her husband back to health, attend to the needs of her three-year-old daughter, and maintain her high academic standing at a college whose establishment was openly hostile toward her efforts.

She went so far as to sit in on Martin's classes at Harvard, to take notes for him so that he wouldn't fall behind during his treatment. She also typed up his third-year paper for him. With her help, he was able to graduate on time.

My wife has the "disadvantage" of doing well at everything.

—Martin Ginsburg

Ginsburg's attitude on such challenges could be summed up as follows: "If you want to do something badly enough, you find a way. Somehow you manage," as quoted by Jack L. Roberts in his book *Ruth Bader Ginsburg: Supreme Court Justice.*

It is also interesting to note that, while at Harvard, Ginsburg honed her prodigious writing skills, studying with no less an important author than Vladimir Nabokov. Nabokov impressed on her the importance of precision, and Ginsburg would strive to express her legal documents with great verbal economy. Even today, "when I write an opinion, I will often read a sentence aloud and [ask] 'Can I say this in fewer words, can I write it so the meaning will come across with greater clarity?'" Ginsburg said.

After two years at Harvard, Ginsburg transferred to Columbia University because Martin Ginsburg had accepted a job in New York City. He would eventually become one of the nation's leading tax attorneys. At Columbia, Ginsburg graduated at the top of her law school class. As Bayer describes the graduation ceremony, "At Columbia's graduation ceremony, hundreds of people in the audience heard four-year-old Jane proudly proclaim, 'That's my mommy!'"

But unlike her male classmates, she would find no law firms knocking at her door to recruit her as an associate, no matter how outstanding her accomplishments. In fact, they refused to hire her, even as they competed fiercely for male candidates with lesser qualifications. When she sought work as a legal clerk, Supreme Court Justice Felix Frankfurter dismissed her as a candidate. He said he didn't hire women and even went so far as to ask if she wore skirts because he didn't like to see girls in pants.

Despite such infuriating and discouraging episodes, Ginsburg always kept a level head about her situation. As Bredesen writes, "When she was asked years later if she was bitter about her lack of success in finding a job, she replied, 'I don't think that being angry or being hostile is very productive. In order to bring about real change, you have to do it through constant dialogue, constant persuasion, and not in shouting matches.'"

Ginsburg persisted until she secured a clerkship with the more open-minded Federal District Judge Edward L. Palmieri in the District Court in New York. She later took part as a research associate in a comparative law project sponsored by Columbia. This project took her to Sweden for several months, where she observed the Swedish courts and eventually cowrote a book on Swedish judicial procedure. In Sweden, she also had the opportunity to observe a society with a more egalitarian attitude toward women in the workplace and law, as well as more open-minded policies toward childcare for working women. As Bredeson noted, "Ginsburg compared the two cultures; she said that feminist feelings were stirred in her for the first time."

Returning to the United States, she joined the teaching faculty of Rutgers University, where she was the second female to join the school's faculty and was among the first twenty female law professors in the entire country. When Ginsburg became pregnant again, she realized that, as a nontenured instructor, she could be dismissed from Rutgers if the school found out about it. She wore oversized clothes (borrowed from Martin's mother) to hide her condition. Ginsburg gave birth to her son, James, and despite the demands of her career she was a devoted and involved mother to both her children.

Countless times during my thirteen years' service on the D.C. circuit, when I attended a social event and was introduced to a stranger as Judge Ginsburg, the person would extend his hand to my husband—who invariably shook it.

—RUTH BADER GINSBURG

As Ginsburg recalled: "In the fifties, the traditional law firms were just beginning to turn around on hiring Jews. . . . They had just gotten over that form of discrimination. But to be a woman, a Jew, and a mother to boot, that combination was a bit much."

While teaching at Rutgers, Ginsburg encountered other forms of discrimination. As Roberts recounts, "Even the law school textbooks at that time often contained shocking statements about women. For example, one textbook on property law stated, 'Land, like woman, was meant to be possessed.'" When asked by her students to teach a course on sex discrimination, Ginsburg had difficulty finding written material about the issue.

This is my dream of the way the world should be. When fathers take equal responsibility for the care of their children, that's when women will truly be liberated.

—RUTH BADER GINSBURG

Then there was the matter of money. In Linda N. Bayer's biography *Ruth Bader Ginsburg*, Ginsburg described the university's rationalization for underpaying her: "The good dean of the [Rutgers] law school carefully explained about the state university's limited resources and then added it was only fair to pay me modestly because my husband had a very good job." She remained at Rutgers until 1972. Ginsburg and other female faculty members eventually sued Rutgers under the Equal Pay Act and won substantial salary increases.

Ginsburg, while never obtaining the status of a senior associate or junior partner in any of the eastern seaboard's established firms, continued to persevere and flourish in her academic assignments. After leaving Rutgers, she taught a course on women and the law at Harvard, but she could not get tenure there, once again because of her gender. Fortunately, a more enlightened Columbia Law School brought her aboard as the first woman to achieve tenured rank in the school's history.

After reading French philosopher Simone de Beauvoir's seminal examination on the status of women, *The Second Sex*, Ginsburg recognized that her firsthand experiences with gender discrimination were mere symptoms of a much larger problem, one that was culturally and historically entrenched even in the world's greatest democracy. In the United States, there were traditions, attitudes, and laws that denied women the

Not a single law firm in the entire city of New York bid for my employment.

—RUTH BADER GINSBURG

choices and opportunities that men enjoyed as their birthright. Ginsburg felt that the law would be the best route to redress these injustices.

Ginsburg turned her formidable intellect and prodigious work ethic to challenge the practice of gender discrimination, also known in legal circles as suspect classification. The civil rights movement of the early to mid-1960s did away with legal racial discrimination and would provide Ginsburg the groundwork to address and defeat the working legal rationalizations for how the sexes were treated differently, mostly to the detriment of the "weaker" sex. Her battle would be an uphill one, but Ginsburg was more than up to the challenge.

She became involved with the New Jersey chapter of the American Civil Liberties Union (ACLU) in litigating sex discrimination cases. Her first big case to make it all the way to the Supreme Court was *Reed v. Reed*. Sally and Cecil Reed were a married couple who had separated. After their adopted son died, both sought to be named administrator of his estate. The Idaho Probate Court dictated that "males must be preferred to females." Ginsburg authored the brief in favor of Sally Reed's appeal, a brief that, Ayer explains, "became known as the 'grandmother brief,' for it was the ancestor of many future legal opinions on women's rights."

When the Supreme Court ruled in favor of Sally Reed, Ginsburg said, "It was the first time the Supreme Court ever overturned a law in response to a woman's complaint of unfair sex-based discrimination." As Jack L. Roberts notes, "As one person pointed out, [Ginsburg] almost 'single-handedly' forced the Supreme Court to end discrimination against women."

The ACLU put Ginsburg in charge of its Women's Rights Project. Initially, she fought on behalf of New Jersey schoolteachers who stood to lose their jobs once they became pregnant—clearly an issue Ginsburg understood from difficult personal experience.

Ginsburg would herself argue several times before the highest court in the land. She advocated and won: *Fronterio v. Richardson*, 411 U.S. 677 (1973), which gave equal dependant benefits for women in the military; *Weinberger v. Wisenfeld*, 420 U.S. 636 (1975), which—argued on behalf of a man who was left to raise his newborn son after his wife died in childbirth—struck down a Social Security Act provision that gave greater survivor benefits to a woman with children; *Edwards v. Healy*, 421 U.S. 772 (1975), one of several cases that invalidated a Louisiana law exempting women from jury service unless they requested otherwise; *Califano v. Goldfarb*, 430 U.S.

199 (1977), striking down a Social Security Act provision that automatically awarded survivors benefits to a woman, but not a man; and *Duren v. Missouri*, 439 U.S. 357 (1979), which struck down a Missouri law that exempted women from jury service upon request.

These decisions were in keeping with Ginsburg's methodology of wearing away precedent and replacing it with new case law, step-by-step. Often, she would wear her mother Celia's earrings when she appeared before the Supreme Court to remind herself how proud her mother would be of her accomplishments.

As a junior justice on the Court, William Rehnquist once remarked, "So, Mrs. Ginsburg, you won't settle for Susan B. Anthony's face on the new dollar, will you?" Ginsburg did not respond at the time, but the perfect response occurred to her later: "No, Justice Rehnquist. Tokens won't do."

Having experienced discrimination, she devoted the next twenty years of her career to fighting it and making this country a better place for our wives, our mothers, our sisters, and our daughters.

—President Bill Clinton

The legacy and effects of these cases, and their progeny, become all the more important when considering the failure to ratify the Equal Rights Amendment. Without the precedents set by Ginsburg's work on behalf of women's (and sometimes men's) rights against gender discrimination, would women in the United States have the significant legal rights that they enjoy today?

In 1980, President Jimmy Carter appointed Ginsburg as a judge on the United States Court of Appeals for the District of Columbia. Ginsburg and her husband moved to Washington, D.C. To the surprise of many, she proved not to be an activist as a judge. As the *Encyclopedia of World Biography* states: "Though Ginsburg has been hailed as the Thurgood Marshall of the women's movement, she unlike Marshall (who saw his judgeship as an opportunity to continue the activism and advocacy he practiced as a lawyer), brought a cautious, measured disposition to the court. Her belief, shared by many conservatives, is that, with few exceptions, the courts should interpret laws and leave policy-making in the electoral, political domain."

During her tenure on D.C.'s appellate court Ginsburg's measured approach also enabled her to take on the role of mediator between judges who took opposing positions on legal issues. As her former clerk Peter Huber, Esq., recalled, Ginsburg "knows how to disagree without being disagreeable and has mastered the art so well she pulls people her way." Biographer Ayers would describe Ginsburg as "respectful of precedent."

In 1993, Supreme Court Justice Byron White announced his retirement from the nation's highest court. Confronted with the choice of appointing the next justice for the Supreme Court, President Bill Clinton sought someone to balance the court's conservative advocate, Justice Antonin Scalia, yet still exhibit the personal and political skills necessary to move the court's left-leaning members to the critical center. While not President Clinton's first choice, Ginsburg caught his eye with her consensus-building skills. Coupled with her intellectual strengths, Ginsburg's respect of precedent and personal integrity won over conservatives. She was confirmed by the Senate in a vote of ninety-six for, three against, with one senator absent.

Remember that I came from a world where women were protected out of everything. Protected out of being lawyers, out of being engineers, out of being bartenders. Women couldn't work in certain occupations that were regarded as dangerous but also happened to pay better.

—RUTH BADER GINSBURG

In announcing Ginsburg's nomination, President Clinton commented, "Throughout her life, she has repeatedly stood for the individual, the person less well-off, the outsider in society, and has given those people greater hope by telling them they have a place in our legal system."

On August 10, 1993, Ruth Bader Ginsburg was sworn in as the Supreme Court's second female jurist. At the swearing in ceremony, Ginsburg accepted her appointment graciously, yet poignantly, invoking her mother's memory by recalling her as "the bravest, strongest person I have known, who was taken from me much too soon. I pray that I may be all that she would have been had she lived in an age when women could aspire and achieve and daughters are cherished as much as sons." Even President Clinton was moved to tears.

As a justice (and currently the only female justice since Sandra Day O'Connor's retirement in 2001), Ginsburg has leaned toward the Court's liberal side, but she does not hesitate to vote with her right-leaning colleagues when she agrees with them. She is, in fact, very close friends with archconservative Justice Scalia and socializes with him outside the Court.

Ginsburg has other interests as well. Unlike other justices, Ginsburg enjoys public speaking. She and her husband are devotees of the opera, and she has appeared on stage in costume as an extra in opera production.

As a footnote to Ginsburg's as-yet unfinished, but still groundbreaking career, Bayer points out that her daughter, Jane, followed in her mother's footsteps by attending Harvard, becoming a lawyer, and then going on to be a law professor at Columbia University. They became the first mother and daughter to serve on the same law faculty in the United States.

Ginsburg is possessed of a keen intelligence, fierce personal discipline, and a strong sense of justice—particularly in matters of gender equality. She has succeeded in all areas of her life—in academia in the country's most competitive colleges, in the practice of law by winning crucial, landmark cases and by reaching the top of her profession as a Supreme Court justice, and in her private family life. Her dedication to what is just carries beyond the law to her personal conduct. She secures her success by maintaining the highest standards in her personal and professional life.

How to Be Like Ruth Bader Ginsburg

1) **Revere education.** While neither of Ginsburg's parents attended college, they impressed upon her the value of education, her mother stoking Ruth's intellectual curiosity with regular trips to the public library. Ginsburg pursued the finest education possible. Her diligence and academic accomplishments earned her a scholarship to Cornell University. She then went on to Harvard and Columbia law schools. While she experienced discrimination even in those elite institutions, her education opened the doors that led to her ruling on laws to end gender discrimination.

2) **Be the best at what you do.** Groundbreakers shake up the status quo and often encounter double standards and more scrutiny than do their peers. Ginsburg could not be shaken from her path because she was unimpeachable as a scholar, as an advocate, as a writer and researcher, as an attorney, and eventually as a judge.

3) **Work hard for what you believe in.** Celia Bader had instilled in her daughter a love of learning and the belief that girls should have the same opportunities as boys. Ginsburg said of her parents, "Both taught me to love learning, to care about people, and to work hard for whatever I wanted or believed in." Ginsburg never accepted the sex discrimination she was subjected to; she helped change the law so other women wouldn't have to go through what she did.

4) **Understand there really are no limitations.** Ginsburg made it through the demands of two topflight law schools while being married, raising a child, and helping her husband through a serious illness, even taking notes in his classes for him so he wouldn't fall behind. "If you want to do something badly enough, you find a way. Somehow you manage."

Cont'd

5) **Cover all the bases.** Lawyers and judges do a lot of writing to fully express their legal arguments and conclusions, and Ginsburg wanted to have expertise in the written word. While at Harvard, she studied with world-renowned writer Vladimir Nabokov, honing her skills and learning the importance of precision and verbal economy.

6) **Be diplomatic.** Ginsburg's measured approach allowed her to act as a mediator between judges during her tenure on D.C.'s appellate court. She "knows how to disagree without being disagreeable."

7) **Be persistent.** Throughout her education and career, Ginsburg faced the gender discrimination that she eventually "single-handedly" forced the Supreme Court to end. Upon graduating from Columbia University at the top of her class, Ginsburg found that no law firms would hire her, even as they competed fiercely for male candidates with lesser qualifications. The combination of being a woman, a Jew, and a mother was too much for firms at that time, Ginsburg said. In addition, she spent much of her career not receiving equal pay for her work, once being told that because her husband made a good salary, it was fair to pay her modestly.

Despite the hypocrisy of the injustices, Ginsburg remained pragmatic in her search for work and opportunity to change the system: "I don't think that being angry or being hostile is very productive. In order to bring about real change, you have to do it through constant dialogue, constant persuasion, and not in shouting matches." And bring about real change is exactly what Ruth Bader Ginsburg did.

18

Ida B. Wells-Barnett
1862–1931

Courage

I am only a mouthpiece through which
to tell the story of lynching.

—IDA B. WELLS-BARNETT

It was an inauspicious beginning for Ida B. Wells-Barnett when she was born on a summer's day in Holly Springs, Mississippi, in 1862. She was born a slave and born into a United States where the Civil War was raging. President Abraham Lincoln's Emancipation Proclamation freeing all of the Confederate states' slaves, of which her parents were two, was still six months in the future. It would be another three years before the convulsive violence of the Civil War would settle the matter of slavery for good.

It was in this convulsive environment that one of the most articulate and courageous voices for civil rights entered the world.

The first of eight children born to James and Elizabeth Wells, who worked as a carpenter and a cook, respectively, little Ida's prospects didn't suggest she'd be a woman who would help change the United States. She was black, the child of slaves, born into a poor family with seven other children, and a female. But she was also intelligent, possessed of a keen sense of responsibility, and was committed to education. All were attributes that would serve her well in her quest for justice and equality for all people.

Wells-Barnett would make her mark and legacy because she had the courage to speak out through her writings, in the South no less, against the heinous injustice and crime of lynching. She documented hundreds of these wanton, bloodthirsty murders, so nobody could say they didn't really happen. In the course of her work, she had the courage to put her personal safety in jeopardy.

Lynching was nothing more than brutal mob violence, in which people appointed themselves judge, jury, and executioner. Blacks in the South were the primary victims—men, women, and children. Their "offenses" could range from simply being accused of doing anything that "insults" a white person to being accused of serious crimes. Clearly outside the due process of law that every citizen is guaranteed under the Constitution, lynching was a way to instill fear and to control blacks in the aftermath of the Civil War.

The Tuskegee Institute in Alabama puts the number of lynchings between 1880 and 1951 at 3,437 black victims and 1,293 white ones. Most of the lynchings happened in the states of Mississippi, Georgia, Alabama, Texas, and Louisiana.

Wells-Barnett reached the conscience of a nation and joined the ranks of black leaders who said that ending slavery was only the beginning, not the end, of the United States' moral and legal obligation to black Americans. They took their fight to the White House doors. When a black postmaster was lynched in South Carolina, Wells-Barnett was part of a delegation in 1898 that went to see President William McKinley to demand government action on the atrocity.

"Why is mob murder permitted by a Christian nation?

—IDA B. WELLS-BARNETT

An activist her entire adult life, she was one of the founders of the National Association for the Advancement of Colored People (NAACP), and an early advocate in the suffrage movement to secure the right to vote for all women. She also worked with Jane Addams to block the segregation of schools in Chicago. "Wells-Barnett was fearless and respected, an uncompromising fighter for the rights of all human beings," wrote the National Women's Hall of Fame on their website. She was a 1988 inductee.

Wells-Barnett described her early childhood as a lighthearted one. After being emancipated, her now free parents managed to buy their own home. But young Ida also caught wind of a dark family secret, the significance of which would resonate in her later work as an antilynching activist.

James Wells had been owned all his life by a single master, who had also been his father. Ida once overheard her father telling his own mother that he refused to visit with the wife of his former owner. The day James's owner/father died, his new widow had forced James's mother to strip off her clothes and whipped her in front of James and the other slaves. As historian James West Davidson recounts in "They Say": *Ida B. Wells and the Reconstructions of Race*: "Significantly, the memory was one of the few Wells retained of her childhood, her ears 'burning' to understand why the white mistress punished her grandmother."

One thing young Ida had going for her, along with the love of her family, was that both her parents advocated education. Her father served on the first board of trustees of Shaw University, later Rust College, where Ida later attended. Elaine Lisandrelli, in *Ida B. Wells-Barnett: Crusader Against Lynching*, notes that "Jim and Lissie Wells had high expectations for their children, and Ida knew these expectations well."

"Our job," Wells-Barnett wrote, "was to go to school and learn all we could." She was an avid reader, and though her mother permitted reading only the Bible on Sunday, she was free to read Shakespeare, every book in the Sunday school library, and newspapers on the other six days.

Tragedy intervened in her life when Wells-Barnett was only sixteen. The yellow fever epidemic in 1878 caused the death of both her parents and two younger brothers, which left Ida in charge of five children. Wells-Barnett biographer Dennis B. Fradin writes in *Ida B. Wells: Mother of the Civil Rights Movement* that when relatives suggested breaking up the family, Ida declared: "You are not going to put any of the children anywhere. It would make my father and mother turn over in their graves to know their children had been scattered. We own our house, and if you will help me find work, I will take care of my brothers and sisters." Because of her educational qualifications she was able to persuade the local school board to hire her as a teacher while convincing them she was eighteen. Her parents' emphasis on education had paid off in a most important manner they couldn't have anticipated: keeping their family together.

In carrying on the tradition of her parents, Wells-Barnett made sure her siblings were educated. She eventually put the older ones into apprenticeships to supplement their educations and took the youngest girls with her to teach in Memphis, where she continued her education at Fisk College in the evenings.

It was during this period that she experienced an event that changed her life. In 1884, she had bought a first-class ticket on a Chesapeake, Ohio, and Southwestern Railroad train, and when she refused to leave the segregated car voluntarily, she was forced off by the conductor. She sued the railroad in a case that won her a $500 judgment and quite a bit of notoriety, including the following headline from the *Memphis Appeal-Avalanche*: "A Darky Damsel Obtains a Verdict for Damages Against the Chesapeake & Ohio Railroad—Verdict for $500." Wells-Barnett's victory was short-lived, as the judgment was overturned in 1887 by the Tennessee Supreme Court. Their reasoning was that her lawsuit constituted harassment since the railroad had provided "like accommodations" for her.

Wells-Barnett wrote of her bitter disappointment in her diary, "I have firmly believed all along that the law was on our side and would, when we appealed to it, give us justice. I feel shorn of that belief and utterly discouraged." She wrote further about this experience in her early writings against segregationist laws for Baptist newspapers throughout the South. If she couldn't always depend on the law, Wells-Barnett learned she had power of her own pen to reach people to do what was right.

As her fame spread, she became more of an activist, attending conventions and becoming involved with a political group. She also joined a literary group, writing and reading essays on many subjects. They were well received, and she was encouraged to write for publication. She began working for a small Baptist weekly, *The Free Speech and Headlight*, which later became *Free Speech* when she became its sole owner.

Wells-Barnett was fearless in writing about the injustices of the school system and the treatment of black students. She saw firsthand in her work that minority schools were not equal and that black children weren't given the same materials and supplies that white schools had. She wrote editorials about these inequities under the pen name Iola. When she included in her charges the allegation that a white member of the school board was having an affair with one of the black teachers, Wells-Barnett was dismissed from her teaching position in 1891. She had been a teacher for thirteen years, but now she had to become a full-time journalist to earn a living. Wells-Barnett later commented, "I thought it was right to strike a blow against a glaring evil and I did not regret it."

She could have been expedient and kept silent for the sake of her job, but she demonstrated she had the courage of her convictions. She was more concerned about the quality of education for others than her own self-preservation.

While still a teacher, she kept a diary from 1885 to 1887, which has been edited by Miriam DeCosta-Willis and titled *The Memphis Diary of Ida B. Wells*. At this time, Wells-Barnett was in her midtwenties and still trying to decide who she was and how to achieve her goals in writing about the injustices against the black people. She was also juggling an active social life as a Victorian lady. The missionary schools she had attended provided her the background of a principled and moral young lady, but Victorian young ladies did not have the drive, "pride, ambition, outspokenness, assertiveness and rebelliousness" that Wells-Barnett had.

During this period, DeCosta-Willis notes, Wells-Barnett struggled with "personal, financial, and professional problems . . . and [she] often complains of exhaustion and frequent bouts of sickness: catarrh, neuralgia, depression, ear problems and colds. Her most difficult struggle, however, is internal. She portrays herself as a fiery, ambivalent, and fiercely independent woman, at war constantly with contrary instincts: an incipient feminism, countered by a straitlaced Victorian femininity; a desire for male companionship, but no wish for marriage, and a longing for personal freedom, checked by a sense of duty to her family."

In 1892, three of her friends, Thomas Moss, Calvin McDowell, and Henry Stewart owned a successful business called Peoples Grocery Company in an area of Memphis known as the Curve. Like Wells-Barnett, they were upwardly mobile, middle-class blacks. There was a white grocery store across the street, and those owners, who weren't pleased to have the competition, made false allegations against its black counterpart. When deputies arrived in plain clothes, the Peoples Grocery Company owners assumed they were thugs sent to harm them, and they began shooting, wounding several. They were hauled off to jail where they were guarded by friends until tempers cooled. Unguarded a few days later, Moss, McDowell, and Stewart were taken out and lynched. As Frederick Douglass put it, "The men lynched at Memphis were murdered because they were prosperous." Wells-Barnett was godmother to Thomas Moss's daughter, and his murder left her outraged.

Brave woman!
You have done your people and mine a service which can neither be weighed nor measured. If American conscience were only half alive . . . a scream of horror, shame, and indignation would rise to Heaven wherever your pamphlet shall be read."

—FREDERICK DOUGLASS

As Fradin recounts, when there was no punishment forthcoming for the perpetrators who denied the victims their legal due process, Wells-Barnett published scathing editorials about the lack of protection for the Memphis citizens, urging them to leave the city to go west:

The city of Memphis has demonstrated that neither character nor standing avails the Negro if he dares to protect himself against the White man or become his rival. There is nothing we can do about the lynching now, as we are outnumbered and without arms. The White mob could help itself to ammunition, but the order was rigidly enforced against the selling of guns to Negroes. There is therefore only one thing left that we can do: Save our money and leave a town which will neither protect our lives and property, nor give us a fair trial in the courts, but takes us out and murders us in cold blood when accused by White persons.

Whole church congregations moved and others followed. Those blacks left behind boycotted white businesses and abandoned the use of public transportation. The city tried to frighten its citizens into staying by telling them Indians or diseases would kill them, but Wells-Barnett refuted these claims by reporting back from areas where the former citizens of Memphis were living. She became a target for angry whites and began carrying a pistol.

She said, "I had already determined to sell my life as dearly as possible if attacked. I felt if I could take one lyncher with me, this would even up the score a little bit."

She pursued her crusade undaunted, conducting her own personal investigations into the lynchings she wrote about. Margaret Truman wrote in *Women of Courage* in 1976, "To call this dangerous work is an understatement. Imagine a lone Black woman in some small town in Alabama or Mississippi, asking questions that no one wanted to answer about a crime that half the Whites in the town had committed."

Only by earnest, active, united endeavors to arouse public sentiment can we hope to put a stop to these demonstrations of American barbarism.

—IDA B. WELLS-BARNETT

A black person could be lynched for any number of perceived offenses: quarreling with whites, being saucy, making threats, and striking a white person in self-defense. Frequently, men were lynched for supposed crimes against white women. Wells-Barnett realized that such alleged crimes were an excuse for lynching, but not the cause. Her investigations uncovered a large number of consensual interracial sexual liaisons, some initiated by white women. While blacks were killed for this behavior, whites seduced and raped black women with apparent impunity. To prove this double standard, Wells-Barnett drew a glaring comparison between a lynch mob that killed a black man from Nashville accused of merely visiting a white woman and another mob that did not harm a white man who had been convicted of raping an eight-year-old black girl.

In one of her most scathing rebukes of lynching, Wells-Barnett wrote in *Free Speech*, "Nobody in this section of the country believes the old thread bare lie that Negro men rape White women. If Southern White men are not careful, they will over-reach themselves and public sentiment will have a reaction; a conclusion will then be reached which will be very damaging to the moral reputation of their women."

Her article triggered a firestorm. The *Memphis Daily Commercial* dubbed her a "Black scoundrel" and rebutted, "There are some things the Southern White man will not tolerate, and the obscene intimations of the foregoing have brought the writer to the outermost limit of public patience." Tellingly, the editorial added that the fact Wells-Barnett had been "allowed to live is evidence as to the wonderful patience of southern Whites. But we have had enough of it." The *Memphis Scimitar* demanded that Wells-Barnett be "tied to a stake at the intersection of Main and Madison streets, branded in the forehead with a hot iron, and tortured with tailor's shears."

Wells-Barnett left for New York after publishing this last article. The *Free Speech* was burned to the ground by an angry mob, and she lost all the money she had invested in her business. When Wells-Barnett arrived in New York, her friend T. Thomas Fortune, publisher of the *New York Age*, greeted her with relief and told her of the "rumpus" she had caused. Wells-Barnett's friends warned her there would be a gunman waiting at every train from the North to kill her if she returned to Memphis.

I expected some cowardly retaliation from the lynchers. I felt that one had better die fighting against injustice than to die like a dog or rat in a trap.

—IDA B. WELLS-BARNETT

"They had destroyed my paper, in which every dollar I had in the world was invested. They had made me an exile and threatened my life for hinting at the truth. I felt I owed it to myself and my race to tell the whole truth," Wells-Barnett said.

Wells-Barnett began writing for the *New York Age* and continued to attack the policy of lynching, hoping to educate the people of the northern states about the atrocities in the South. She began to publish pamphlets such as *Red Record: Tabulated Statistics and Alleged Causes of Lynching in the United States, 1892, 1893, and 1894* and *Mob Rule in New Orleans*. Her public appearances to read her work packed houses.

Invited by the British Anti-Lynching Society, she went to England to garner support from powerful people there to pressure the South to end lynching. Surprised by the courtesy and civility with which she was treated, she remarked, "It was the first time I had met any members of the White race who saw no reason why they should not extend to me the courtesy they would have offered to any lady of their own race."

The *London Sun* published this description of her during her visit, encapsulating both her dynamism and the very horrors that she faced down at home:

Miss Ida B. Wells is a negress, a young lady of little more than twenty years of age, a graceful, sweet-faced, intelligent, courageous girl. She hails from Memphis, Tenn. She is not going back there just now, because the White people are anxious to hang her up by the neck in the market place and burn the soles of her feet, and gouge her beautiful dark eyes out with red-hot irons. This is what the Southern American White man does with a negro or negress for preference, when he wants a holiday sensation; and when he finds a charming victim, such as this sweet girl would make, the mayor of the town orders the schools to be closed, and the parents don their Sunday-go-to-meeting best, and lead the youngsters out by the hand. They all go out to see the gun, and have their photographs taken at the scene of the martyrdom, and there is much rejoicing over the Black sinner that repenteth not."

Wells-Barnett's writing served to educate more than the white establishment. As Fradin documents, no less a figure in black leadership than Frederick Douglass, then seventy-five years old, "visited Ida to tell her that her article had been a 'revelation' to him." While he had disapproved of lynching, Douglass confessed, he had assumed that the victims were guilty. If the greatest living black leader was so misinformed, Wells-Barnett realized, then there must be millions of black and white northerners who didn't know the facts about lynching.

In 1893, Wells-Barnett attended the World's Columbian Exposition in Chicago, and she organized the first black women's club. They were able to raise money to prosecute a white policeman for killing an innocent black man, and later they established the first black orchestra and the first kindergarten for black children.

Wells-Barnett settled in Chicago, where she met Ferdinand I. Barnett, a successful, widowed lawyer and newspaperman. He owned and edited the *Chicago Conservator*, a black weekly newspaper. She, Barnett, and Frederick Douglass wrote a booklet on the exclusion of blacks from the Columbian Exposition titled "The Reason Why the Colored America is Not Represented in the World's Columbian Exposition." Ten thousand copies were distributed during the fair.

In 1895 she married Ferdinand Barnett. She was thirty-three then, late for most women to marry in those times. As Fraden observes, "The marriage was unusual by the standards of a century ago. To begin with, the bride refused to give up her birth name. She was one of the first married women to hyphenate her name, becoming known as Ida B. Wells-Barnett."

The couple were ahead of their time in other ways as well. When most men expected their wives to remain at home and not be involved politically, Barnett encouraged his wife to continue her work. He was also a crusader, and they continued the campaign for equal rights for African-Americans. He did not expect her to handle domestic chores, hiring others to handle the cleaning and laundry. Cooking chores he personally enjoyed and performed himself. By all accounts, it was a happy marriage, and it lasted for the rest of their lives.

Wells-Barnett gave birth to her first child exactly nine months after their wedding. She devoted herself to raising her family with as much vigor and passion as she had for her work. As quoted by Suzanne Freedman, author of *Ida B. Wells-Barnett and the Anti-Lynching Crusade*, Wells-Barnett wrote, "Motherhood is a profession just like school teaching and lecturing, and once I am launched on such a career, I owe it to myself to become as expert as possible in the practice of that profession." Indeed, Wells-Barnett distinguished herself once more by making her fiery political speeches with a nursing baby in tow. Ultimately, the couple produced four children, and Ferdinand Barnett already had two children from a previous marriage, making Wells-Barnett the mother of six.

Even as she devoted more of her time than ever to raising her family, Wells-Barnett continued to work for women's groups and to lead campaigns to expand freedoms for blacks, attacking such Jim Crow restrictions as segregated seating on buses and in theaters. When she exposed segregationist policies of the YMCA, many wealthy donors withdrew their support and gave instead to organizations supporting black causes. Wells-Barnett remained uncompromising in her pursuits, withdrawing from a number of organizations, including the NAACP and the Afro-American Council because she believed them to be appeasers or not activists.

Her editorial style remained as biting and feisty as ever. She called for blacks to be armed to protect themselves, and for punishment to a town where a lynching took place. It was during the time that Wells-Barnett was pregnant with her second child that the Barnetts sold the *Conservator*, and she retired to private life. Her retirement was abbreviated after yet another brutal lynching—this time of a black postmaster—provoked her to lobby Congress and President William McKinley for an antilynching law in 1898. She said unequivocably, "We refuse to believe this country, so powerful to defend its citizens abroad, is unable to protect its citizens at home."

Lynchings continued through the 1890s, some of which Wells-Barnett personally witnessed. It took an extraordinary focus on her mission to countenance so much of the evil that she encountered during her crusade. A lynching could be cause for a huge community party, with people cultivating a carnival-like atmosphere, bringing their children, and posing for souvenir photographs next to the corpses of victims. Fradin presents an especially chilling conversation that Wells-Barnett uncovered during one of her investigations: "Ida B. Wells learned of a seven-year-old witness who was overheard bragging, 'I saw them burn the nigger, didn't I, Mama?' 'Yes, darling,' answered her mother, 'you saw them burn the nigger.'"

Agitate and act until something is done.

—IDA B. WELLS-BARNETT

Her outrage unabated, Wells-Barnett remained a firebrand against such inhumanity. She couldn't go along with Booker T. Washington's quiet racial diplomacy, and she began supporting the more militant W. E. B. DuBois. She had her third and fourth children during this time but continued to investigate and write about the lynchings and race riots that erupted in Illinois and Arkansas. While in Elaine, Arkansas, she listened for hours while a group of men sentenced to die for their part in a riot prayed about dying and being received in heaven. She counseled them to, "Quit talking about dying. If you believe God is all-powerful, believe he is powerful enough to open these prison doors. Dying is the last thing you ought to think about, much less talk about. Pray to live and believe you are going to get out." Indeed, the men did not die. Her pamphlet, *The Arkansas Race Riot*, helped to free them. It became one of her proudest accomplishments. The *Chicago Defender* wrote, "If we only had a few men with the backbone of Mrs. Barnett, lynching would soon come to a halt in America."

People began to disassociate themselves from Wells-Barnett when she refused to compromise on issues of right and wrong, and often her friends and associates would disagree with her. She worried that taking a less aggressive (and more appeasing) stance would only serve to postpone civil rights and, she believed, would only foster more lynchings and perpetuate the lie that blacks were inferior to whites. Historian Thomas C. Holt called her "a lonely warrior." Booker T. Washington was a detractor and influenced others to stand against her. While readily acknowledging that "My temper has always been my besetting sin," Wells-Barnett could not understand why some black organizations chose to marginalize her and exclude her from the decision-making process.

Some did see her as inflexible, but Wells-Barnett believed it was essential for her to remain uncompromising about such life-and-death matters as liberty and justice for blacks in the United States. Mary White Ovington, white founder of NAACP said, "She was a great fighter, but we knew she had to play a lone hand. And if you have too many players of lone hands in your organization, you soon have no game." She also wrote that Wells-Barnett was "fitted for courageous work, but perhaps not fitted to accept the restraint of organization."

Wells-Barnett continued to demonstrate on behalf of women's right to vote, organizing Chicago's Alpha Suffrage Club in 1915, and chairing the Chicago Equal Rights League. She marched in parades and was with the suffragists when they marched to the Republican National Convention and demanded that women be given the right to vote. She played an active role in the National-American Suffrage Association.

The ballot is the right which safeguards all our rights.

—IDA B. WELLS-BARNETT

In biographer Richard M. Haynes's book *Ida B. Wells: Antilynching Crusader*, Wells-Barnett said, "With no sacredness of the ballot there can be no sacredness of human life itself. For if the strong can take the weak man's ballot, when it suits his purpose to do so, he will take his life also. . . . The more complete the disenfranchisement, the more frequent and horrible has been the hanging, shootings and burnings." She argued that blacks were given inferior schools because they had no ballot with which to protest.

In her last years Wells-Barnett ran unsuccessfully for the Senate, then worked as a probation officer in 1913, using her salary to support a branch of the National Urban League in Chicago, which provided lodging, a reading room, and an employment center to serve the needs of the black community. When a new mayor was elected in Chicago, Wells-Barnett lost her job, forcing her to close the doors to the center. It was at this point that she began her autobiography, *Crusade for Justice*, which would not be published until decades later.

In the book, Wells-Barnett expressed her disappointment in the results of her efforts and the ingratitude she experienced at the hands of her fellow blacks: "All at once the realization came to me that I had nothing to show for all those years of toil and labor." She had risked her life, fortune, and companionship throughout her early years to bring justice and equality to the black community, and thought she had wasted her time.

She was rushed to the Daly Hospital on March 21, 1931, and died two days later at the age of sixty-nine from kidney disease. She was buried in Oakwood Cemetery in Chicago.

With all of her years of working tirelessly, speaking endlessly, and writing volumes about the horrors of lynching, the practice went on into the mid-twentieth century, with mob rule in control. Wells-Barnett undertook an enormous task, and she did not live to see that even as formidable a power as President Harry S. Truman could not entirely end the practice of lynching. She did have something to show for her work, but it didn't become obvious until thirty-four years after her death. It wasn't until the 1955 murder of Emmett Till (a fourteen-year-old from Chicago who was murdered because he supposedly whistled at a white woman), and the subsequent acquittal of his killers by an all-white jury that legislation was introduced to Congress, passed, and signed into law in 1965 by President Lyndon Baines Johnson as the Civil Rights Act.

Many times people go unappreciated during their lifetimes, and such was the case with Ida B. Wells-Barnett. In 1941 the Chicago Housing Authority opened the Ida B. Wells Housing Project, and in 1950 the City of Chicago named her one of twenty-five outstanding women in the city's history.

In 1987, the Memphis Community Relations Commission dedicated an historical marker at the former site of the *Free Speech* newspaper offices. In

1990, during the Black History Month observance, the United States Postal Service issued a stamp honoring Ida B. Wells-Barnett.

During her lifetime, Wells-Barnett was a polarizing figure whom newspapers and individuals would alternately praise or attack. While the *New York Times* maintained an adversarial editorial stance against Wells-Barnett throughout her career and dubbed her a "slanderous and nasty-minded mulattress," the *Manchester Guardian* lauded: "Her quiet, refined manner, her intelligence and earnestness, her avoidance of all oratorical tricks and her dependence upon the simple eloquence of facts makes her a powerful and convincing advocate." The *Cleveland Gazette* criticized her for "trying to be pretty as well as smart." Her good friend T. Thomas Fortune wrote: "She has plenty of nerve, she is as smart as a steel trap, and she has no sympathy with humbug."

As Patricia A. Schechter summarized Wells-Barnett in *Ida B. Wells-Barnett and American Reform, 1880–1930*, "She was described as unsexed and supersexed, unladylike and too feminine, a paragon and a prostitute, a 'Black' woman and a 'mulatress,' a martyr and a savior. Uncomfortable with the message, most opponents criticized the messenger." Indeed, Wells-Barnett was a Cassandra of her age: clear-sighted, speaking the uncomfortable truths, and forever struggling against a populace—both black and white—that would not hear her.

A briefer, but no less eloquent summation of Wells-Barnett's efforts came from New Orleans poet Victor-Ernest Rillieux, who immortalized her thusly: "Tout pour l'humanité! Tout pour Dieu! Rien pour soi!" (All for humanity! All for God! Nothing for herself!)

How to Be Like Ida B. Wells-Barnett

1) **Be brave.** Wells-Barnett had the courage to speak out through her writings and activism against the heinous crime of lynching. She also documented hundreds of these murders, so nobody could deny they were happening. In the course of her work, she put her personal safety at risk, but she never second-guessed herself. She was true to her cause, and courage became a logical extension of it. "I felt I owed it to myself and my race to tell the whole truth."

2) **Encourage and seek education.** Education is the great equalizer. Wells-Barnett's parents were slaves at the time of her birth, but they both advocated education and had high expectations for their children. Her father served on the first board of trustees of Shaw University, later Rust College, where Wells-Barnett later attended. "Our job was to go to school and learn all we could," Wells-Barnett wrote.

3) **Take responsibility.** When tragedy struck and Wells-Barnett lost both parents to the yellow fever epidemic of 1878, she rose to the occasion. She vowed, as the oldest sibling, that her family would not be broken up, and she took responsibility for not letting that happen. She persuaded the local school board that she was eighteen and was hired as a teacher because of her strong educational background. In carrying on the tradition of her parents, Wells-Barnett made sure her siblings were educated.

4) **Hone your talents.** As Wells-Barnett's voice and fame as a writer spread, she joined a literary group, writing and reading essays on many subjects. They were well received, and she was encouraged to write for publication.

5) **Have the courage of your convictions.** Wells-Barnett was fearless in writing about the injustices of the school system and the

Cont'd

treatment of the African-American students, witnessing first-hand in her work as a teacher that the schools were not equal. More concerned about the quality of her students' education than preserving her own livelihood, her essays exposed the duplicity of a white school board member and resulted in Wells-Barnett being dismissed from her job. "I thought it was right to strike a blow against a glaring evil and I did not regret it."

6) **Expose hypocrisy.** A black person could be lynched, murdered in cold blood, for any number of perceived minor offenses, including striking a white person in self-defense. Frequently, black men were lynched for alleged sexual crimes against white women, while whites seduced or raped black women with apparent impunity. Wells-Barnett's investigations uncovered a large number of consensual interracial sexual liaisons. She published a glaring comparison of a lynch mob that killed a black man accused of merely visiting a white woman and another mob that did not harm a white man convicted of raping an eight-year-old black girl. Her writings triggered a firestorm. Wells-Barnett escaped to New York, while her newspaper was burned to the ground.

7) **Surround yourself with supportive people.** Wells-Barnett's husband supported her activist work and encouraged her to continue it. She had married another crusader, and together they continued their campaign to fight for the civil and moral rights of blacks in the United States.

19

Mary Kay Ash
1915–2001

Dream Maker

People are definitely a company's greatest asset.
It doesn't make any difference whether the product
is cars or cosmetics. A company is only
as good as the people it keeps.

—Mary Kay Ash

The devoutly religious Mary Kay Ash, founder and chairwoman of Mary Kay Inc., believed in applying the Golden Rule, "Do unto others as you would have them do unto you," to her business practices. The Golden Rule itself was ingrained in Ash by her mother. Mary Kay Ash's story is Horatio Alger-esque in that she risked her life savings of $5,000 to start her company in 1963, against the advice of her accountant and attorney. That amount was worth about $33,000 in today's dollars. Part of the money was used to buy the rights to the first Mary Kay products, which were skin-care formulas she purchased from the family of a cosmetologist she had met about ten years prior and who had recently passed away.

Today, the company sells over $2.4 billion worth of cosmetics wholesale through 1.8 million Mary Kay Independent Beauty Consultants. Mary Kay Inc. is headquartered in Dallas, Texas, and has about thirty-five hundred employees. It has manufacturing facilities in Dallas and China that produce over two hundred different products worldwide.

"Mary Kay never craved fame or wealth—she simply wanted to improve the lives of women. She used her considerable abilities to go about doing that. Over the course of her lifetime and after, her brilliance, generosity, and timeless philosophies brought many honors her way," said Yvonne Pendleton, Independent National Sales Director, Mary Kay Inc.

Ash was the recipient of the Horatio Alger Distinguished American award, as well as being named Lifetime Television's most influential businesswoman of the twentieth century. In an academic study by Baylor University, Ash was named the greatest woman entrepreneur in American history.

"Mary Kay wasn't born into wealth. Her formal education stopped at high school. She became a working woman out of necessity after her husband left her in sole support of three children. She didn't marry into or inherit her business," Pendleton said. "What she did was to take all of her life experiences after a twenty-five-year career [in direct selling], and shape this into something that would forever alter the business landscape for women. In so doing, she would also shatter the notion of glass ceilings for generations of women," Pendleton added.

During her lifetime Mary Kay did everything in her power to assure that women could aspire to greatness in their lives while keeping their priorities in order. She believed in women and she created for women, with her marketing plan, a company not only to enrich their lives but to motivate them to greatness most never believed they could achieve.

—YVONNE PENDLETON

Prior to starting her company, Ash's twenty-five years of direct selling experience include a long association with World Gift, where she'd been their national training director. When her male assistant was promoted over her, at twice her salary, she resigned. She had planned to write a book about what the perfect company attributes should be and instead discovered that she had created her own business plan.

In today's business world, people often spend most of their waking hours at work. Companies have a great power to make their employee's lives better through compassion and basic fairness, or conversely, they can treat employees like personal property. Many people live paycheck to paycheck today, wholly dependent on their salary and other benefits such as health care. Ash believed that people in management have a sacred responsibility to be fair with employees and not unduly, out of pettiness or unfairness, throw their lives into turmoil either through making the workplace a stressful, unhappy place to be, or through unfair terminations.

In *Mary Kay: You Can Have It All*, Ash wrote: "Before our doors opened for business, I vowed that no one associated with my company would ever be subjected to unfair treatment or unjust management. I can say unequivocally that every decision we make at Mary Kay . . . is based on the Golden Rule." Given her success, Ash proved there doesn't have to be a choice between running a company properly and acting responsibly and morally toward those who depend on it for their livelihood.

Ash wrote that she wasn't saying an employee can never be terminated or laid off, but that in these situations a leader should still exercise extreme compassion. "There's even a right way to discharge an employee by the Golden Rule," she said.

> *[Ash] developed people by setting the pace, by educating and encouraging them. Inspiring them to do more and building their confidence through their accomplishments. She was a point of accountability without micromanaging.*
>
> —BARBARA SUNDEN,
> INDEPENDENT NATIONAL SALES
> DIRECTOR, MARY KAY INC.

"A person who lacks compassion is not an admirable leader. . . . It is a mistake to view benevolence as a weakness in business. Real strength entails being considerate and supportive of people's feelings," Ash wrote.

Ash also wrote that leaders are teachers, in addition to being motivators and individuals who demonstrate compassion through caring. She said leaders make the road map to success for others easy to understand and to follow.

"She was such a great leader that the learning was easy, effortless and so natural. Just being around Mary Kay . . . you were learning to become a leader. It was through her example," said Barbara Sunden, Mary Kay

*Mary Kay was one of the
most powerful women I have
ever met but that power was
cloaked in kindness, humility
and compassion.*

—BARBARA SUNDEN,
INDEPENDENT NATIONAL SALES
DIRECTOR, MARY KAY INC.

independent elite executive national sales director. Sunden is currently Mary Kay's number one executive national sales director.

Sunden said Ash's teachings can be broken down to: "She told us how to do it—she showed us how to do it. And then she let us do it. This was one of Mary Kay's major training tips: Tell them how; show them how; and then let them show you how."

While some companies first build themselves through their products, Mary Kay Inc. was built first with motivated people selling great products. It is a people-driven business. It is not an exaggeration to say that Ash determined, all things being equal in products, that caring employees and company representatives could make the distinctive difference. That is not surprising given that one of Ash's most important precepts was that "every person is special." The importance of the individual wasn't simply rhetoric with her; it was a living, breathing reality.

In the new book issued by Mary Kay Inc., *The Mary Kay Way: Timeless Principles from America's Greatest Woman Entrepreneur*, Pendleton wrote in the acknowledgments, "Mary Kay dedicated the original version of this book to 'all those who still believe that *people* and *pride* are the two foremost assets in building a successful business.'"

*Mary Kay led us to know
what to do—what the goal was.
She encouraged us to
formulate a plan and then
to be responsible to take
action on the plan.*

—BARBARA SUNDEN,
INDEPENDENT NATIONAL SALES
DIRECTOR, MARY KAY INC.

Ash was committed to personally greet groups of new employees at the company's Dallas headquarters, to "welcome them into our family," she said. How serious was she about that? Enough to turn down an invitation from the president of the United States. Ash declined an invitation from President Ronald Reagan to attend a White House gala to keep her commitment to greet new employees in Dallas. Jim Underwood, author of *More Than a Pink Cadillac: Mary Kay Inc.'s 9 Leadership Keys to Success*, said Ash believed it was more important to keep her commitment to her new employees than to socialize with the president of the United States.

"I never cease to be amazed at how positively people react when they're made to feel important," Ash said Her attitude was rooted in the flawless logic that "God didn't have time to create a nobody—just a somebody." She believed that everyone has a talent just waiting to be brought out in them if they aren't already employing their gifts.

Mary Kay had more of a leadership style rather than a management style. Managers usually have their people reporting to them often. Managers stay on top of people telling them every step to take and when.

—Barbara Sunden,
INDEPENDENT NATIONAL SALES DIRECTOR, Mary Kay Inc.

"I remember going to her home, during new director's training, [and] was I scared; it was like going to Queen Elizabeth's palace or something of that magnitude," said Sabrina Goodwin Monday, a Mary Kay independent national sales director from Garland, Texas. "Upon our meeting, within minutes, I felt as if I was in a family member's home, warm, sweet, and comfortable. Mary Kay's genuine spirit put me at ease immediately. I felt as if I was special, near and dear to her heart, even though I was one of 300 in her home at the time."

Darlene Berggren of Monument, Colorado, is an independent senior national sales director who has been working with Mary Kay Inc. since 1980. She has helped expand Mary Kay into other countries, including countries in Eastern Europe. "Mary Kay always practiced 'make people feel important.' When she traveled to other countries, she would always try to speak at least a few words in their languages. For one of my meetings, she even recorded a message in Polish saying 'dziekuje' (dzyehn-KOO-yeh), which translates to 'thank you' for the work we were doing sharing the opportunity with Polish women here in the [United States]."

I feel Mary Kay is a woman of influence and power simply for what she stood for. Her strength, humility, and inspiration. Her ability to move women beyond themselves. Her courage and hope-filled dreams that she so beautifully passed on to others.

—Sabrina Goodwin Monday,
INDEPENDENT NATIONAL SALES DIRECTOR, Mary Kay Inc.

Hand in hand with making people feel important, Ash believed you praise people to success. "I believe praise is the best way for a leader to motivate people. At Mary Kay, we think praise is so important that our entire marketing plan is based on it," Ash wrote. "I believe that you should praise people whenever you can; it causes them to respond as a thirsty plant responds to water."

In a survey done of independent national sales directors by Mary Kay Inc. for the release of *The Mary Kay Way*, 60 percent named the company's "Praise People" approach as having the greatest influence on their careers.

Cheryl Warfield, an independent national sales director, said in *The Mary Kay Way*, "by praising people to success . . . we awaken sleeping giants that are within people. And huge success happens from there."

"It's so true that in the workplace, people are always told what they are doing wrong, seldom what they do right," wrote independent national sales director Yvonne Williams.

The motto Ash chose for the company was "God first, family second, career third." She felt family and personal happiness couldn't and shouldn't be sacrificed for professional success. "Mary Kay taught us to put our faith first, our family second and our career third. She said that if we lose our family in the process of our quest for success that we have missed the point," said Karen Piro, a Mary Kay independent executive national sales director who started working with the company in 1975.

"I believe she represents the epitome of womanhood, The BEST of ALL Worlds," Sabrina Goodwin Monday said. "Being a stay-at-home-Mom with an executive income, and maintaining balance and harmony in one's life. The priorities of God first, family second and career third. I'm enjoying the journey totally! Giving women permission to have it all, because of Mary Kay's shared principles in business/life. I LOVE MY LIFE, my family LOVES their LIFE!! Mary Kay used to say, 'If mama ain't happy, ain't nobody happy!'"

Ash's positive attitude wasn't just something she espoused for others, but something she lived by even in the most trying of circumstances. Shortly after deciding to start her company in 1963, her husband died of a heart attack. He was going to play an important role in the new business. It was a devastating blow, but Ash persevered in spite of it.

"She made it clear that one of the reasons she got to where she was, was that she never gave up! I think back to the fact that she started her company one month to the day after her husband passed away at the breakfast table. Every time I have gone through a frustration and think I have it bad (which isn't often) I remember what she persevered through at the very beginning of this company. Many women would not have kept going, especially in 1963. That was just one example of her perseverance," said Lisa Madson, an independent national sales director who began working with the company in 1986.

Sunden said the number one life lesson she learned from Ash was to never give up. "She taught us to find a way or make one—keep on keeping on. A positive attitude was her major teaching, to focus on a positive outcome, to find the seed of greatness in every adversity. She talked about positive thinking all the time. If you think you can, you will, and if you think you can't, you're right."

Nan Stroud, an independent elite executive national sales director whose association with the company dates back to 1968, counts Ash's advice of never giving up the most important advice she received from her, but one that was used in a very personal way. "Our oldest child had many developmental challenges and we were told when she was eight that we should institutionalize her," Stroud said. "Mary Kay encouraged me through conversations and letters to work with all the resources I had to give our daughter a better future. Her encouragement and training empowered me to search for every possible answer . . . and to find many. Today our daughter is a fully-functioning young married woman, with a wonderful, spiritual family and professional life. Every time I see her, I am again so thankful for Mary Kay's continual encouragement and gentle nudging to find a positive solution to a difficult life challenge."

Mary Kay believed in never giving up, and being a victor and not a victim to your circumstances.

—SABRINA GOODWIN MONDAY, INDEPENDENT NATIONAL SALES DIRECTOR, MARY KAY INC.

Stroud added that Ash taught her to "accept what you cannot change and work to make everything else better. I learned that life will not always be what I want it to be, but my attitude and willingness to work through the challenges will always bring victory. I learned to love life as it is and work to make it better for all those around me."

Ash, of course, didn't limit her application of the Golden Rule exclusively to members of Mary Kay, or restrict her philosophy of letting people know they were important to her. "I think Mary Kay resonates with people today because she was someone who was always thinking of and helping other people, female or male, to grow. She modeled the purest of characters. She lived the Golden Rule, and constantly helped others to believe in themselves. She put others' needs before her own, and she always spoke honestly and taught us integrity and the value of each human being," Piro said.

Yvonne Pendleton relates a story that took place the day of Ash's funeral, a very cold day in Dallas in November 2001. "One of our executives noticed a gentleman in short sleeves, and it was obviously very cold. He was standing outside the church, and then someone who was very active in the Direct Selling Association recognized he was a businessman who'd been very successful in founding his own company in the Carolinas. So, someone just went up to him and welcomed him from the company," Pendleton said.

His name was Joe L. Dudley, and he owned Dudley Products Inc. in North Carolina. Pendleton recalled that Dudley said, "'When I heard the news, and when I heard the memorial service was in Dallas today, I had to get here. I took the first flight I could get. I didn't even think about the weather. The reason is I am where I am because Mary Kay took a personal interest in my small start-up company, and all my many questions.'"

One of the most inspiring entrepreneurial leaders, Mary Kay always understood the importance of people and the value they can bring to an organization.

—J. W. MARRIOT JR., CHAIRMAN AND CEO, MARRIOTT INTERNATIONAL, INC.

He had made it a point to sit by Ash at an event where she was being honored to ask her some questions. "She gave him more information than he could ever dream and told him to call her if he had any questions or ran into any obstacles," Pendleton said. "Mary Kay just took a real [as she would with many people], personal interest in his success. Nobody knew he was coming to the funeral. He just came to pay his respects. It just touched all of us. Because there were lots of industry officials there; this story really touched our hearts, because he said he just came to say 'thank you' to her one last time."

How to Be Like Mary Kay Ash

1) **Live by the Golden Rule.** We benefit by being on the receiving end of those who practice the Golden Rule. Consequently, we should all live by its principles when it come to dealing with other people, whose lives and feelings are just as important as ours. The devoutly religious Ash believed in applying the Golden Rule to her life and business practices. "I can say unequivocally that every decision we make at Mary Kay . . . is based on the Golden Rule." Given her success, Ash proved there doesn't have to be a choice between running a company properly and acting responsibly and morally toward those who depend on it for their livelihood.

2) **Trust your instincts.** File this also under "Knowing what you want." Ash risked her life savings of $5,000 to start her company in 1963, against the advice of her accountant and attorney. Estee Lauder did something similar, saying while accountants and lawyers are great at what they do, she and her family made the business decisions.

3) **Set an example.** Ash wrote that leaders are teachers, and that leaders make the road map to success for others easy to understand and to follow. According to independent sales director Barbara Sunden, Ash "was such a great leader that the learning was easy, effortless and so natural. Just being around Mary Kay . . . you were learning to become a leader. It was through her example." Sunden said Ash's teachings can be broken down to: "She told us how to do it—she showed us how to do it. And then she let us do it."

4) **Understand the value of people.** "People are definitely a company's greatest asset," Ash wrote. "It doesn't make any difference whether the product is cars or cosmetics. A company is only as

Cont'd

good as the people it keeps." Ash also wrote, "I never cease to be amazed at how positively people react when they're made to feel important."

5) **Set your priorities.** The motto Ash chose for her company was "God first, family second, career third." She felt family and personal happiness couldn't and shouldn't be sacrificed for professional success. "Mary Kay taught us to put our faith first, our family second and our career third. She said that if we lose our family in the process of our quest for success that we have missed the point," said Karen Piro, independent executive national sales director who started working with the company in 1975.

6) **Never give up.** Ash got to where she was because she never gave up. She believed in being a victor, not a victim. Independent national sales director Barbara Sunden said the number one life lesson she learned from Ash was to never give up. "She taught us to find a way or make one. . . . A positive attitude was her major teaching, to focus on a positive outcome, to find the seed of greatness in every adversity. She talked about positive thinking all the time. If you think you can, you will, and if you think you can't, you're right."

7) **Take an interest in people.** Ash's interest in people wasn't limited to those who worked for her or with her. She impacted the life of Joe Dudley so much so that he felt compelled to pay his respects to her at her funeral, just to say thank you one last time.

8) **Praise people to success.** "I believe praise is the best way for a leader to motivate people. At Mary Kay, we think praise is so important that our entire marketing plan is based on it," Ash wrote. "I believe that you should praise people whenever you can; it causes them to respond as a thirsty plant responds to water." In a survey of independent national sales directors, 60 percent named the "Praise People" approach as having the greatest influence on their careers.

20

Barbara Walters
1929–

Ambition

I listen. . . . that's the most important thing.

—BARBARA WALTERS

For Barbara Walters, success did not come easily. When she decided to make her career in television news back in the 1950s, the industry was male-dominated and chauvinistic, lacking any significant female presence. And Walters's accent and diction would also seem to exclude her from on-camera work. All in all, she was an unlikely prospect to be the woman to break through the gender barrier in television news and pave the way for others.

But newswomen Joan Lunden, Diane Sawyer, Connie Chung, and Oprah Winfrey, among others, have credited Walters with opening doors to opportunities that they might not otherwise have had. While there were other women who had made advances in television news and served as an example before Walters, she is arguably the most important woman in television journalism history.

"I don't think Barbara knows how enormous of an impact she's had on this industry, on women in particular. I don't think she'll ever really fully get it," Oprah Winfrey said to Martin Clancy and Christina Caron in an ABC News online article. "I don't think we'd be here, if it weren't for Barbara. When I first auditioned for my first television job, I got through [it] pretending to be Barbara Walters. . . . I mean, the spirit of Barbara, the image of Barbara, for the first year of my television career, I thought I was Barbara—Black!"

"I never set out to be a trailblazer. I never said, I'm gonna do this, you know, for women. I had no mentors," Walters said, as quoted by Clancy and Caron.

What she had, instead, was a love for the business and a drive to succeed. After becoming established as a well-respected presence on NBC, Walters caught the public's attention with her then-unheard-of $1 million a year salary in 1976 when she moved to ABC. Walters became the highest-paid and the first female network television news anchor when she cohosted the *ABC Evening News* with Harry Reasoner.

"One does not work for money; one works for love," Walters said to Egyptian president Anwar Sadat when, on her first network news broadcast for ABC, he made reference to her salary and his ($12,000) at the end of an interview.

While the ABC news pairing with Reasoner would prove to be one of the most difficult times of her professional life, the *New York Times* said after her first broadcast that she was a "thorough professional, a remarkable woman who has risen to the top in what was once almost exclusively a man's world."

I was the kind nobody thought could make it. I had a funny Boston accent. I couldn't pronounce my R's. I wasn't a beauty.

—BARBARA WALTERS

Two years prior to her ABC move, Walters became the first woman in history to cohost NBC's *Today Show*, and in the process became the first woman ever to cohost on a TV network news show.

America has been watching Barbara Walters for more than forty years. She's made her mark and resonated with the American public through her series of celebrity and newsmaker interviews. In addition to the countless people she's gotten to open up about themselves on national television, she's interviewed every American president since Richard Nixon and brought many of them into the nation's homes through her *Barbara Walters Specials*.

When Egyptian president Anwar Sadat and Israeli prime minister Menachem Begin met after Sadat's historic visit to Israel in November 1977, it was Walters who conducted the first joint interview with them. She has ridden in jeeps with U.S. presidents, such as Ronald Reagan, and with dictators, such as Fidel Castro, with whom she conducted an unprecedented interview. She has run the query-gamut from asking Russian president Boris Yeltsin point-blank if he drank too much, to asking legendary actress Katharine Hepburn what kind of tree she would like to be. In all, she has interviewed heads of state and world leaders, movie stars and celebrities, people in all walks of life. She's even explored the dark side of life by interviewing criminals and the infamous.

Both viewers and interviewees place their trust in Walters. When she makes a promise or gives her word, she does everything in her power to keep it. On her first day coanchoring the ABC network news, she had two interviews prerecorded and ready to go. One was with former Israeli prime minister Golda Meir and the other with Anwar Sadat. Meir wanted a promise that hers would air first, so she could wish all Jewish people (of which Walters is one), a special Yom Kippur greeting in addition to trumping Sadat. Walters agreed to Meir's wishes, but when her producer saw the interviews, he wanted Sadat's first. "I told him about my promise to Golda Meir and argued vehemently against the change, but he was adamant and as this was my first broadcast, I had to go by his decision," Walters said. Meir was furious and never did another interview with her. But Walters did everything she could to keep her promise and vowed to never allow this to happen again.

> *It's a fact that it is much more comfortable to be in the position of the person who has been offended than to be the unfortunate cause of it.*
>
> —Barbara Walters

Katie Couric, the former cohost of the *Today Show* and now the anchor of the *CBS Evening News*, said a few years ago to *Working Woman* magazine that she admires how hungry and competitive Walters is, even after achieving so much. "She will never rest on her laurels," Couric said. "It gives all women a real boost." The late ABC News president Roone Arledge said, too, that Walters continued to improve even after she came to ABC with an already established career and record salary.

Among the awards Walters has garnered: In 1990 she became the first woman inducted into the Academy of Television Arts and Sciences' Hall of Fame "for being acknowledged worldwide as one of television's most respected interviewers and journalists." The Overseas Press Club gave her their highest award, the President's Award, in 1988. She received a Lifetime Achievement Award from the International Women's Media Foundation in 1991.

To connect with her subjects and public, Walters employs a lost art in her interviews: she listens. To prepare for her signature work, she puts herself in the mind of the viewer and asks herself what they really want to know about people like Ronald Reagan, Bill Clinton, Martha Stewart, Margaret Thatcher, Gloria Steinem, Oprah Winfrey, Lucille Ball, and Mel Gibson. She has said that some journalists ask questions to make themselves look smart rather than keeping in mind what is interesting to their viewers. Walters will ask controversial questions, but she tries to keep them within the bounds of good taste.

Wait for those unguarded moments. Relax the mood and, like the child dropping off to sleep, the subject often reveals his truest self.

—Barbara Walters

Meticulous and detailed, Walters writes an average of 250 questions per interview subject in preparation for speaking with them. Many times she will start the interview asking about the subject's childhood because she says it is a safe area and tends to open up all kinds of memories for people.

In 1970 Walters wrote *How to Talk with Practically Anybody About Practically Anything*. "The idea was that there were all kinds of situations in which people just didn't know what to say. These situations included not only when talking to a celebrity, but to someone you don't know at a dinner party; to a person who has just lost a loved one; to a child; to an athlete when you know nothing about sports, to a tycoon—even to a bore," Walters explained in her autobiography, *Audition*.

The 1970 book sold well and has been through eight printings. She offers, then and now, advice on how to get people to open up. One surefire question that will accomplish this, she says, is asking someone about their very first job. "Trust me: everyone, from presidents and movie stars to policemen and moving men, remembers his or her first job and will relate it in minute detail," she wrote.

Walters ended the book with what she called other surefire conversation starters. Some of her favorites that she still uses today are: "If you were not doing the work you are now doing, what would you most like to be doing?" "If you could live at any time in history, when would you have wished to live?" "If you were suddenly given a million dollars and told that you had to spend it just on yourself, what is the first thing you would buy?" "If you were hospitalized for three months but not really too sick whom—and it can't be a relative—would you want in the next bed?"

"[Walters] is intelligent, informed, and charismatic. . . . Her own vulnerability and charisma allow you to be vulnerable with her. She's not trying to get some preconceived notion of what she wants in an interview. . . . She goes into the interview with good and informed questions. She's not interested in burning you, but relentlessly searches for something new," said actress Sharon Stone, as quoted in *Barbara Walters* by Henna Remstein.

Actor Christopher Reeve, paralyzed during a tragic horse-riding accident, said of his famous 1995 interview with Walters that included his wife, Dana: "She made us feel unself-conscious. And that allowed the television audience to see two people as they really are. . . . Barbara gave us room to express [the despair I once felt] and also to talk about how much joy, hopefulness, laughter and love remain in our life." Walters received the prestigious George Foster Peabody Award for her interview with the Reeves.

It was Reeve, Superman on the big screen, who chose Walters to tell his story to. He told her he'd watch her interviews and was impressed that she didn't interrupt her subjects, and that was important to him because his ability to talk was dependent on a respirator. "He could speak as long as the breath held. Then he had to wait for the respirator to generate another breath before he could speak again. It was a slow process, and the interviewer had to be patient. Because I seemed to listen, Reeve chose me to be the person to whom he would tell his story," Walters wrote.

Walters interviewed Reeve several times between September 1995 and November 2003, her last interview eleven months before his death. Reeve and Walters shared the same birthday, September 25, and spent many of them together after they met.

Walters was greatly touched by Reeve's courage and desire to continue his life the best he could after the accident. With the love and support of his wife, Dana, he made many contributions after his accident, including establishing the Christopher Reeve Foundation, which searches for cures to paralyzing spinal cord injuries and seeks to improve the quality of life of those afflicted.

Reeve told Walters that he hoped to walk again and that he would keep working through setbacks. "It's like a game of cards. If you think the game is worthwhile, then you just play the hand you're dealt. Sometimes you get a lot of face cards; sometimes you don't. But I think the game is worthwhile. I really do."

Walters wrote Reeve was one of the celebrities who most affected her life: "Whenever I feel even a little bit of despair, I think of Chris and I tell myself once more how lucky I am and that the game is worthwhile."

Walters began her career in 1953 when the young Sarah Lawrence College graduate was given the job of producing a daily, live, fifteen-minute children's show called *Ask the Camera*. In 1954, she was hired on to CBS's *Morning Show* to research and book guests. Her first opportunity to be in front of the camera came when a runway model failed to show up to host a fashion segment and Walters took her place.

"I never minded doing the so-called female things—fashion shows, cooking spots, whatever . . . but at the same time, it did bother me I wasn't allowed to participate in a Washington [political] interview. . . . That's why I started going out and getting my own interviews," Walters said, as quoted in Remstein.

For example, in July 1956, she went out and got the stories of some of the surviving passengers from the deadly collision of the ocean liners *Stockholm* and *Andrea Doria*. This earned her more challenging work.

Walters was "ambitious, determined. You could see it in her eyes," said *Morning Show* producer Charlie Andrews. "She always knew she wanted to be in front of the camera," said features coordinator Madeline Amgott, also in Remstein's book.

In 1957, CBS canceled their morning show and Walters was unemployed. The marriage to her first husband ended in 1958. Then her father,

Lou Walters, the owner and creative force behind the legendary Latin Quarter nightclubs in Boston, Miami, and New York City, went bankrupt when his cabaret, Café de Paris, closed. Walters, who'd grown up in privileged circumstances that included an eighteen-room house in Newton, Massachusetts, saw her father lose everything, including his Fifth Avenue penthouse, due to his poor financial investments and a tax evasion scandal.

It was Lou Walters's connections that helped get his daughter's foot in the door to start her career in television news. She wrote that her father was sensitive and amusing, well-read, and never without a book. "If I have any writing ability, I get it from him," she said.

Walters took on the responsibility for her family's welfare: "Suddenly, I had to work. . . . I not only had to support myself but my parents and my sister. . . . I knew I'd have to work all my life so I'd never feel financial pressure," she said.

Walters's sister, Jacqueline, was a key person in her life. She was three years older but born, as Walters wrote in *Audition*, mildly mentally retarded. "Just enough to prevent her from attending regular school, from having friends, from getting a job, from marrying. Just enough to stop her from having a real life."

Walters said that she knew from a very early age that at some point Jackie would become her responsibility. "That awareness was one of the main reasons I was driven to work so hard," she wrote, "but my feeling went beyond financial responsibility."

Early on in her life she felt both ashamed of Jackie and guilty because she had so much and her sister had so little. Her relationship with her sister had all the complications that one might expect in Walters's formative years. For example, Walters's mother would often ask her to take Jackie, who was very lonely, with her when she went out with a girlfriend or on a date. Walters loved her sister, but she resented being made to feel different and having restraints put on her life because of Jackie.

Walters supported Jackie until her sister died from ovarian cancer in 1985. "She always loved me. She taught me compassion and understanding. (In later years these feelings would be important to me in interviewing.) Often frustrated herself, often cranky and prone to tantrums, she never expressed resentment or jealousy of me," Walters wrote.

Due to her experiences with Jackie, Walters developed a real empathy for people who've had to overcome obstacles. Because of this, her favorite interviews are not with celebrities or heads of state but with people who have overcome physical, mental, or emotional challenges.

After the CBS morning show was canceled and Walter was without a job, she found herself on the outside of the television industry looking in. She went to work at the public relations firm Tex McCrary Inc. for $60 a week. Her job as a publicist was to book clients on television shows and generate positive press.

Although she was out of the news business, she made the best of it and honed her related journalistic skills by writing client profiles and press releases. Her outstanding work with Tex McCrary led her back into television news in 1961, when she got a temporary thirteen-week contract writing for the *Today Show* for $300 a week.

Her on-air career began in earnest when she covered fashion week in New York City for the *Today Show*. That performance led to Walters being hired on as a full-time writer and being sent to France to cover the Paris fashion show. She delivered on that, too, and was then sent as a member of the press corps to travel with first lady Jacqueline Kennedy on her 1962 trip to India and Pakistan. Walters continued to build her credentials by doing both feature segments and hard news interviews, such as those she did in the aftermath of the assassination of President John F. Kennedy. In 1964 she earned a promotion to full reporter, and in 1974 she was promoted to cohost of the *Today Show*.

According to Walters, initially she was not allowed to write for the male correspondents or to ask questions in "male-dominated" areas such as economics or politics, and she was forbidden to interview guests on-camera until all of the men on the *Today Show* had finished asking questions. Thanks in part to Walters's contributions, these commandments no longer apply, wrote Susan McLeland for the Museum of Broadcast Communications.

Walters credits *Today Show* host Hugh Downs, who anchored it from 1962 to 1971, with being her champion and encouraging producers to give Walters a bigger role. "If Hugh had not fought for my opportunity to appear regularly on *Today*, I would not have happened in this business," Walters said to *Good Housekeeping* magazine in 1992.

Downs said, "In truth, she discovered herself. . . . With her talents, she would have eventually happened without me."

When Downs departed the show in 1971, Walters had to deal with new host Frank McGee, a man she says felt threatened by the thought of a woman as his professional equal.

McGee, Walters wrote, didn't consider the *Today Show* a serious news program. He arranged a meeting with NBC president Julian Goodman and asked Walters to attend. At the meeting he complained that Walters's participation in interviews diminished their importance. "He felt my role on the show should be restricted to, as he called them 'girlie' interviews." McGee didn't want Walters to join in on news-making interviews.

When Goodman instantly agreed to McGee's requests, Walters was shocked. She'd built impressive credentials to that point and decided she needed to stand up for herself and against sexism toward female reporters.

"I was nervous in front of these two formidable men, but somehow I summoned up my courage and found my voice. I told Goodman that I hadn't been on the program all those years and contributed all the interviews I'd done to go back to the era of the tea-pouring girl. I just couldn't accept his decision . . . looking back, I consider that day to be one of the milestones of my career. I cannot imagine what my future would have been had I just swallowed my feelings and restricted my work to the 'girlie' assignments."

The only compromise Walters won was to be able to ask the fourth question of an important newsmaker, after McGee had asked the first three. To counter this, Walters set her sights on going outside of the studio to get interviews that she would conduct. She read three or four newspapers a day as well as magazines to generate ideas.

To contact her would-be interview subjects, Walters wrote letters. "What I tried to do in the letters—and still do—is not to tell the people why I want to do the interview, but why they should want to do the interview. Do they feel they are being misunderstood or maligned? Would they like the opportunity to tell their side of the story?" Walters said.

Some of the notable interviews Walters went out and got were with Henry Ford II of the Ford Motor Company, Tricia Nixon, daughter of President Nixon, Dean Rusk, former secretary of state, and H. R. Haldeman, Nixon's chief of staff.

Veteran newsman Sam Donaldson, who worked with Walters at ABC, admired her go-getter style, as he wrote in his book *Hold On, Mr. President!* "Barbara Walters was someone who would come driving up to a story in a limousine, dressed expensively and fashionably, dive into the [muddy water] and swim to the story, grab it in her teeth, swim back to her limousine with it, and drive off to the studio with an exclusive—while the rest of us were still hopping from rock to rock trying to keep our trousers dry."

One of Walters's most difficult professional challenges came with her $1 million annual contract—hosting *ABC Evening News* with veteran newsman Harry Reasoner in 1976.

Reasoner saw Walters as more of a celebrity interviewer than pure journalist, and his disdain for her style was evident subtly on the air and blatantly in private. Remstein said that in his 1981 autobiography, *Before the Colors Fade*, Reasoner claimed his problem was not with Walters on a personal level but with the perception of her hire. "Whether it was a stunt or not, it was going to be perceived as a stunt," he wrote.

Sam Donaldson recalled the first night of the Reasoner-Walters pairing. "We had a big audience. Everyone came to see the million-dollar baby. . . . Barbara was a little stiff, but who wouldn't be? Harry was standoffish, and treated her as if 'Who is this dame' who he has to sit with."

While the *New York Times* wrote that Walters hadn't "faltered or fumbled embarrassingly on the new job," other critics weren't as kind as time went on. Even her first two interviews, with Sadat and Meir, a current and former head of state, were actually dismissed by some as "celebrity interviews." Although they gained seven hundred thousand new viewers during her first seven weeks on the air, and their Nielsen rating went up to 10.5 from 9.9, ABC's network news was still entrenched in third place behind CBS and NBC.

As Reasoner's and Walters's on-air tension became obvious, and stories emerged about the difficult pairing, hundreds of letters from female fans who'd observed Reasoner's antagonism toward Walters offered her support. These women, Walters wrote, "related their experiences of harassment and discrimination, their own inability to climb the ladder to success in their all-male environments. 'Hang in there,' they wrote. 'If you can make it, we can make it.'" She tried to reply personally to as many of the letters as possible.

During this period of time, Walters flaw-
lessly moderated the third 1976 presidential
debate between Governor Jimmy Carter and
President Gerald Ford. Still, criticism came
when she interviewed the victor, Carter,
shortly after the election for the first *Barbara
Walters Special.* Some of the questions and a
final comment by Walters, "Be wise with us, Governor. Be good to us," had
Morley Safer of *60 Minutes* say on his radio commentary, "The interview
with Governor Carter is really what ended Ms. Walters's brief career as a
journalist and placed her firmly in the ranks of . . . the Merv Griffins and
Johnny Carsons."

*You know, you really are
an inspiration to women
all over America.*

—FORMER PRESIDENT
LYNDON JOHNSON TO
BARBARA WALTERS

Overall the move to network cohost proved to be a public relations disaster. Low ratings and criticism of an "infotainment mentality" was
thought to be taking over the broadcast, McLeland wrote. The experiment
ended in mid-1978. Reasoner went back to CBS, three anchors now made
up ABC's network news, and Walters, valued by network news president
Roone Arledge, was given the title of "chief correspondent for special
events," which she found preferable to anchoring the news. Rather than
complain or make excuses, she took the high road and set about reinventing herself in addition to winning the respect of her colleagues.

"It's six o'clock in the morning, she'd be out on the rope line with the
rest of us," Donaldson said. "She was going to work hard, never mind
that she had been demoted and it was all in the press. And she was going
to demonstrate that she had the right stuff, as Tom Wolfe would say. And,
for me, ever since that day, she's had the right stuff. . . . She demonstrated
that she wanted to be serious. . . . And she was gonna prove that she could
do it."

Walters reinvented herself with her *Barbara Walters Specials.* While she
did interview celebrities, she also continued to reveal her hard news credentials during interviews with heads of states and newsmakers. Besides Sadat
and Begin and the U.S. presidents, Walters interviewed British prime minister Margaret Thatcher and business giant and presidential contender Ross
Perot. You name the person, and there is a reasonable chance Barbara
Walters has interviewed him or her.

In addition to her specials, in 1979 Walters became a regular contributor to the ABC newsmagazine show *20/20*, and in 1984 she was officially reunited with Hugh Downs as his cohost on the show. Walters left the show in 2004. In 1997 she became executive producer and cohost of the popular morning program on ABC, *The View*.

Success can make you go one of two ways. It can make you a prima donna, or it can smooth the edges, take away the insecurities, let the nice things come out.

—Barbara Walters

As she looks back on her career, Walters wrote, "On the negative side there were the Frank McGees and the Harry Reasoners, who were threatened by the thought of a woman as their professional equal. On the positive side there have been plenty of men and women who had no concerns whether it was a man or a woman interviewing them."

One somewhat sore spot for Walters during her difficult times at ABC was the *Saturday Night Live* parody of her by comedienne Gilda Radner. Radner as "Baba Wawa" would overexaggerate Walters's speech impediment, substituting Ws for Rs and Ls. Walters herself offers an example of Radner's routine in: "Hewwo! This is Baba Wawa hewe to say fawewell. . . . This is my wast moment on NBC and I want to wemind you to wook for me awong with Hawwy Weasoneh weeknights at seven o'cwoc. . . . dewivering wewevant news stowies with cwystal cwahity."

While many found the *Saturday Night Live* skit very funny, and it became a signature of the show during that time period, Walters was not amused. "I found it extremely upsetting. I was feeling so down that I probably wouldn't have found anything funny," she wrote. Walters said people started calling her "Baba Wawa" behind her back *and* to her face.

"I felt they were laughing at me rather than laughing at Gilda's characterization of me," she wrote. Walters credits her daughter Jackie with setting her straight. "Oh Mom. Lighten up," Jackie said. Walters's daughter helped her realize she was losing perspective. "Where was my sense of humor?" Walters said.

She eventually met Radner and the two had a nice meeting and parted as friends. When Radner died of ovarian cancer in 1989 at age forty-two, Walters sent a note to her husband, actor Gene Wilder, in which she paid tribute to Radner. It read: "She made me laugh. I will miss her. Baba Wawa."

Remstein writes that while Walters recognizes her role as a barrier breaker in television journalism, she credits the contributions of others who were at the forefront of change in the roles and opportunities for women. "My contributions were relatively small," Walters modestly said, as quoted by Remstein. "Because I was able to go off and interview a head of state and do a serious, good job, people could no longer say, 'Only a man can do that, because the head of state won't take it seriously.' But the success of women in TV and in other fields is because of the whole women's movement and the changes in this country. It's much more [women's rights activists] Gloria Steinem and Betty Friedan than it is Barbara Walters."

How to Be Like Barbara Walters

1) **Work at what you love.** Walters knew that she wanted to work in the television news even though the industry was male-dominated and chauvinistic. She wasn't trying to be a trail-blazer; she just wanted to do her job well, and that led her to the top. "One does not work for money, one works for love."

2) **Don't let others set limitations for you.** "I was the kind nobody thought could make it. I had a funny Boston accent. I couldn't pronounce my R's. I wasn't a beauty." But Walters didn't let the opinions of others keep her from pursuing her dreams. In the end, she became arguably the most important woman in television journalism history.

3) **Always strive to improve.** Walters is not known for resting on her laurels. In spite of all her successes, she continues to work at improving her craft. Katie Couric told *Working Woman* magazine that she admires how hungry and competitive Walters is, even after achieving so much.

4) **Be a good listener.** Walters attributes much of her success as an interviewer to her willingness to listen. Christopher Reeve appreciated Walters's approach; he noted that she didn't inter-rupt him, and that's why he agreed to be interviewed by her. "Because I seemed to listen, Reeve chose me to be the person to whom he would tell his story."

5) **Understand your audience.** Walters doesn't ask questions to make herself look smart, as other journalists sometimes do. Instead, she keeps her audience in mind, asking herself what it is they really want to know. She also considers the interview from her subjects' viewpoint. Instead of telling them why she wants to do the interview, Walter instead tells them why she thinks they will want to do it. "Do they feel they are being

Cont'd

misunderstood or maligned? Would they like the opportunity to tell their side of the story?"

6) **Use a personal touch.** There is still power in a personal letter, as Walters demonstrates. She prefers a personal letter to a phone call when trying to arrange an interview. And she's in good company. Mother Teresa, Margaret Thatcher, and Eleanor Roosevelt, among others, utilized the power of personal letters.

7) **Be prepared.** Walters is meticulous and detailed when preparing for interviews, coming up with an average of 250 potential questions per interview subject. Obviously she can't ask that many questions, but going through this process helps her be thoroughly prepared for the interview.

8) **Take responsibility for others.** Walters knew from an early age that she would someday be responsible for the care of her sister, Jacquelyn. She willingly took on that responsibility, and it was one of the reasons she was driven to work so hard. After her father lost everything, Walters supported her parents and her sister. She supported Jacquelyn until she died in 1985, never considering her a burden. "She taught me compassion and understanding."

9) **Know what you want.** Walters's goal was always to be in front of the camera, rather than work as a behind-the-scenes writer. When she ran into resistance from her on-air cohosts, she went outside of the studio to conduct interviews on her own.

10) **Stand up for yourself.** Walters was a successful reporter for the *Today Show* when new host Frank McGee arrived in 1971. Claiming that Walters's participation in serious interviews diminished their importance, McGee demanded that her role be limited to, as he called them, "girlie" interviews. Although she was nervous, Walters stood up to McGee and NBC president Julian Goodman, insisting that she had earned her place

Cont'd

on the *Today Show* and refused to go back to the "era of the tea-pouring girl." Walters considers that day one of the milestones in her career. "I cannot imagine what my future would have been had I just swallowed my feelings and restricted my work to the 'girlie' assignments."

11) **Don't give up because of setbacks.** When CBS canceled their morning show in 1957 and Walter was without a job, she wasn't too proud to look for work outside of the television industry. She used her new job as a publicist for a public relations firm to further hone her journalistic skills and as a springboard back into television news.

12) **Fight through adversity.** When Walters was taken off the ABC network news, some saw it as a demotion or downright failure. Rather than complain or make excuses, Walters set about reinventing herself, winning the respect of her colleagues in the process. "She was going to work hard, never mind that she had been demoted and it was all in the press. And she was going to demonstrate that she had the right stuff," Sam Donaldson recalled.

Walters reinvented herself with her *Barbara Walters Specials*, went on to cohost *20/20*, and in 1997 she became executive producer and cohost of the popular morning program on ABC, *The View*.

13) **Laugh at yourself.** Don't take yourself too seriously. At first, Gilda Radner's "Baba Wawa" sketch on *Saturday Night Live* bothered Walters. But in time, with the help of her daughter, Jackie, Walters was able to laugh at herself. She paid tribute to Radner after her death with a condolence note to Radner's husband, Gene Wilder, which she signed "Baba Wawa."

21

Rachel Carson
1907–1964

Naturalist

We cannot have peace among men whose
hearts find delight in killing any living creature.
By every act that glorifies or even tolerates such
moronic delight in killing, we set back
the progress of humanity.

—RACHEL CARSON

Even before Rachel Carson's book *Silent Spring* was published in 1962, it was sending shock waves through offices and boardrooms of the nation's largest chemical manufacturing giants. Carson wrote in *Silent Spring* that every day insecticide sprays, dusts, and aerosols were being applied indiscriminately to our forests and to people's farms, homes, and gardens. She called them "nonselective chemicals" that wipe out both the insects they're intending to and ones they're not.

She wrote that these chemicals possess the power "to still the song of birds and the leaping of fish in the streams, to coat the leaves with a deadly film, and to linger on in soil—all this though the intended target may be only a few weeds or insects." Carson then asked the question for everyone to ponder: "Can anyone believe it is possible to lay down such a barrage of poisons on the surface of the earth without making it unfit for all life?" She said these chemicals shouldn't be called *insecticides*, which wipe out pests, but that they should be termed *biocides*, because they wipe out living organisms—and therefore life.

Silent Spring was a stunning indictment of the proliferation of chemical pesticides such as DDT and their deadly effects on wildlife, the environment, and human health. Meticulously researched and eloquently written, it was the first work of its kind to alert the public about a danger that was not widely known.

Velsicol, Monsanto, American Cyanamid, in fact the whole chemical industry, supported no less by the U.S. Agricultural Department, the American Medical Association, and segments of the media, tried to squash the serialized version of the book, which was appearing first in the *New Yorker* magazine that spring. But Carson was no bug, and a showdown between an entire industry and her eloquent and moving presentation of her findings in *Silent Spring* was in motion.

From the time she was a child, Carson was imbued with a love of nature. She was born in 1907 in Springdale, a town in the Allegheny Valley of Pennsylvania. Her parents, Robert Warden and Maria McLean Carson, lived on a sixty-five-acre farm surrounded by beautiful woods and not far from the shores of the Allegheny River. Maria Carson instilled in her bright, precocious daughter a love of reading and learning. She used long walks through the wondrous laboratory of the woods, streams, and fields to ignite her daughter's passion for nature.

"I can remember no time when I wasn't interested in the out-of-doors and the whole world of nature. Those interests, I know, I inherited from my mother and have always shared with her. I was rather a solitary child and spent a great deal of time in woods and beside streams, learning the birds and the insects and flowers," Carson recalled in *The House of Life* by Paul Brooks.

Socializing with people was never a top priority for Carson. She always preferred to spend her time exploring the local countryside or caring for her farm animals. It became second nature to her to be alone often.

Another passion Maria Carson fostered in her daughter was a love of writing, and Rachel Carson pursued it fervently as a child. Carson's literary career got off to an auspicious and early start when her short story, "A Battle in the Clouds," was published by *St. Nicholas* literary magazine for children. Carson was only ten when she joined the ranks of such authors as Stephen Vincent Benét, Ring Lardner, Edna St. Vincent Millay, Sterling North, Cornelia Otis Skinner, and Eudora Welty, all of whom were published for the first time in the pages of *St. Nicholas*.

Carson continued writing throughout her teen years, submitting her poetry to periodicals, and eventually attending the Pennsylvania College for Women as an English major. Her "sense of wonder" for the natural world was reawakened in her junior year when she took a required biology course; she immediately switched her major to zoology. At the time, Carson felt that she was effectively abandoning her fledgling career as a writer. She didn't know it then, but her twin passions for writing and science would complement each other in the years to come.

The value Carson placed on intellectual achievement paid off as she graduated magna cum laude in 1929 and then earned her master's degree in zoology, a subject she taught for a few years at the University of Maryland.

While teaching at the University of Maryland, Carson, now in her twenties, began taking summer courses at the prestigious Marine Biological Laboratories in Woods Hole, Massachusetts. And as with everything else she had an interest in, Carson became engrossed in study. She explained, "I had never seen it. I dreamed of it and I longed to see it, and I read all the sea literature I could find."

It was in the rocky intertidal zone of the coastline at Woods Hole that Carson first encountered—and became enchanted with—the intriguing creatures and mysteries of the sea.

By 1935, Carson slowly started to combine her two great passions of writing and science by taking part-time work for the U.S. Bureau of Fisheries. She penned radio scripts to educate the public about undersea life, which led a year later to a full-time position as an aquatic biologist. At the same time, she contributed feature articles, mostly relating to marine zoology, to the *Baltimore Sun* to supplement her meager income.

The strong, lyrical prose that characterized even the most scientific of Carson's writing didn't go unnoticed by an editor for one of her pieces for a government publication. He thought the writing so elegant, so unusual, that he insisted that she submit it to the *Atlantic Monthly*, which she did.

To Carson, the important things in life were intellect and achievement. And as long as she was true to those values, she felt, life would provide whatever she needed.

—E. A. TREMBLAY,
RACHEL CARSON: AUTHOR/ECOLOGIST

Carson would never have her poetry published, but in September 1937, the *Atlantic Monthly* published her essay "Undersea," her first publication in a popular well-known national magazine. As excerpted here, "Undersea" featured the same theme and tone that would inform her later works:

To sense this world of waters known to the creatures of the sea we must shed our human perceptions of length and breadth and time and place, and enter vicariously into a universe of all-pervading water. For to the sea's children nothing is so important as the fluidity of their world. It is water that they breathe; water that brings them food; water through which they see . . . water through which they sense vibrations equivalent to sound.

She decided to build on her success by combining "Undersea" with another article titled "Chesapeake Eels Seek the Sargasso Sea" as a starting point for her first book. The moment arrived when both her passions could be brought together for a single purpose and vision. Carson explained, "It dawned on me that by becoming a biologist I had given myself something to write about."

Carson had a specific goal in mind when she set out to write her first book: she wanted to make the sea and the life that depended on it come alive for her readers as vividly as it had in reality for her. That book, *Under the Sea-Wind*, was published in 1941. The *Scientific Book Club Review* set the tone of its critical notices: "Not since the publication of *Salar the Salmon* has there been a volume so replete with information about sea life. There is poetry here, but no false sentimentality. There is ruthlessness as well as beauty in nature." Carson would later say that *Under the Sea-Wind* was her favorite among her books. But in spite of the positive reviews, it would not make much of a splash in the literary world, and hence, no money to speak of.

Meanwhile, Carson continued working for what eventually became the U.S. Fish and Wildlife Service. With her writing talent and strong work ethic came an increase in her editorial duties. The service promoted her, first to information specialist in 1946 and then to chief editor of publications in 1949.

Undeterred by the lack of public interest in her first book, Carson soon had a second work in progress that would deal with the origins and geologic aspects of the sea. As usual, Carson's research on the subject was exhaustive. "I believe I consulted, at a minimum, somewhat more than a thousand separate printed sources," she noted.

Carson was a slow, painstaking writer, preferring to revise paragraph by paragraph, sometimes even sentence by sentence, before she went on to the next.

—LINDA LEAR,
RACHEL CARSON: WITNESS FOR NATURE

Despite all the hard work, Carson's agent circulated this work in progress, only to have it rejected by no fewer than fifteen magazines, including the *National Geographic* and the *Saturday Evening Post*. It finally reached the *New Yorker*, which immediately recognized its value and serialized it as "A Profile of the Sea."

The entire manuscript was published in 1951 as *The Sea Around Us*, which sold over two hundred thousand copies in hardcover within the year. The book garnered for Carson the John Burroughs Medal and the National Book Award.

In his book *Rachel Carson: Author/Ecologist*, biographer E. A. Tremblay documents that during her acceptance speech for the 1952 National Book Award, Carson delineated her overall goal in writing: "The aim of science is to discover and illuminate truth. And that, I take it, is the aim of literature, whether biography or history or fiction." As to her writing style, she explained, "If there is poetry in my book about the sea, it is not because I deliberately put it there, but because no one could write truthfully about the sea and leave out the poetry."

Carson had stepped into the national spotlight. Her "arrival" on the public scene, with all the attendant success, would allow Carson to financially leave the U.S. Fish and Wildlife Service to concentrate on writing full time. She retired from the department in 1952.

Carson was able to buy some land that summer on the coast of Maine, near West Southport. It was a magical place for Carson, one she had been visiting with her mother since 1946. She built a cottage on the Sheepscot River so that she could remain enmeshed in nature and be near the sea she loved.

She could have spent the rest of her life writing at her leisure of the astonishing beauty of the natural world, and for her, it would have been a perfect life. Her writing would support her, and she would be able to stay close to the sea she loved, doing the thing she loved most: writing about nature. But Carson's unique sensitivities to nature were about to put her at the forefront of exposing a new and serious danger that was invisible to most everyone else: the poisoning of America's fragile and vital ecosystems by chemical pesticides.

Carson's new mission arrived in the form of a letter she received from Olga Owens Huckins of Duxbury, Massachusetts. In the letter, Huckins lamented that DDT, which was being sprayed almost indiscriminately where Huckins lived, was killing the local songbirds. Answering the call, Carson decided her pen would be her best weapon to fight this war, and she began exhaustive research into the matter.

To this point, no one really knew how serious the matter was. DDT had been peddled to the agricultural and pest abatement industries as an effective control against insects that destroyed crops, harmed livestock, and spread such dreaded diseases as malaria. In fact, the inventor of DDT, Swiss chemist Paul Hermann Müller, had been awarded the Nobel Prize for Physiology or Medicine in 1948 for creating what seemed to be an invaluable tool in the fight against disease and starvation worldwide.

It took the truly keen observers of nature—scientists, birdwatchers, and other kindred souls of Carson's to stumble upon the fact that DDT was undermining the delicate structure of the world's ecosystems. It was killing smaller creatures—insects, birds—at the bottom of the food chain, and it was winding up in more concentrated and dangerously toxic doses at the very top of the food chain, where human beings reside.

The more she learned about pesticides, their use and effects, the more appalled Carson became about what they were doing to the environment. "What I discovered was that everything which meant the most to me as a naturalist was being threatened, and that nothing I could do would be more important," Carson said.

Carson decided to use her celebrity to shed light on an issue that she felt needed to be pushed to the forefront of our national consciousness. She started writing what would become *Silent Spring*. And as she embarked on her sacred crusade, she was met by resistance and apathy at every turn.

As she sent out her essays, they were universally rejected by numerous publications, including *Reader's Digest*. The scale of the danger Carson was calling to their attention was too great for these publishers to believe. Some thought she was an alarmist and a scaremonger. However, what Carson was saying was true, and she would not allow her message to be ignored.

Undaunted, Carson kept pushing forward, amassing voluminous amounts of research and documentation to back up her arguments. Her persistence finally paid off when the *New Yorker* decided to run the serialized version of *Silent Spring* in June 1962.

Because of her stellar reputation for painstaking research and literary eloquence, and armed with her newfound fame, Carson believed she would be able to count on sizable support from a variety of sources. Conservation organizations of the day, as well as leading scientists in numerous fields, would back her to the hilt. They might even be able to command investigations and hearings.

The discipline of the writer is to learn to be still and listen to what his subject has to tell him.

—RACHEL CARSON

The battle was now underway. Carson's opening barrage from the very first chapter reverberates as much today as it did when *Silent Spring* was released in 1962. Opening her masterwork, she wrote:

> *There was once a town in the heart of America where all life seemed to live in harmony with its surroundings. . . . Then a strange blight crept over the area and everything began to change. . . . There was a strange stillness. . . . The few birds seen anywhere were moribund; they trembled*

violently and could not fly. It was a spring without voices. On the mornings that had once throbbed with the dawn chorus of scores of bird voices there was now no sound; only silence lay over the fields and woods and marsh.

Not surprisingly, the chemical industry, which was reaping huge profits from the worldwide manufacture and distribution of pesticides, wanted to maintain the status quo. What was surprising was the degree to which they would go to fight Carson.

They threatened Carson with lawsuits. They derided her in public information pamphlets and through the media as a "hysterical woman" who wasn't qualified to write such a book. One review accused her of downright errors, oversimplifications, and unsound generalizations. They tried to portray her as an alarmist.

Yet the "hysterical woman" at the center of this firestorm was already a bestselling author and National Book Award winner for *The Sea Around Us*. This author they deemed "unqualified" was an accomplished scientist with a master's degree in zoology from Johns Hopkins University. She had worked as a marine biologist for the U.S. Fish and Wildlife Service. Rachel Carson was no "lightweight."

I am a slow writer, enjoying the stimulating pursuit of research far more than the drudgery of turning out manuscript.

—RACHEL CARSON

Carson also knew she had the facts on her side; they were gleaned from her own studious and meticulous research even before she had begun to write *Silent Spring*. Her high work standards as a researcher served as one of her most effective means of defense.

Carson also had the backing of her colleagues in the scientific community as well as the *Audubon and National Parks Magazine*, which published additional excerpts from *Silent Spring* that summer. And Carson was not one to back down from what she saw as her duty to educate the world about what she now knew. As activist author Marty Jezer recounted in his book, *Rachel Carson: Biologist and Author*, Carson vowed that "there would be no peace for me if I kept silent."

The industry smear campaign, which had actually managed to dupe the

American Medical Association into coming out on their side, eventually backfired. The bad publicity only served to bring more public awareness to Carson's book, and *Silent Spring* became a runaway bestseller.

The brouhaha over *Silent Spring* was reaching epic proportions. "Perhaps not since the classic controversy over Charles Darwin's *The Original of Species* had a single book been more bitterly attacked by those who felt their interests threatened," said author Paul Brooks.

Over time, both the public and government would get involved. It was the television age, and people not only read the book, but would hear about it in the news and on TV. *CBS Reports* scheduled an hour-long program about it as sales for *Silent Spring* passed the half-million mark. Despite two major corporate sponsors withdrawing their support, the network, refusing to bow to outside pressure, went ahead with the broadcast. It drew an estimated viewing audience of 10 to 15 million.

The show won few friends for the chemical industry and eroded public confidence in government officials. What it did do was allow Carson, not her critics, to define the issue. She explained on *CBS Reports*: "Man's attitude toward nature is today critically important simply because we have now acquired a fateful power to alter and destroy nature. But man is a part of nature and his war against nature is inevitably a war against himself. . . . Now I truly believe that we in this generation must come to terms with nature, and I think we're challenged as mankind has never been challenged before to prove our maturity and our mastery, not of nature, but of ourselves."

After the broadcast, President John F. Kennedy discussed the book at a press conference. He called for a special panel to be appointed with the sole purpose of examining its conclusions. The findings the panel reported were a complete and total validation of Carson's writings of the potential dangers of pesticides as well as a scathing indictment of corporate and bureaucratic indifference to those very same hazards, prompting eventual congressional hearings.

And through it all, Carson withstood the slings and arrows with dignity and grace, as well as a few well chosen one-liners aimed at her critics who, on top of everything else, would try to brand her as a "Communist." Twisting their paranoid precepts right back at them, she said, "It is one of the ironies of our time that, while concentrating on the defense of our country against enemies from without, we should be so heedless of those who would destroy it from within."

Silent Spring has been compared in this respect to Harriet Beecher Stowe's *Uncle Tom's Cabin*: both books, in rare company, have transformed society. Slavery was already a hot-button issue in pre–Civil War America by the time *Uncle Tom's Cabin* saw publication, while *Silent Spring* jump-started environmental protection as an important issue worthy of national debate. It could be easily argued that Carson's crusade to put her issue in the public awareness was harder won. But both books, authored by women of strong vision and singular dedication, withstood criticism from powerful and moneyed forces that the authors were unqualified to press their cases. And both books—and their authors—prevailed for the betterment of the nation.

The writer must never attempt to impose himself upon his subject. He must not try to mold it according to what he believes his readers or editors want to read. His initial task is to come to know his subject intimately, to understand its every aspect, to let it fill his mind. Then at some turning point the subject takes command and the true act of creation begins.

—RACHEL CARSON

When Harriet Beecher Stowe met President Abraham Lincoln at the height of the Civil War, he reportedly said to her, "So you're the little lady who started this whole thing." Exactly a century later, when Carson was testifying before Congress in 1963, after the release of *Silent Spring*, Senator Abraham Ribicoff's welcome echoed Lincoln's words. "Miss Carson," he said, "you are the lady who started all this."

At the time of her greatest battle and greatest triumph, Carson was fighting a two-front war. Her enemies included not only the corporate interests and their government and media lackeys seeking to crush and defame her but also breast cancer. Carson, who was diagnosed while writing *Silent Spring*, had been given very little information about her condition early into the battle. Her physician at the time did not believe that women needed to hear the truth about their disease if it could not be successfully eradicated. Eventually, she underwent a radical mastectomy and radiation treatment, and she often wrote while fighting against intolerable physical pain and exhaustion. She wrote because she felt time was running out for the environment. Time, it turns out, was also running out for her.

As she battled the cancer, Carson derived strength to carry on both fights from her mother, one of her biggest influences, who, Carson said, "could fight fiercely against anything she believed wrong, as in our present Crusade! Knowing how she felt about that will help me to return to it soon and to carry it through to completion."

Carson won her battle with her critics and brought the dangers of chemical pesticides to a national audience. But she would lose her battle with breast cancer in 1964 at the age of fifty-seven. Ironically enough, new research indicates a link between this disease and exposure to toxic chemicals, including DDT. Rachel Carson lived, and may have died, for her life's work.

Al Gore, former vice president, Academy Award winner for his eco-disaster documentary *An Inconvenient Truth*, and 2007 Nobel Peace Prize winner for his global efforts on behalf of the environment, writes in his introduction to the 1994 edition of *Silent Spring*: "Carson brought two decisive strengths to this battle: a scrupulous respect for the truth and a remarkable degree of personal courage. She had checked and rechecked every paragraph in *Silent Spring*, and the passing years have revealed that her warnings were, if anything, understated."

Gore adds: "*Silent Spring* came as a cry in the wilderness, a deeply felt, thoroughly researched, and brilliantly written argument that changed the course of history. Without this book, the environmental movement might have been long delayed or never have developed at all."

Carson's legacy sparked more than a few grassroots environmental movements. In her "Essay on the Biological Sciences" from 1958, she leaves us with words any environmental movement can be based on, as well as a warning:

> *Awareness of ecological relationships is—or should be—the basis of modern conservation programs, for it is useless to attempt to preserve a living species unless the kind of land or water it requires is also preserved. So delicately interwoven are the relationships that when we disturb one thread of the community fabric we alter it all—perhaps almost imperceptibly, perhaps so drastically that destruction follows.*

How to Be Like Rachel Carson

1) **Do what you love.** Carson's heart was always with the outdoors. From an early age she invested her time in nature. She found wonder in the woods and streams and in all living things, such as birds, insects, and flowers. Eventually she added the natural wonders of the sea to her interests. It is hardly a surprise her life's work became protecting these treasures.

   Carson was also an accomplished writer whose prose brought her subjects to life. She started early on that, too, having published a short story at age ten. Nature and writing were her two great passions, and they eventually culminated in her seminal work, *Silent Spring*.

2) **Express your passion.** In writing her first book, *Under the Sea-Wind*, Carson's goal was to make the sea and the life that depended on it vividly come alive for her readers. In marrying her two loves, writing with nature, she produced a passion she could share with the world.

3) **Don't allow others to discourage you.** Carson was not deterred by the lack of public interest in her first book and soon began working on a second one. This early work in progress was rejected repeatedly until it was finally picked up the *New Yorker* magazine. When it was published in book form as *The Sea Around Us*, it sold over two hundred thousand copies within the year and won Carson the John Burroughs Medal and the National Book Award.

4) **Work from your heart.** Carson had an innate honesty in her writing, her goal being to present the natural world truthfully to her readers. She believed that the aim of both science and literature should be to illuminate the truth. In accepting the 1952 National Book Award, Carson said, "If there is poetry in my

Cont'd

book about the sea, it is not because I deliberately put it there, but because no one could write truthfully about the sea and leave out the poetry."

5) **Seek to make a difference.** With the success of *The Sea Around Us,* Carson had financial security for the first time. She could have spent the rest of her life enjoying nature and writing at her leisure, but when she became aware of the serious threat pesticides posed to fragile ecosystems, Carson knew she had to act. She began investigating the effects of DDT on the environment. "What I discovered was that everything which meant the most to me as a naturalist was being threatened, and that nothing I could do would be more important."

6) **Do your homework.** Facts have a way of winning out. When Carson tried to publish the essays that would eventually form the basis of *Silent Spring,* they were consistently rejected because publishers would not believe the scale of the danger she was exposing. Many called her an alarmist or a scaremonger. But Carson had the facts on her side. She had carefully and meticulously researched and documented her arguments, and when the *New Yorker* ran the serialized version of *Silent Spring,* her research stood up to the vicious attacks of the industry most threatened by her facts.

7) **Carry on in the face of adversity.** Carson's courage was significant. Diagnosed with breast cancer while writing Silent Spring, she continued to press on to warn society about the danger to the environment. She died only two years after its publication at the age of fifty-seven, leaving behind a legacy of the finest social responsibility.

Power Points

We trust this book has inspired you and given your spirits a lift,
As you have studied the lives of great women, and perhaps discovered your gift.
Maybe like J. K. Rowling, you have the talent to write,
Or like Martha Stewart, you can whet any appetite.
You can be like Lucille Ball, with skills to entertain,
Mirror Estée Lauder, makeup a cosmetic domain.
Katharine Graham posted great reviews, as a publisher first-rate,
Madeleine Albright became our first female U.S. secretary of state.
Barbara Jordan fought for equal rights and was willing to sacrifice,
You can make your mark on the international stage like Condoleezza Rice.
Teaching may be your strength, learn from Mary McLeod Bethune,
Shirley Chisholm blazed a trail for equality, call her "Danielle" Boone.
Crusading and caring for the environment were Rachel Carson's goals,
Jane Addams's life's mission was to serve downtrodden souls.
Danica Patrick drives herself to win each NASCAR race,
There's Rachael Ray and her culinary way, who succeeds with charm and grace.
Meg Whitman found success on the information highway,
Generating billions of dollars and happy customers for the online auction, eBay.
If you're athletic like Lorena Ochoa, it's great to be well-below par,
Take a page from Suze Orman's financial books, so your investments will go far.
Persevere like Ida Wells-Barnett did, stand your ground and fight,
Question and listen like Barbara Walters and you will develop great insight.
Nurture supreme judgment and, like Ruth Bader Ginsburg, study to be wise,
Be values-oriented like Mary Kay Ash and never compromise.
These twenty-one women created opportunities, worked hard, and never quit.
They maximized their time, making the most of every minute.
Because they did they became *The Women of the Hour*,
And now it's your turn to follow their leads and become
A Woman of Power!

—Ken Hussar

❦ Epilogue ❧

As we put this book together, we noticed some common threads evident in the lives of these amazing women. They all sought and found their passions in life, then made commitments to follow those passions to major accomplishments. They remained focused in the pursuit of their dreams, and when they encountered tough challenges, they never lost sight of their purpose and mission. These women all demonstrated an enormous work ethic and persevered, no matter what obstacles they faced.

One final thought struck us: none of these women achieved their dreams alone. They surrounded themselves with great mentors, role models, and colleagues, proving that no man—or woman—is an island. We firmly believe that as you apply the life lessons learned from these women that you, too, can carve out your niche and realize your full potential.

Pat and Ruth Williams
Orlando, Florida

References

Jane Addams

Addams, Jane. *Peace and Bread in Time of War*. Urbana: University of Illinois Press, 2002.

Addams, Jane. *Twenty Years at Hull-House*. Urbana: University of Illinois Press, 1990.

Fradin, Judith Bloom, and Dennis Brindell Fradin. *Jane Addams: Champion of Democracy*. New York: Clarion Books, 2006.

Harvey, Bonnie Carman. *Jane Addams: Nobel Prize Winner and Founder of Hull House*: Berkeley Heights, NJ: Enslow Publishers, 1999.

Kramer, Barbara. *Trailblazing American Women: First in Their Fields*. Berkeley Heights, NJ: Enslow Publishers, 2000.

Polikoff, Barbara Garland. *With One Bold Act: The Story of Jane Addams*. Chicago: Boswell Books, 1999.

Madeleine Albright

Albright, Madeleine Korbel, with Bill Woodward. *Memo to the President Elect: How We Can Restore America's Reputation and Leadership*. New York: Harper, 2008.

Albright, Madeleine Korbel, with Bill Woodward. *Madame Secretary*. New York: Random House, 2003.

Dobbs, Michael. *Madeleine Albright: A Twentieth-Century Odyssey*. New York: Henry Holt and Co., 1999.

Hasday, Judy L. *Madeleine Albright*. Philadelphia: Chelsea House, 1999.

Kramer, Barbara. *Madeleine Albright: First Woman Secretary of State*. Berkeley Heights, NJ: Enslow Publishers, 2000.

Lippman, Thomas W. *Madeleine Albright and the New American Diplomacy*. Boulder, CO: Westview Press, 2000.

Mary Kay Ash

Ash, Mary Kay. *Mary Kay, You Can Have It All : Lifetime Wisdom from America's Foremost Woman Entrepreneur*. Rocklin, CA: Prima Pub., 1995.

Ash, May Kay, with Yvonne Pendleton. *The Mary Kay Way: Timeless Principles From America's Greatest Woman Entrepreneur*. Hoboken, NJ: John Wiley & Sons, Inc., 2008.

Buchholz, Todd G. *New Ideas from Dead CEOs: Lasting Lessons from the Corner Office*. New York: Collins, 2007

Lucille Ball

Arnaz, Desi. *A Book*. Cutchogue, NY: Buccaneer Books, 1976.

Ball, Lucille, with Betty Hannah Hoffman. *Love, Lucy*. New York: Berkley Boulevard Books, 1997, 1996.

Brady, Kathleen. *Lucille: The Life of Lucille Ball*. New York: Billboard Books, 2001.

Davis, Madelyn Pugh, with Bob Carroll Jr. *Laughing with Lucy: My Life with America's Leading Lady of Comedy*. Cincinnati, OH: Emmis Books, 2005.

Sanders, Coyne Steven, and Tom Gilbert. *Desilu: The Story of Lucille Ball and Desi Arnaz*. New York: HarperEntertainment, 2001, 1993.

Mary McLeod Bethune

Broadwater, Andrea. *Mary McLeod Bethune: Educator and Activist*. Berkeley Heights, NJ: Enslow Publishers, 2003.

Halasa, Malu. *Mary McLeod Bethune*. New York: Chelsea House, 1989.

Rachel Carson

Brooks, Paul. *The House of Life: Rachel Carson at Work*. Boston: Houghton Mifflin, 1989.

Carson, Rachel. *Silent Spring*. (With introduction by Al Gore.) Boston: Houghton Mifflin Co., 1994.

Jezer, Marty. *Rachel Carson*. New York: Chelsea House, 1988.

Lear, Linda A. *Rachel Carson: Witness for Nature*. New York: Henry Holt, 1998, 1997.

Locker, Thomas, and Joseph Bruchac. *Rachel Carson: Preserving a Sense of Wonder*. Golden, CO: Fulcrum Pub., 2004.

Tremblay, E. A. *Rachel Carson: Author/Ecologist*. Philadelphia: Chelsea House Publishers, 2003.

Shirley Chisholm

Brownmiller, Susan. *Shirley Chisholm: A Biography*. Garden City, NY: Doubleday, 1970.

Chisholm, Shirley. *Unbought and Unbossed*. Boston: Houghton Mifflin, 1970.

Haskins, James. *Fighting Shirley Chisholm*. New York: Dial Press, 1975.

Hicks, Nancy. *The Honorable Shirley Chisholm, Congresswoman from Brooklyn*. New York: Lion Books, 1971.

Scheader, Catherine. *Shirley Chisholm, Teacher and Congresswoman*. Hillsdale, NJ: Enslow Publishers, 1990.

Ruth Bader Ginsburg

Ayer, Eleanor H. *Ruth Bader Ginsburg: Fire and Steel on the Supreme Court*. New York: Dillon Press; Toronto: Maxwell Macmillan Canada; New York: Maxwell Macmillan International, 1994.

Bayer, Linda N. *Ruth Bader Ginsburg*. Philadelphia: Chelsea House Publishers, 2000.

Bredeson, Carmen. *Ruth Bader Ginsburg: Supreme Court Justice*. Springfield, NJ: Enslow Publishers, 1995.

Italia, Bob. *Ruth Bader Ginsburg*. Minneapolis, MN: Abdo & Daughters, 1994.

Roberts, Jack L. *Ruth Bader Ginsburg: Supreme Court Justice*. Brookfield, CT: Millbrook Press, 1994.

Katharine Graham

Asirvatham, Sandy. *Katharine Graham*. Philadelphia, PA: Chelsea House Publishers, 2002.

Graham, Katharine. *Personal History*. New York: Vintage, 1998.

Barbara Jordan

Blue, Rose, and Corrine Naden. *Barbara Jordan*. New York: Chelsea House, 1992.

Holmes, Barbara A. *A Private Woman in Public Spaces: Barbara Jordan's Speeches on Ethics, Public Religion, and Law*. Harrisburg, PA: Trinity Press International, 2000.

Jeffrey, Laura S. *Barbara Jordan: Congresswoman, Lawyer, Educator*. Springfield, NJ: Enslow Publishers, 1997.

Jordan, Barbara, and Shelby Hearon. *Barbara Jordan, A Self-Portrait*. Garden City, NY: Doubleday, 1979.

Estee Lauder

Lauder, Estee. *Estee: A Success Story*. New York: Random House, 1985.

Buchholz, Todd G. *New Ideas from Dead CEOs: Lasting Lessons from the Corner Office*. New York: Collins, 2007.

Lorena Ochoa

Official Lorena Ochoa website
  http://www.lorenaochoa.com/site_ing.html

Lorena Ochoa by Nancy Lopez
  http://www.time.com/time/specials/2007/article/0,28804,1733748_1733756_1736207,00.html

Paul Forsyth, golf correspondent
  http://www.timesonline.co.uk/tol/sport/golf/article4406448.ece
  http://golf.about.com/od/golferswomen/p/lorena_ochoa.htm

Alan Shipnuck, senior writer, *Sports Illustrated*
  http://www.golf.com/golf/tours_news/article/0,28136,1811420-0,00.html
  http://www.golfdigest.com/instruction/swing/2008/08/photos_ochoa

Suze Orman

Orman, Suze. *The Courage to Be Rich: Creating a Life of Material and Spiritual Abundance*. New York: Riverhead Books, 2002.

Orman, Suze. *The 9 Steps to Financial Freedom: Practical & Spiritual Steps So You Can Stop Worrying*. New York: Three Rivers Press, 2000.

Orman, Suze. *Women & Money: Owning the Power to Control Your Destiny*. New York: Spiegel & Grau, 2007.

Orman, Suze. *The Laws of Money, the Lessons of Life*. New York: Free Press, 2003.

Danica Patrick

Patrick, Danica, with Laura Morton. *Danica: Crossing the Line*. New York: Simon & Schuster, 2006.

Rachael Ray

www.rachaelray.com/bio.php - 20k

www.rachaelrayshow.com

www.rachaelraymag.com

www.time.com/time/magazine/article/0,9171,1187293,00.html - 34k

Patrick Cain, *Investor's Business Daily*, May 2008

Liza Hamm and Michelle Tauber, *People Magazine*, May 2007

Beverly Keel, Rachel Ray's Recipe For Success, http://www.americanprofile.com/article/4962.html

Condoleeza Rice

Brown, Mary Beth. *Condi: The Life of a Steel Magnolia*. Nashville, TN: Thomas Nelson, 2007.

Ditchfield, Christin. *Condoleezza Rice: National Security Advisor*. New York: Franklin Watts, 2003.

Mabry, Marcus. *Twice As Good: Condoleezza Rice and Her Path to Power*. New York: Modern Times, 2007.

Wade, Mary Dotson. *Condoleeza Rice: Being the Best*. Topeka, KS: Bindery, 2003.

J. K. Rowling

Fraser, Lindsey. *Conversations with J. K. Rowling*. New York: Scholastic, 2001 Edition.

Kirk, Connie Ann. *J. K. Rowling: A Biography*. Westport, CT: Greenwood Press, 2003.

Sexton, Colleen A. *J. K. Rowling*. Minneapolis: Lerner Publications Co., 2006.

Shapiro, Marc. *J. K. Rowling: The Wizard Behind Harry Potter*. New York: St. Martin's Griffin, 2000.

Martha Stewart

Stewart, Martha. *The Martha Rules: 10 Essentials for Achieving Success as You Start, Build, or Manage a Business.* Emmaus, PA: Rodale, 2005.

Stewart, Martha, edited by Bill Adler. *The World According to Martha.* New York: McGraw-Hill, 2006.

Price, Joann F. *Martha Stewart: A Biography.* Westport, CT: Greenwood Press, 2007.

Barbara Walters

Remstein, Henna. *Barbara Walters.* Philadelphia: Chelsea House, c. 1999.

Walters, Barbara. *Audition: A Memoir.* New York: Alfred A. Knopf, 2008.

Ida B. Wells-Barnett

Davidson, James West. *They Say: Ida B. Wells and the Reconstruction of Race.* Oxford; New York: Oxford University Press, 2007.

Fradin, Dennis Brindell, and Judith Bloom Fradin. *Ida B. Wells: Mother of the Civil Rights Movement.* New York: Clarion Books, 2000.

Freedman, Suzanne. *Ida B. Wells-Barnett and the Antilynching Crusade.* Brookfield, CT: Millbrook Press, 1994.

Haynes, Richard M. *Ida B. Wells: Antilynching Crusader.* Austin, TX: Raintree Steck-Vaughn, 1994.

Lisandrelli, Elaine Slivinski. *Ida B. Wells-Barnett: Crusader Against Lynching.* Springfield, NJ: Enslow Publishers, 1998.

Schechter, Patricia A. *Ida B. Wells-Barnett and American Reform, 1880–1930.* Chapel Hill: University of North Carolina Press, 2001.

Van Steenwyk, Elizabeth. *Ida B. Wells-Barnett: Woman of Courage.* New York: F. Watts, 1992.

Meg Whitman

Horvitz, Leslie Alan. *Meg Whitman: President and CEO of eBay.* New York: Ferguson, 2006.

Acknowledgments

With deep appreciation we acknowledge the support and guidance of the following people who helped make this book possible:

Special thanks to Alex Martins, Bob Vander Weide and Rich DeVos of the Orlando Magic.

Thanks also to our writing partner Michael Mink for his superb contributions in shaping the manuscript.

Hats off to three dependable associates—Pat's assistant Latria Graham, Pat's trusted and valuable colleague Andrew Herdliska, and our ace typist Fran Thomas.

We would like to offer a heartfelt thanks to Ken Hussar. Without Ken's editing, this book would have never been completed. Ken, thank you for everything you have done. We could not have done it without you.

Hearty thanks also go to our friends at Health Communications. Thank you all for believing that we had something important to share and for providing the support and the forum to say it. Special thanks to Allison Janse for your continued support and encouragement.

And finally, special thanks and appreciation go to our wonderful and supportive children and grandchildren. They are truly the backbone of our lives.

—Pat and Ruth Williams

Developing a book like this is no easy task. I have experienced the hard work of research and the joys of digging deeply into the lives of accomplished women. I am grateful to the following individuals who assisted and inspired me on this project:

First, I thank Amelie Frank, a Los Angeles-born and based writer, editor, publisher, and poet whose biography appears in *Who's Who of American Women* and *Who's Who in America*. She helped me with much of the research and writing on Mary McLeod Bethune and Suze Orman, and did a great job helping with the editing. She was enthusiastic and tireless in her efforts, and demonstrated a positive can-do attitude.

Keith Ravye, my long-time friend and a talented writer, contributed to the chapters on Madeleine Albright and Rachael Carson. Keith has written freelance articles for national publications and currently writes for the political Blog ofpoliticsandmen.com. *How to Be Like Women of Power* is his first book project contribution.

Shirley Oliver, another friend, helped with the chapter on Ida Barnett Wells. Shirley has a BA in Psychology and an MA in Marriage and Family Therapy.

Nancy Sokoler Steiner helped with the chapter on Barbara Jordan. Nancy is a freelance writer and author based in Los Angeles. Specializing in health, education and human interest pieces, she is a contributing writer to *The Jewish Journal of Greater Los Angeles* and has been published in *The Los Angeles Times Magazine, UCLA Magazine,* and *Lifestyles Magazine* among others. She is the author of the children's book *On This Night: The Passover Seder in Rhyme (Hachai)*. For more information, visit her website at www.nancy-steiner.com

—*Michael Mink*

About the Authors

*P*at Williams is the senior vice president of the NBA's Orlando Magic. One of America's top motivational, inspirational, and humorous speakers, he has addressed employees from many of the Fortune 500 companies and the Million Dollar Round Table. Pat has been featured in *Sports Illustrated, Reader's Digest, Good Housekeeping, Family Circle, The Wall Street Journal, Focus on the Family, New Man Magazine,* plus all of the major television networks, The Maury Povich Show and Dr. Robert Schuller's *Hour of Power.*

Ruth Williams is an inspirational and motivational speaker and a consultant with the FranklinCovey organization. She has trained and managed thousands of people in various aspects of professional and personal development. She has worked with such companies as American Express, Chase Manhattan Bank, CitiBank, Nextel Communications, the U.S. Navy and Air Force, Home Shopping Network, World Omni Lease, Lockheed Martin, Ryder Trucks, the PGA Tour and State Farm Insurance. She is currently pursuing a Ph.D. in organizational leadership.

Michael Mink is a freelance writer who has written hundreds of special feature profiles for the "Leaders and Success" page in *Investors Business Daily.*

You can contact Pat and Ruth Williams at:

Pat and Ruth Williams
^{c}/o Orlando Magic
8701 Maitland Summit Boulevard
Orlando, FL 32810
407-916-2404
pwilliams@orlandomagic.com

Visit Pat Williams's website at:

www.PatWilliamsMotivate.com

If you would like to set up a speaking engagement for Pat and/or Ruth Williams, please call Andrew Herdliska at 407-916-2401 or e-mail him at aherdliska@orlandomagic.com.

We would love to hear from you. Please send your comments about this book to Pat Williams at the above. Thank you.

The gift of literacy

Foreword by Phil Jackson,
Head Coach of the Los Angeles Lakers

READ FOR YOUR LIFE

11 Ways to Transform Your Life with Books

PAT WILLIAMS
with Peggy Matthews Rose

Code #5458 • $14.95

Pat Williams, senior vice president of the Orlando Magic, marathon runner and father of 19, is on a mission to help you fully access and enjoy the power of reading.

"Every so often a book comes along that is an essential read. How to Be Like Jesus is one of those rare books. . . ."

—Tim LaHaye, coauthor, Left Behind

How to Be Like Jesus

LESSONS ON FOLLOWING IN HIS FOOTSTEPS

Pat Williams
With Jim Denney
Foreword by Jerry B. Jenkins, coauthor, New York Times bestselling Left Behind series

Code #0693 • $14.95

Succeeding with Integrity in Business and Life

How to Be Like Rich DeVos

Cofounder of Amway and owner of the Orlando Magic

Pat Williams
with Jim Denney

Code #1584 • $14.95

"Of all the books written about Walt Disney, this may be the most important."
From the Foreword by Art Linkletter

How to Be Like Walt

Capturing the Disney Magic Every Day of Your Life

Code #2319 • $13.95

How to Be Like Women of Influence

LIFE LESSONS FROM 20 OF THE GREATEST

Pat and Ruth Williams
With Michael Mink

Code #0545 • $12.95

To order direct: Telephone (800) 441-5569 • www.hcibooks.com
Prices do not include shipping and handling. Your response code is BKS.

How to Be Like **MIKE**

LIFE LESSONS ABOUT BASKETBALL'S BEST

Pat Williams
With Michael Weinreb

Code #9551 • $12.95

Foreword by
Bill Walton

How to Be Like **Coach WOODEN**

Life Lessons
from Basketball's
Greatest Leader

Pat Williams
with David Wimbish

Code #3919 • $14.95

32 Women at the Top of Their Game
and How You Can Get There Too

How to Be Like **Women Athletes of Influence**

Pat Williams with Dana Pennett O'Neil

Code #6772 • $14.95

How to Be Like
Jackie Robinson

Life Lessons from
Baseball's Greatest Hero
Pat Williams with Mike Sielski

Foreword by
Bud Selig

Code #1738 • $14.95

Precious life lessons

Pat Williams and bestselling author Karen Kingsbury have teamed up to bring graduates a big, little book of ten invaluable faith-driven lessons from inspiring to hilarious.

Forever Young
Ten Gifts of Faith for the Graduate

Pat Williams and Karen Kingsbury

Code #253X • $14.95

The Takeaway

14 Unforgettable Lessons Every Father Should Pass On to His Daughter

Pat Williams and Karyn Williams
with Peggy Matthews Rose

Code #3892 • $14.95

The Takeaway promises to feed valuable information into your heart and life that is rich in nutritional value for raising children who will go out and impact the world.